Classroom Assessment of Reading Processes

Classroom Assessment of Reading Processes

SECOND EDITION

Rebecca Swearingen
Southwest Missouri State University

Diane Allen
University of North Texas

Houghton Mifflin Company
Boston New York

Senior Sponsoring Editor: Loretta Wolozin
Associate Editor: Jennifer Roderick
Senior Project Editor: Kathryn Dinovo
Senior Manufacturing Coordinator: Marie Barnes
Associate Marketing Manager: Jean Zielinski DeMayo

Cover design: Nina Wishnok/Dynamo Design
Cover image: Laura Ljungkvist represented by Art Department

Printed in the U.S.A.

Library of Congress Catalog Card Number: 99-71893

ISBN: 0-395-96415-6

123456789-QD-03 02 01 00 99

Contents

Preface ..... *xiii*

SECTION A Basic Information **1**

PART 1 Orientation **3**

The Classroom Assessment of Reading Processes 3

Theoretical Framework 4

Comparisons to Other Informal Reading Inventories 5

General Information on IRIs 5

Strengths of the CARP vs. Traditional IRIs 6

Scope of This Tool 7

Development of the Classroom Assessment of Reading Processes 8

Validity and Reliability 8

Selection of Test Materials 9

PART 2 Administering the Classroom Assessment of Reading Processes **11**

When to Use the Classroom Assessment of Reading Processes 11

Deciding Which Sections Are Appropriate 12

Narrative Retelling Administration 13

What Is a Retelling? 13

Practice Session 13

Word List Administration 13

Narrative Retelling Directions 14

Establishing Levels 15

Sample Narrative Retelling 16

Expository Retelling Administration 18

Expository Retelling Directions 19
Establishing Levels 21
Sample Expository Retelling 21
Think-Aloud Administration 24
What Is a Think-Aloud? 24
Think-Aloud Directions 25
Sample Think-Aloud 26

PART 3 ***Analyzing Results*** **29**

Narrative Retelling Rubric Analysis 29
Types of Information Gained 29
Sample Rubric and Discussion 29
Expository Retelling Rubric Analysis 31
Types of Information Gained 31
Sample Rubric and Discussion 32
Miscue Analysis 35
What Is a Miscue Analysis? 35
Patterns of Errors 38
Think-Aloud Rubric Analysis 38
Types of Information Gained 38
Sample Rubric and Discussion 39
References 41

PART 4 ***Using Portfolio Assessment*** **43**

What Are Portfolios? 43
Establishing a Baseline 43
Measuring Growth over Time 44
Sample Portfolio (Kyle, Fifth Grade) 44

SECTION B ***The Assessment Tool*** **71**

PART 5 ***Classroom Assessment of Reading Processes Assessment Materials*** **73**

Word Lists 74
Word List 1 74
Word List 2 75
Word List 3 76
Word List 4 77
Word List 5 78
Word List 6 79

Word List 7 ... 80
Word List 8 ... 81
Word List 9 ... 82
Word List Scoring Sheet ... 83
Narrative Retelling ... 86
Brief Directions for Administering Retelling Passages ... 86

Narrative Passages and Rubrics Form A 88

First Grade Narrative ***Penny Gets Wheels***
Form A—Teacher's Copy ... 88
Retelling Protocol ... 89

Second Grade Narrative ***Ray's Best Friend***
Form A—Teacher's Copy ... 90
Retelling Protocol ... 91

Third Grade Narrative ***Sports Day***
Form A—Teacher's Copy ... 92
Retelling Protocol ... 94

Fourth Grade Narrative ***A Special Trade***
Form A—Teacher's Copy ... 95
Retelling Protocol ... 96

Fifth Grade Narrative ***The Tortoise Who Talked Too Much***
Form A—Teacher's Copy ... 97
Retelling Protocol ... 98

Sixth Grade Narrative ***A Name for a Kitten***
Form A—Teacher's Copy ... 99
Retelling Protocol ... 101

Seventh Grade Narrative ***Maria and the Coquis***
Form A—Teacher's Copy ... 102
Retelling Protocol ... 104

Eighth Grade Narrative ***Matt's Gift***
Form A—Teacher's Copy ... 105
Retelling Protocol ... 107

Ninth Grade Narrative ***Roberto's Encounter in the Field***
Form A—Teacher's Copy ... 108
Retelling Protocol ... 110

First Grade ***Penny Gets Wheels*** Student's Copy ... 111
Second Grade ***Ray's Best Friend*** Student's Copy ... 114
Third Grade ***Sports Day*** Student's Copy ... 116
Fourth Grade ***A Special Trade*** Student's Copy ... 118
Fifth Grade ***The Tortoise Who Talked Too Much*** Student's Copy ... 119
Sixth Grade ***A Name for a Kitten*** Student's Copy ... 120
Seventh Grade ***Maria and the Coquis*** Student's Copy ... 122
Eighth Grade ***Matt's Gift*** Student's Copy ... 124
Ninth Grade ***Roberto's Encounter in the Field*** Student's Copy ... 126

Narrative Passages and Rubrics Form B **_128_**

First Grade Narrative **_Walter and the Mall_**
Form B—Teacher's Copy . . . . . **_128_**
Retelling Protocol . . . . . **_130_**

Second Grade Narrative **_Skunk Baby_**
Form B—Teacher's Copy . . . . . **_131_**
Retelling Protocol . . . . . **_133_**

Third Grade Narrative **_Leaving Nicodemus_**
Form B—Teacher's Copy . . . . . **_134_**
Retelling Protocol . . . . . **_135_**

Fourth Grade Narrative **_Mighty Mini_**
Form B—Teacher's Copy . . . . . **_136_**
Retelling Protocol . . . . . **_137_**

Fifth Grade Narrative **_Making French Toast_**
Form B—Teacher's Copy . . . . . **_138_**
Retelling Protocol . . . . . **_139_**

Sixth Grade Narrative **_Amelia and the Lemonade Stand_**
Form B—Teacher's Copy . . . . . **_140_**
Retelling Protocol . . . . . **_142_**

Seventh Grade Narrative **_Samantha and the Envelope_**
Form B—Teacher's Copy . . . . . **_143_**
Retelling Protocol . . . . . **_145_**

Eighth Grade Narrative **_Annie's Fourteenth Birthday_**
Form B—Teacher's Copy . . . . . **_146_**
Retelling Protocol . . . . . **_148_**

Ninth Grade Narrative **_The Trip Home_**
Form B—Teacher's Copy . . . . . **_149_**
Retelling Protocol . . . . . **_151_**

First Grade **_Walter and the Mall_** Student's Copy . . . . . **_152_**
Second Grade **_Skunk Baby_** Student's Copy . . . . . **_156_**
Third Grade **_Leaving Nicodemus_** Student's Copy . . . . . **_159_**
Fourth Grade **_Mighty Mini_** Student's Copy . . . . . **_161_**
Fifth Grade **_Making French Toast_** Student's Copy . . . . . **_162_**
Sixth Grade **_Amelia and the Lemonade Stand_** Student's Copy . . . . . **_163_**
Seventh Grade **_Samantha and the Envelope_** Student's Copy . . . . . **_165_**
Eighth Grade **_Annie's Fourteenth Birthday_** Student's Copy . . . . . **_167_**
Ninth Grade **_The Trip Home_** Student's Copy . . . . . **_169_**

Expository Retelling 171
Brief Directions for Administering Expository Passages 171

Expository Passages and Rubrics Form A 172

First Grade Expository ***Who Helps Bear Cubs?***
Form A—Teacher's Copy 172
Retelling Protocol 173

Second Grade Expository ***Trees and Animals Need Each Other***
Form A—Teacher's Copy 174
Retelling Protocol 175

Third Grade Expository ***How Big Is Big?***
Form A—Teacher's Copy 176
Retelling Protocol 177

Fourth Grade Expository ***Antarctica***
Form A—Teacher's Copy 178
Retelling Protocol 179

Fifth Grade Expository ***How the Electric Eel Makes Electricity***
Form A—Teacher's Copy 180
Retelling Protocol 181

Sixth Grade Expository ***Rice***
Form A—Teacher's Copy 182
Retelling Protocol 183

Seventh Grade Expository ***A Mom with a Mission***
Form A—Teacher's Copy 184
Retelling Protocol 186

Eighth Grade Expository ***The How and Why of Fingerprints***
Form A—Teacher's Copy 187
Retelling Protocol 189

Ninth Grade Expository ***The Decision That Led to Civil War***
Form A—Teacher's Copy 190
Retelling Protocol 192

First Grade ***Who Helps Bear Cubs?*** Student's Copy 193
Second Grade ***Trees and Animals Need Each Other*** Student's Copy 195
Third Grade ***How Big Is Big?*** Student's Copy 197
Fourth Grade ***Antarctica*** Student's Copy 199
Fifth Grade ***How the Electric Eel Makes Electricity*** Student's Copy . . 200
Sixth Grade ***Rice*** Student's Copy 201
Seventh Grade ***A Mom with a Mission*** Student's Copy 202
Eighth Grade ***The How and Why of Fingerprints*** Student's Copy 204
Ninth Grade ***The Decision That Led to Civil War*** Student's Copy 205

	Expository Passages and Rubrics Form B	207
First Grade Expository	*Different Kinds of Bears*	
	Form B—Teacher's Copy	207
	Retelling Protocol	208
Second Grade Expository	*Animal Homes*	
	Form B—Teacher's Copy	209
	Retelling Protocol	210
Third Grade Expository	*Bird Migration*	
	Form B—Teacher's Copy	211
	Retelling Protocol	212
Fourth Grade Expository	*Japan*	
	Form B—Teacher's Copy	213
	Retelling Protocol	214
Fifth Grade Expository	*Nocturnal Animals*	
	Form B—Teacher's Copy	215
	Retelling Protocol	216
Sixth Grade Expository	*How Tornadoes Behave*	
	Form B—Teacher's Copy	217
	Retelling Protocol	218
Seventh Grade Expository	*Tsunami*	
	Form B—Teacher's Copy	219
	Retelling Protocol	220
Eighth Grade Expository	*The Origin of Agriculture*	
	Form B—Teacher's Copy	221
	Retelling Protocol	223
Ninth Grade Expository	**Brown *v.* Board of Education:** *Desegregating America's Schools*	
	Form B—Teacher's Copy	224
	Retelling Protocol	226

First Grade	*Different Kinds of Bears* Student's Copy	227
Second Grade	*Animal Homes* Student's Copy	229
Third Grade	*Bird Migration* Student's Copy	231
Fourth Grade	*Japan* Student's Copy	233
Fifth Grade	*Nocturnal Animals* Student's Copy	234
Sixth Grade	*How Tornadoes Behave* Student's Copy	235
Seventh Grade	*Tsunami* Student's Copy	236
Eighth Grade	*The Origin of Agriculture* Student's Copy	237
Ninth Grade	**Brown *v.* Board of Education:** *Desegregating America's Schools* Student's Copy	239

Think-Alouds ... 241

Brief Directions for Administering Think-Aloud Passages ... 241

Think-Aloud Passages and Rubrics 242

First and Second Grade Think-Aloud
Teacher's Script ... 242
Think-Aloud Protocol ... 244
Student's Copy ... 245

Third and Fourth Grade Think-Aloud
Teacher's Script ... 251
Think-Aloud Protocol ... 253
Student's Copy ... 254

Fifth and Sixth Grade Think-Aloud
Teacher's Script ... 259
Think-Aloud Protocol ... 261
Student's Copy ... 262

Seventh Through Ninth Grade Think-Aloud
Teacher's Script ... 267
Think-Aloud Protocol ... 269
Student's Copy ... 270

Portfolio Checklists ... 275

SECTION C **Resources** 283

PART 6 *Annotated Bibliography of Children's Literature* 285

First Grade ... 285
Second Grade ... 289
Third Grade ... 294
Fourth Grade ... 299
Fifth Grade ... 302
Sixth Grade ... 306
Seventh Through Ninth Grade ... 309

Glossary ... 321
Brief Guide to Administering the CARP ... 324

Preface

Every teacher has questions about the reading processes used by students in the classroom. What strategies does a student use to figure out unfamiliar words? How does a student use the organization of the text to aid comprehension? What is the role of a student's prior knowledge in understanding the author's message? What are the specific reading needs of each student? We developed the *Classroom Assessment of Reading Processes* (CARP) to help teachers find the answers to such questions.

The CARP emerged from our extensive experience teaching and doing research with children in classroom and clinical settings. We searched for answers to many of the questions that other teachers had asked about students and reading, but we did not find one comprehensive tool that helped teachers assess the variety of reading processes used by students. Thus, our goal in developing this tool, the CARP, was to provide a set of assessments in one text based on our view of reading as a cognitive process, focusing on helping teachers link assessment with instruction.

Intended Audience

The CARP is an appropriate assessment tool for several audiences.

- Graduate students majoring in reading and/or studying for reading specialist certification may use the CARP in both classroom and clinical settings. Such students may have opportunities to use this instrument with students who experience difficulties with reading.
- Preservice teachers will learn to use it in their teacher education settings.
- Novice teachers will observe that it matches current reading theory taught in their teacher preparation courses and offers them a tool to use in their future classrooms with all students.
- Practicing teachers will find that the CARP is easy to adapt to their classroom needs; they may select a few or all sections to administer.

Special Features of *Classroom Assessment of Reading Processes*

The CARP offers a qualitative view of a student's reading processes. Rather than determining numbers or scores, teachers can use the CARP to describe specific reading behaviors related to the underlying processes of the reading act. By focusing on these processes, teachers will be able to develop specific reading activities to support students' progress in reading. The following special features will assist teachers in documenting students' reading behaviors and processes:

1. ***Narrative Retellings:*** The narrative retelling section requires students to read a story and then to retell the story in their own words. The teacher evaluates students' responses according to their use of story structure to make sense of the text. The CARP provides teacher marking sheets to assist in analyzing students' knowledge and use of story structure to comprehend the passage.

2. ***Expository Retellings:*** Research indicates that students read expository text in different ways and at different levels than narrative text. Therefore, the CARP provides a separate section to assess expository reading processes. This is done by a modified K-W-L format. The K-W-L requires students to respond to a topic by telling (1) what they know; (2) what they want to find out; and (3) what they learned from reading the text. In the CARP, students are given the topic of the story that they will read and asked to tell what they know. Following the reading of the text, they tell what additional information they learned about the topic. The teacher marking sheets allow teachers to determine if the students have prior knowledge on the topic and if that knowledge assisted with the comprehension of the text.

3. ***Think-Alouds:*** The think-aloud stories in the CARP are divided into sections that allow the teacher to stop periodically and ask students to talk about what has happened in the story and to predict what might happen later in the story. Students confirm or reject predictions by referring to specific information in the story. Think-alouds give teachers a window into students' thinking processes and metacognitive strategies as they make sense of the text.

4. ***Portfolio Checklists:*** Checklists are provided to assist the teacher in using the CARP to measure growth over time.

5. ***Annotated Bibliography of Children's Literature:*** A bibliography of quality children's literature is provided for grade levels one through nine. The bibliography presents the books by grade level and provides source information and an annotation to help teachers make connections between assessment and instruction.

6. ***Instructor's Resource Manual (IRM):*** To accompany the CARP, we developed an Instructor's Manual to provide additional support to professors or staff development leaders as they train students and in-service teachers in the use of the CARP. The IRM includes additional case studies, black line masters for transparencies, and documentation regarding validity and reliability issues.

Highlights of the Second Edition

In response to comments from users of the CARP, we have made some additions and changes to the text for this edition. The most significant additions and changes follow:

- The CARP now includes narrative, expository and think-aloud passages for grade levels one through nine. This makes the CARP appropriate for use in the middle grades with all students and in the high school grades for students who are reading below level.
- The Annotated Bibliography of Children's Literature in Part 6 also has been expanded to include books of interest to adolescents.
- The Think-Aloud section has been modified. The purpose of this section is to provide easy reading material that will allow students to articulate their own reading processes to the examiner or teacher. Rather than have passages for the individual grade levels, the passages have been grouped. For example, there is one passage for use with first- and second-grade-level readers, one for third- and fourth-grade-level readers, etc.
- Narrative passages for first grade, second grade, and sixth grade have been changed. The new stories more clearly demonstrate a solid story structure and more closely match the purposes of the CARP.
- New information has been provided throughout the text to indicate how the CARP can be used effectively in a balanced reading program. While the CARP maintains a focus on reading processes related to meaning, some teachers may need to document students' understanding and implementation of decoding strategies as part of a balanced reading program. Part 1 provides the Betts Criteria to assist the teacher in determining word recognition scores for each of the narrative and expository passages. The Miscue Analysis section demonstrates how teachers can examine the word errors that a child makes in order to design appropriate strategy lessons.

Acknowledgments

We are indebted to many colleagues and friends. Their feedback, support, and encouragement are greatly appreciated. The students and teachers with whom we have worked through the years have had a tremendous impact on the development of this text. They have asked questions about reading and helped us figure out solutions, and have provided honest feedback to earlier versions of this text. Our university colleagues have challenged our thinking and supported our efforts. A special thanks goes to colleagues from the University of North Texas, Madge Craig, Jean Greenlaw, and Alexandra Leavell; and to Genny Cramer and Janet Doelling from Southwest Missouri State University, who believed in the project and cheered us on. Dana Arrowwood performed library research and provided many books for the bibliography. Also, a special thanks to Diane's summer EDRE 5190 class who helped to review and modify several of the new passages for the middle grades.

We would like to thank the following reviewers for their feedback through the development process:

Judith E. Craig, University of Alaska, Anchorage
Marguerite K. Gillis, Southwest Texas State University
Jessica L. Grant, Christensen Elementary School
Roberta Kaufman, Concordia University
Joseph E. Mahony, University of Nebraska, Kearney
Karen Mandernach, Sac Elementary School
Sherry Markel, Northern Arizona University
Virginia McCormack, Ohio Dominican College
Marvis D. Ward, Florida Atlantic University
Carol D. Wickstrom, Texas Woman's University
Marilyn Wikstrom, Buena Vista University

We would especially like to thank Loretta Wolozin from Houghton Mifflin, who believed in this project from the beginning, and Lisa Mafrici and Jennifer Roderick from Houghton Mifflin, who gently prodded and poked until this manuscript was complete.

Classroom Assessment of Reading Processes

Basic Information

PART 1

Orientation

The Classroom Assessment of Reading Processes

Reading is a constructive process. Readers construct their own meaning of a text by combining their **schemata** with clues and concepts that the author provides. Therefore, readers must actively participate in the reading process. Most reading assessments disregard this theory of reading when they evaluate only discrete skills and subskills. The Classroom Assessment of Reading Processes (CARP) is a tool that teachers can use to evaluate students' construction of knowledge and involvement with print.

To evaluate a student's reading processes, the CARP uses the following special elements:

1. ***Narrative Retellings:*** The student reads a story. The teacher then asks the student to retell the story. The retelling allows the teacher to determine whether the student can recall story elements in the appropriate sequence. This provides a measure of the student's comprehension. The teacher uses the **protocols** provided to analyze student responses and assess independent, instructional, and frustration reading levels.

2. ***Expository Retellings:*** The expository portion of the CARP is developed around a modified **K-W-L** (Ogle, 1986) format. The teacher first asks the student about his or her prior knowledge of the topic. Then the student reads the text, and the teacher asks the student to retell information gained from the text. Using the protocols, the teacher is able to determine how the student uses prior knowledge to gain information from text, as well as independent, instructional, and frustration reading levels.

3. ***Think-Alouds:*** Think-aloud passages provide the teacher with a procedure for determining *metacognitive* processing. A checklist helps the teacher analyze the student's ability to develop, confirm, modify, and reject predictions.

4. ***Portfolio Checklists:*** A variety of checklists simplify the recording of assessment analyses. Checklists that document

the student's use of metacognitive strategies, **miscues,** and word analysis techniques are among those included.

5. ***Annotated Children's Literature Bibliography:*** The bibliography provides a concrete link between assessment and instruction. Books in this resource are organized by reading level.

Theoretical Framework

"Making sense of print is what reading is all about" (Goodman, 1984, p. 112), or reading is constructing meaning. To construct meaning, the reader interacts with and responds to the text based on prior experience, implied meaning of the author, and the context in which that interaction occurs (Cooper, 1997; Walker, 1996; Rosenblatt, 1983; Valencia & Pearson, 1987). The CARP is based on the theory that the reader is an active participant in the construction of meaning.

In accordance with the theory of reading as constructing meaning, key sections of the CARP focus on assessing the student's ability to obtain meaning from the text in a variety of contexts. Word knowledge and decoding skills play an important role in the construction of meaning in that they are analyzed in terms of the effect they have on the construction of meaning. The CARP thus does not measure word knowledge as a subprocess. This treatment of word errors is supported by research (Allen & Swearingen, 1992; Klesius & Homan, 1985; D'Angelo & Mahlios, 1983), which indicates that children may be placed for instruction in material that is too easy if placement is based on the number of word errors made in oral reading. Some word errors, such as insertions, may indeed have little impact on the comprehension of the material (Ekwall & Shanker, 1993; D'Angelo & Mahlios, 1983).

Traditional reading assessment does not take into account the interactive nature of the reading process. During traditional reading assessment, students are asked to provide specific responses that are subsequently evaluated as correct or incorrect. Teachers do not obtain information related to the process that the students used to formulate their responses (Valencia & Pearson, 1987; Readence & Martin, 1988; Winograd, Paris, & Bridge, 1991; Collins & Cheek, 1993). **Authentic reading assessment** is an attempt to evaluate reading in a way that more closely aligns to actual classroom instruction. Teachers who use authentic reading assessment are interested in determining students' thinking processes as well as their reading performance. The CARP helps teachers obtain a measure of students' thinking processes related to reading (Brozo, 1990; Henk, 1987).

Increased literacy is one goal of education reform. As a result of this emphasis, more attention is being focused on appropriate reading assessments that address the literacy goals set by the teacher. Many teachers are discovering that informal classroom assessments of reading, such as informal reading inventories, provide more relevant information for planning personalized instruction to meet proposed outcomes and goals than do traditional assessments. Teachers who use informal measures of reading can determine a child's use of comprehension, vocabulary, and word identification strategies within contexts that more closely resemble classroom activities. Teachers can combine the information gained through these informal measures with their identified literacy goals to plan appropriate instruction.

Vygotsky's **Zone of Proximal Development** encompasses "the gap between the child's level of actual development determined by independent problem solving and her level of potential development determined by problem solving supported by an adult or through collaboration with more capable peers" (Dixon-Krauss, 1996, pp. 14–15). This definition suggests that teachers can best help students learn if they understand where the students are in their actual reading development. With the retellings (narrative and expository) and think-alouds in the CARP, teachers can identify the actual reading development of their students. These procedures also can help teachers design appropriate instruction, enabling the students to approach their potential reading development level.

Comparisons to Other Informal Reading Inventories

General Information on IRIs

The informal reading inventory (IRI) is probably the most widely used of informal assessments for reading (Searles, 1988; Collins & Cheek, 1993). The IRI consists of grade-level stories that the child may read either orally or silently. The stories are followed by questions, which are sometimes divided into categories of comprehension skills; for example, main idea, cause-effect relationships, details, or inference. Word miscues (Caldwell, 1985) and comprehension errors allow teachers to determine a suggested reading level for a child, such as third grade or fourth grade. Teachers can then use this grade level to determine placement in instructional materials. For a more extensive description of IRIs, see the review of commercial IRIs by Pikulski (1990). This review covers the types of items included and the specific means of determining levels in IRIs. Because the IRI is administered individually, the teacher can also obtain qualitative information on the child's reading behaviors, such as patterns of word errors and reading attitudes. This additional information is valuable to the teacher who wants to provide personalized instruction for students.

Strengths of the CARP vs. Traditional IRIs

The assumptions of traditional IRIs predate current understandings drawn from cognitive research. Many researchers question the validity of these assumptions, focusing on the following four areas:

1. Many IRIs do not assess the interactive nature of reading. The organization of most IRIs does not encourage a reader to use his or her own knowledge to derive meaning from textual information (Henk, 1987). The CARP, however, assists students in activating prior knowledge through the use of purpose-setting statements and through the modified K-W-L format for expository passages.

2. IRI passages contain little or no variety in the types of text structures. Studies have shown that students read different types of text, such as narrative and expository, in different ways. Many IRIs do not provide the option of varying texts (Caldwell, 1985). IRIs that do include various text structures score the responses for each type in exactly the same way (Gillis & Olson, 1986). The CARP, however, is designed to assess narrative and expository passages not only separately, but also differently, because the two types of text are written in different ways. Students' performance on narrative text is assessed through retelling. Their performance on expository text is assessed by first activating prior knowledge and then comparing this to the information the students glean from the text.

3. Administrative and scoring time constraints limit the number of comprehension questions (5 to 10) on IRIs. Some researchers challenge the placement of students based on so few questions (Schell & Hanna, 1981). In addition, other researchers have found that many IRI questions are mislabeled (Allen & Swearingen, 1991). For example, most IRIs have questions labeled as main idea, but many of them actually ask for the topic as opposed to the main idea, and some ask for the main idea of passages that do not have a main idea (Dufflemeyer & Dufflemeyer, 1987; 1989). Because the CARP assesses reading process rather than specific skills, questions that isolate or introduce other constructs are not appropriate. The format of the CARP allows the teacher to explore the child's reading performance more holistically.

4. IRIs are formatted so that students alternately read one passage silently and the next orally (Warren, 1985). The CARP allows the teacher greater flexibility in how the passages will be read. Based on the type of information the teacher seeks, the CARP offers a variety of options. Inclusion of two narrative and two expository passages at first through sixth grade levels allows the teacher to analyze oral reading miscues, compare narrative and expository reading processes (oral and/or silent), and/or measure reading growth over time.

In summary, the CARP was designed to address the four validity issues in the following ways:

- **Traditional IRIs are not organized to encourage the reader to use his or her own knowledge to derive meaning.** *The CARP helps activate prior knowledge through purpose-setting statements and the modified K-W-L.*
- **Most traditional IRIs do not take into account the different strategies a reader uses based on text structure.** *The CARP assesses narrative and expository text separately and in different ways.*
- **Traditional IRIs limit or mislabel comprehension questions.** *The CARP allows for a more open-ended evaluation by assessing process through retelling rather than measuring specific skills through questioning.*
- **Traditional IRIs require students to alternately read an oral passage, followed by a silent passage.** *The CARP allows greater flexibility. It includes two forms for both narrative and expository text, allowing the teacher to administer whichever portions more closely fit his or her needs.*

Scope of This Tool

The CARP is intended primarily for use with students in grades one through six, with special uses for middle school or other readers. By using the CARP, teachers assess

1. Student reading levels for both expository and narrative text
2. Student use of metacognitive strategies
3. Student use of prior knowledge to gain new information
4. Student understanding of story structure

The CARP is specifically designed to allow teachers to choose which sections to administer and in what order. Teachers also choose the method of reading: oral and/or silent. Although the CARP is designed to provide teachers with a wide variety of information concerning the reading processes their students use, it is not designed to evaluate knowledge of discrete comprehension skills.

Word recognition levels are not considered for determining independent, instructional, and frustration reading levels. However, to calculate the word recognition level of any passage, the teacher can easily apply the Betts criteria (1954) to the percentage of miscues.

Betts Criteria		
READING LEVEL	**WORD RECOGNITION**	**COMPREHENSION**
Independent	99%	90%
Instructional	95%	75%
Frustration	90% or less	50% or less

The CARP does not allow teachers to ascertain information regarding attitude and interest directly. However, as teachers administer the CARP, they will have many opportunities to note students' responses to text and the reading task. These observational notes will provide invaluable information when compiling portfolios.

The CARP is intended for use with children who have already received reading instruction and who would be expected to have knowledge of reading and of story structure. When working with children who are at the emergent level, the teacher might consider using an instrument specifically designed for assessing print concepts and phonemic awareness, for example, Clay's Concepts About Print Test (1985).

Although the CARP's passages are written at first through ninth grade levels, this does not preclude assessing older readers with this instrument. Teachers working with tenth, eleventh, and twelfth grade at-risk readers may find the CARP helpful for assessing student needs and for planning instruction.

Development of the Classroom Assessment of Reading Processes

Validity and Reliability

Because validity and reliability issues are central to any good assessment instrument, they were considered an important aspect in the development of the CARP. Research indicates that many IRIs have failed to report tests of reliability (Helgren-Lempesis, 1986) and have not always established adequate validity (Klesius & Homan, 1985). Two types of validity were established for this assessment: **content validity** and **concurrent validity.**

Content validity is established if the assessment instrument measures content that reading experts deem to be central to the process of reading. As mentioned earlier, the authors developed the CARP based on the theory of reading as an interactive, constructive process, a view that recent reading research supports. Concurrent validity was established by comparing the assessment results of readers on the CARP to the test results of those readers on achievement tests and individualized standardized reading tests.

Reliability is the consistency of the assessment instrument to produce the same results each time it is administered. Two types of reliability were examined for the CARP: interscorer reliability and alternate forms reliability. Interscorer reliability was established by comparing the results that several different scorers obtained on the same passages. Alternate forms reliability implies that a student will make approximately the same score on a Passage A story as on a Passage B story. The CARP provides two forms for narrative and expository retellings. Alternate forms reliability was established by independent judges who scored students' results on both forms of the CARP for independent, instructional, and frustration levels.

Selection of Test Materials

A second area of concern in the development of the CARP was the selection of materials for the test passages. Many of the passages were adapted from basal reading programs that were out of print. This was done to avoid using passages with which students would be familiar. Other passages were selected from popular children's magazines, such as *Highlights* and *Child Life*. Both authors carefully read all the passages to ensure that characters and settings were not culturally biased. Knowing that classrooms are diverse, the authors chose culturally neutral passages that would appeal to *all* children. The Fry Readability Formula (Fry, 1977) was used to establish reading levels for each passage.

Administering the Classroom Assessment of Reading Processes

When to Use the Classroom Assessment of Reading Processes

Decisions about appropriate placement in reading materials or special programs for at-risk readers are often based on scores from a standardized reading test. Although standardized tests provide a reliable and valid numerical reading score, they offer very little information that can help the classroom teacher design appropriate instruction for each student. Instead, teachers should choose additional assessments that give information related to (1) the strategies a child uses to decode unfamiliar words, (2) the child's specific areas of reading difficulties, (3) the highest level of understanding for placement in the appropriate level of materials, (4) the child's ability to use prior knowledge for better understanding of text, (5) other thinking and metacognitive reading processes, and (6) an estimation of the child's fluency.

Teachers who collect this type of information are able to create a classroom curriculum based on an **instructional-assessment cycle.** By using the data gathered from initial informal assessments, the teacher can plan instruction for individual students, small groups, or the whole group. During implementation of the planned instruction, the teacher can assess the students' reading performances, behaviors, and processes. These new assessments, conducted during the instruction, will help the teacher modify the instruction to meet the needs of the individual students.

Traditional informal reading inventories allow teachers to assess decoding skills and the child's level of reading ability. Teachers should choose the CARP when they need to assess an individual child's reading skills and processes to plan the appropriate instruction. The teacher will find this information useful for any child in the classroom, the gifted as well as the struggling.

Deciding Which Sections Are Appropriate

The CARP is designed so that the teacher can administer any one part of it to satisfy a specific purpose. It is helpful in most cases to begin with the word lists because determining a level on these lists facilitates entry into the other sections of the test. The following guidelines can help teachers decide which other parts of the CARP to administer.

Guidelines for Administering Sections of the CARP

TO ASSESS . . .	ADMINISTER . . .
Independent, instructional, and/or frustration reading levels	• Narrative retelling passages • Expository retelling passages
Understanding of story structure	• Narrative retelling passages
Use of prior knowledge	• Narrative retelling passages • Expository retelling passages • Think-aloud passages
Metacognitive skills	• Think-aloud passages
Decoding strategies	• Narrative retelling passages with a miscue analysis • Expository retelling passages with a miscue analysis
Differences between oral and silent reading levels	• Narrative retelling passages • Expository retelling passages
Differences in ability to handle a variety of text	• Narrative retelling passages *and* • Expository retelling passages
Ability to construct meaning	• Narrative retelling passages • Expository retelling passages • Think-aloud passages

The CARP passages may be administered either orally or silently. Because two forms of the test are provided, the teacher may choose to administer one form orally to establish levels and then administer the other form silently to compare the student's responses on the two modes of reading.

Narrative Retelling Administration

What Is a Retelling?

"Retelling or free recall is the process of recalling text after hearing or reading it" (Smith & Keister, 1996, p. 17). The CARP assesses independent, instructional, and frustration narrative reading levels through the use of retelling. During a **retelling** procedure, the teacher asks the student to either read or listen to a piece of text. The teacher then asks the student to recall as much information as he or she can. The teacher records this information. Retellings can focus on the number of story elements recalled, the type of story elements recalled, or a combination of number and type. The CARP measures reading level by identifying the number and type of story elements recalled.

To help students understand the task, the students first participate in a practice session.

Practice Session

Prior to beginning the narrative retelling portion of the CARP, it is important to make sure the student is familiar with the task that is being asked of him or her. This practice session teaches the child the task and makes the child comfortable with the examiner and the task. Choose a familiar fairy tale, such as *Little Red Hen,* and discuss the story with the student to make sure that he or she is familiar with the story and then fill out the sample protocol. Fill in the protocol as you discuss the important elements of the story such as characters, setting, episodes, and conclusion.

Word List Administration

Be certain that the student understands the task before you begin testing. To determine where to begin the narrative passages, use the graded word lists that are provided. Starting one grade level below the student's grade placement, begin to administer the word lists. If the first word list administered is not at the student's independent level, move down one grade level. Continue moving down one grade level at a time until you reach the student's independent level. Then continue forward until a frustration level is reached. (See page 15 for establishing and scoring levels.)

Because administration of the graded word lists is essentially a test of **automaticity** (LaBerge & Samuels, 1974) or sight words, the teacher must not wait too long for a student to provide the word. A maximum five-second wait is most appropriate. Teachers can mark the graded word lists with a simple plus or minus. However, because a miscue analysis may be performed on the mispronounced words, teachers may want to record the student's response above the word missed.

The word lists start on page 74.

Narrative Retelling Directions

Having determined the student's independent, instructional, and frustration levels on the word lists, the teacher may begin the graded narrative passages. Begin the passages at the highest independent level the student achieved on the word lists. Tell the student, **"I am going to ask you to read some stories. Please read them carefully because I am going to ask you to tell me as much as you can remember from the story."** At this point, remind the student of what he or she did in the practice session and what parts of the story were identified.

Prior to having the student start the passage, read the purpose-setting statement. Two forms are provided for the narrative retelling. The teacher may want to use Form A for oral reading and Form B for silent reading. If Form A is used for oral reading, a marking copy of the passage is provided for the teacher to mark word recognition errors for a miscue analysis. The following marking system is recommended as a fast and accurate way to mark miscues.

TYPE OF STUDENT ERROR	TEACHER'S MARKING	EXAMPLE
Substitutions/ mispronunciations	Write the student's response above the text word.	bun burn
Insertions	Write the added word(s) above the text line and indicate the location of the insertion using the symbol ^ .	big the ^ brown dog
Omissions	Circle the omitted word(s).	the (big) boy
Teacher provided	Write "TP" above any word that is pronounced or provided for the student.	TP elephant
Repetitions	Draw a straight line above all words and phrases that are repeated.	down the street
Self-corrections	When the student corrects any error, mark the correction by writing a "C" over the miscue.	moCose mouse

When the student has finished reading the story, say, **"Tell this story as if you were telling it to a friend who has not heard it before."** Mark the student's responses on the protocol sheet. Remember that the responses suggested on the protocol sheet are merely *suggestions* of what a student might say; they are not to be taken as verbatim responses. For example, the Form A Second Grade passage protocol sheet refers to the girl's first day, second day, third day, and so on.

New Girl at School

PLOT (14 points each)

______ 1. Marcia starts at new school.

______ 2. She has bad first day (nobody notices grasshopper shirt, children call her Martha, doesn't know where lunchroom is, and doesn't know subtraction).

______ 3. She has bad second day (no one sat with her on bus and was by herself at lunch).

______ 4. She has a better third day (did not want to go to school, teacher does not hold up her picture, was not chosen as captain, but made it to second base).

______ 5. She has an even better fourth day (teacher displays airplane, someone notices grasshopper shirt, and Karen asks her to sleep over).

The student must understand that the events occur over a period of time, but the student does not have to specifically refer to first day, second day, and so on. Another example is the Sixth Grade passage, in which several advisors to the king suggest names for the kitten. Knowing that the suggestions came from several advisors is important, but the student does not need to identify each advisor by title.

Establishing Levels

After the student retells the story, fill out the scoring matrix at the bottom of the page. Using this matrix, the teacher can determine the student's independent, instructional, and frustration reading levels. The **independent reading level** is the level at which a student can read without assistance. The **instructional reading level** is the level at which the student can read with assistance from the teacher. This is the level at which reading instruction should occur. The **frustration reading level** is the level at which a student cannot achieve success even with assistance from a teacher. A score of 85 or above represents an independent level passage, 70 or above represents an instructional level passage, and below 70 represents a frustration level passage.

SCORE	LEVEL
≥85 points	Independent
70 to 84 points	Instructional
<70 points	Frustration

If the student's performance falls in the independent level, have the student repeat the process with the next higher level of text. The student should continue reading and retelling the stories until he or she reaches the frustration level. If the first text is at the instructional level, the teacher should have the student read the next lower level passage and continue backward, one grade at a time, to find the independent level before continuing higher to find the frustration level. If the first text is at the frustration level, the teacher should proceed backward until instructional and independent levels of reading have been reached.

Sample Narrative Retelling

Jessica is a fifth grade student. Her highest independent level on the word lists was third grade; therefore, the starting level for the narrative retelling is third grade. The passage selected for the assessment is the Form B Third Grade passage, "Leaving Nicodemus."

The teacher begins the retelling session by saying to Jessica, **"I am going to ask you to read some stories. Please read them carefully because I am going to ask you to tell me as much as you can remember from each story."** She continues, **"This story tells about three young boys who are on a trip on their own from one home to another. Read this story to find out what happens to them on their trip."** Jessica reads the story silently.

When Jessica finishes, the teacher says, **"Tell this story as if you were telling it to a friend who has not heard it before."** Jessica responds:

> *There are these boys that had to go away . . . these three brothers that went away and they said really we can do that and stuff. They went camping. They said if we keep the fire going and the gun stocked the wild animals won't come get us in the middle of the night. Well, they did . . . then they remembered about wild rattlesnakes like the one and stuff so his brother Willie said not to move and stuff and he was, like, why not? He's, like, look beside you, don't look but there is a rattlesnake beside you. Johnny said so he didn't, and he was trying to think what his Dad was telling him about rattlesnakes and he kept on thinking, 'cause he couldn't breathe or move. He was so scared and his little brother was asleep, but the other two were up and he was telling them that he thought let the fire go out and it will go away, finally the fire went out, and it went away and the wild rattlesnake went into the dark night again and they started back out and went on a deer trail and they took that and they kept on following it and they saw a little house and a man came outside and they thought it was Daddy and so they all ran to him and there was hugs, kisses, laughs, cries and all that they were doing and stuff and that was their journey and that's all I can say.*

The teacher then prompts with, **"Is that all you can remember?"** Jessica responds, *"Yes."*

The teacher then marks the protocol sheet as follows:

Leaving Nicodemus

CHARACTERS (2.5 points each)

__✓__ Willie __✓__ Johnny

__✓__ Little Brother __✓__ Daddy

SETTING (3 points each)

__✓__ On the road from Nicodemus __✓__ New house

PLOT (14 points each)

__✓__ 1. Willie, Little Brother, and Johnny leave Nicodemus.

_____ 2. The boys followed the map.

__✓__ 3. At night they built fires and fired the gun to scare wild animals.

__✓__ 4. There was a rattlesnake by the fire.

__✓__ 5. After the fire went out, the rattlesnake left.

RESOLUTION (14 points)

__✓__ 6. After twenty-two days, they came to their new house and found their father.

Jessica recalled all of the characters and both settings. She recalled all but one of the plot points ("The boys followed the map"). This means that Jessica received 86 points on this passage. This passage is at her independent level.

		READING LEVELS	
Character Total	10	Independent	Above 85 Points
Setting Total	6	Instructional	70–84 Points
Plot Total	56	Frustration	Below 70 Points
Resolution Total	14		
TOTAL POINTS	86		

Finally, the teacher completes the Observations checklist for this passage.

OBSERVATIONS

	Inappropriate				Appropriate
Includes detail	1	2	3	4	(5)
Uses prior knowledge to establish story line	1	2	3	(4)	5
Infers beyond text	1	2	3	4	(5)
	Out of Sequence				**In Sequence**
Tells story in correct sequence	1	2	3	4	(5)
	Verbatim				**In Own Words**
Restates story verbatim	1	2	3	(4)	5

Expository Retelling Administration

In the CARP, the expository retelling passages and protocols differ significantly from the narrative retelling passages and protocols. The purpose of narrative text is to tell a story. When children retell narrative stories, they have one basic framework from which to work: characters, setting, plot, and resolution. Assessment of a child's narrative reading, then, should measure how well a child understands and interprets a story within the story framework. Expository text, on the other hand, informs the reader and may be written in a variety of structural formats, for example, cause and effect, descriptive, or listing. Assessment of expository reading should determine first what the child already knows about the topic and then how well the child combines the new information in the text with his or her prior knowledge.

Each type of text requires the reader to process ideas in very different ways and should be assessed differently. In other IRIs, narrative text and expository text are often mixed together and assessed in the same ways. Using the CARP, the teacher can assess each type of text independently of the other but can compare the results. For instance, the expository passages allow the teacher to gather specific information about how the student uses prior knowledge. At the same time, they allow the teacher to compare the student's performance on narrative text with performance on expository text.

Expository Retelling Directions

Teachers may use the expository retelling passages to establish reading levels for children. If the child has read the narrative retelling portion of the CARP, the teacher may use the highest independent reading level achieved as a starting point for the expository retellings. For example, if the child read the second grade narrative passage independently, this next part of the assessment should begin with the second grade level expository passage. In some cases, the teacher may choose to give only the expository section of the CARP. In that instance, the teacher should have the child begin with a passage that is one year below the child's placement in school. For example, a third grader would begin with a second grade passage. If, after the child reads, the teacher determines that the beginning passage was at the instructional or frustration level, the child should read subsequently lower levels of passages until he or she reaches an independent level. Having determined the independent level, the teacher should return to a passage one level higher than the beginning passage. The child should continue to read until instructional and frustration levels have been determined.

Once the beginning level has been decided, the teacher is ready to introduce the assessment to the child. Begin by saying, **"Tell me everything you know about (the topic)."** As the child responds, the teacher should mark responses in the Prior column on the protocol sheet if that information appears in the text. (A sample protocol sheet is shown on page 20.) In some cases, the child may give information that is not a part of this particular text. The teacher should note this additional information in the space in the middle of the page. This is important information because it may indicate the accuracy of the child's information and the child's ability to activate prior knowledge. If the child tells the teacher 90% or more of the information that is in the text, choose a Form B passage at the same level.

Who Helps Bear Cubs? (Level 1.0)

TOPIC: Bear Cubs

PRIOR	RECALL	
		1. Bear cubs are so little.
		2. Bear cubs can't see well.
		3. Bear cubs can't get things to eat.
		4.* Mother bear gives her cubs all that they need.
		5. Soon bear cubs go out with their mother.
		6. Bear cubs want to see everything.
		7. Bear cubs jump, roll, and play.
		8. Mother bear helps the cubs find things to eat.
		9. Mother bear helps the cubs know all the things that bears do.
		10. Someday the Mother bear will not help the cubs.

*Stated main idea

OBSERVATIONS					
	Inadequate				Adequate
Has prior knowledge	1	2	3	4	5
Recalls information	1	2	3	4	5
Uses prior knowledge to infer	1	2	3	4	5
Recognizes stated main idea	1	2	3	4	5
	Verbatim				In Own Words
Restates text verbatim	1	2	3	4	5

OTHER FACTUAL INFORMATION GIVEN BY THE STUDENT

When the student has completed the Prior Knowledge section, the actual reading of the passage should begin. Tell the student, **"I am going to ask you to read some stories. Please read them carefully because I am going to ask you to tell me as much as you can remember from each story."** Because the expository section is not used to develop a miscue analysis, the passages should be read silently. This provides the teacher with another possible comparison to the child's performance on the narrative retelling passages.

After the reading, the teacher should assess what the student learned from the passage by asking, **"What information about (the topic) did you learn from reading this passage?"** Place check marks in the Recall column on the protocol sheet to indicate which pieces of information the student remembers. The teacher should note any additional information that the student recalls. The teacher should also complete the observation checklist at the bottom of the page.

Establishing Levels

Reading levels for the expository passage are established by combining prior knowledge information with the information learned from the reading. Use the following criteria to establish each level:

SCORE	LEVEL
≥90% combined prior and recall	Independent
75% to 89% combined prior and recall	Instructional
<75% combined prior and recall	Frustration

Sample Expository Retelling

Kyle is a fifth grade student. His highest independent level on the narrative retelling was third grade; therefore, the starting level for the expository retelling is third grade. The passage selected for the assessment is the Form A Third Grade passage, "How Big Is Big?"

The teacher begins the assessment session by saying to Kyle, **"Tell me everything you know about big animals."** Kyle's responses include *"The biggest animal is the elephant"; "I think the whale is the biggest one in the ocean"; "The giraffe is the tallest."* With these responses, the teacher places check marks in the Prior column on the protocol sheet beside the following items:

2. The tallest animal is the giraffe.
7. The elephant is the biggest animal on land. (Note that Kyle did not give the totally accurate response; however, his response is very close and he should be given some credit.)

14. The biggest animal that has ever lived on land or sea is the blue whale. (Again note that Kyle's answer does not include all of the information. This should be noted on the protocol.)

Kyle has some basic information but not 90% of the information in the article, so the teacher continues with this passage. The teacher instructs Kyle, **"This passage is about big animals. Read it to yourself as carefully as you can. We will talk about what you learned when you have finished."**

After Kyle has read the passage, the teacher asks him, **"What information about big animals did you learn from reading this passage?"** In response, Kyle gives the following information:

> *Well, some animals are so big you can't even imagine how big they are. A giraffe is tall as three grown-ups. It has a really long neck and really long legs. The giraffe can see so far away that it can get away before it's killed. Elephants weigh as much as 60 grown-ups. They're really big! They live in herds. Sometimes the herds are big and sometimes they're little. The blue whale was the biggest animal that ever lived and it weighed like 1000 grown-ups. It was way bigger than an elephant. A shark is big too.*

The teacher marks the Recall column on the protocol sheet as follows:

PRIOR	RECALL	
	✓	1.* Some animals are so huge that it's hard to even picture them in your mind.
✓		2. The tallest animal is the giraffe.
	✓	3. It is as tall as three grown-up people.
	✓	4. It has a very long neck and very long legs.
	✓	5. A giraffe is so tall that it can see things far away.
	✓	6. If it sees something frightening, the giraffe has time to run away.
✓		7. The elephant is the biggest animal on land.
	✓	8. An elephant can weigh as much as sixty grown-up people!
	✓	9. Elephants live in herds.
	✓	10. Some herds have as few as four or five elephants, but others have as many as 1000.
		11. The whale shark is longer than four cars.
		12. It weighs as much as two elephants.
		13. The whale shark is gentle and eats only small plants and fish.
✓		14. The biggest animal that has ever lived on land or sea is the blue whale.
	✓	15. The blue whale weighs more than 1000 grown-up people and is longer than seven cars.

*Stated main idea

By combining the number of correct responses in the Prior column with those in the Recall column, the teacher determines that Kyle knows 85% of the material (12 responses out of a possible 15 responses). This passage is at Kyle's instructional level for expository text.

The teacher next completes the Observations checklist.

OBSERVATIONS

	Inadequate				Adequate
Has prior knowledge	1	2	(3)	4	5
Recalls information	1	2	3	(4)	5
Uses prior knowledge to infer	1	2	(3)	4	5
Recognizes stated main idea	1	2	3	4	(5)
	Verbatim				**In Own Words**
Restates text verbatim	1	2	3	(4)	5

Because Kyle is in the fifth grade, his teacher wants to know if he can also comfortably read expository text closer to his grade level material. She administers the Form A Fourth Grade and Fifth Grade passages. Kyle scores within the instructional range on both passages.

Think-Aloud Administration

What Is a Think-Aloud?

Think-alouds are defined by Wade (1990) as "readers' verbal self-reports about their thinking processes." The think-aloud portion of the CARP consists of passages that are divided into sections and a scripted teacher section. As the student completes each section, he or she is asked to predict what is going to happen and to confirm or reject previous predictions. Five types of readers can be identified using a think-aloud procedure (Wade, 1990):

1. A *good comprehender* makes reasonable predictions and rejects predictions when new material contradicts a previous prediction.
2. A *non–risk taker* is not comfortable making predictions. This reader looks for confirmation from the teacher when making a prediction or may simply state that he or she does not know what will happen.

3. The *nonintegrator* does not connect one part of a story to other parts. This reader may make separate, unconnected predictions for each part of the story.
4. A *schema imposer* sticks with his or her initial prediction despite new, conflicting information.
5. The *storyteller* relates the sections of the story to him- or herself and relies heavily on prior knowledge.

More specific characteristics and behaviors of these five types of readers are given in the following table.

Types of Comprehenders	
Good Comprehender	• Constructs meaning • Monitors comprehension • Makes reasonable inferences • Recognizes the need for more information • Abandons an original idea for a new, better one
Non–Risk Taker	• Is a bottom-up processor • Fails to go beyond the text • May look for clues from the examiner • Often claims not to know • May repeat words or phrases verbatim • Guesses in a questioning manner
Nonintegrator	• Develops a new hypothesis for every section • Never relates new section to previous sections • Is guided by the schema of the moment
Schema Imposer	• Holds onto initial hypotheses despite new, conflicting information • Is unaware of alternative hypotheses
Storyteller	• Draws far more on prior knowledge or experience than on text information • Identifies strongly with characters in the story • Makes casual inferences based on what the character does

Adapted from Wade, S. E. (1990). Using think-alouds to assess comprehension. *The Reading Teacher,* 43(7), 442–451. Copyright by the International Reading Association. All rights reserved.

Think-Aloud Directions

A teacher might choose to administer the think-aloud passage in two ways. First, use the *highest* independent reading level identified with the retelling passages. Second, use a level that is at least one year below the student's grade placement.

The teacher first chooses the passage to be administered and then consults the script for that passage. This script is designed to help the teacher prompt the student to make predictions, to discuss predictions, and to confirm or reject predictions. Only one passage is usually administered to the child.

Once the passage is completed, the teacher fills in the protocol sheet.

Think-Aloud Protocol

OBSERVATIONS

	Inadequate				Adequate
Uses prior knowledge to establish story line	1	2	3	4	5
Makes logical predictions	1	2	3	4	5
Discards inappropriate predictions as new information is presented	1	2	3	4	5
Connects pieces of text into a whole text that makes sense	1	2	3	4	5
Offers predictions willingly	1	2	3	4	5
Requires prompting	1	2	3	4	5

COMMENTS

Sample Think-Aloud

Jessica is asked to read the third grade think-aloud passage because third grade was found to be her highest independent level on the narrative passages. The teacher begins the session by saying, **"Read the following paragraph to yourself."** When Jessica has finished reading the paragraph, the teacher asks her to make a prediction based on what she has read. Jessica replies, *"I think they will be given a spelling test."* The teacher asks Jessica to read the next section. Jessica then gives the following predictions:

> *Mrs. Fuller finds a surprise in her desk. I'm not sure what it will be. I think they will try to catch the mouse, probably with a trap. I hope they don't kill it. I think they should keep the mouse. I think they will get Jack one of those big cage things. You know, the one with all the tubes and things. But they will have to send him home with someone for the summer since school is out.*

Finally, the teacher asks Jessica, **"Did you guess what was going to happen? Why or why not?"** Jessica replies, *"I still think they should send the mouse home with someone for the* *summer. They probably will get a cage for him next year. Otherwise he would just stay in the old classroom."*

The teacher completes the checklist as follows:

Think-Aloud Protocol

OBSERVATIONS

	Inadequate				Adequate
Uses prior knowledge to establish story line	1	2	3	4	(5)
Makes logical predictions	1	2	3	4	(5)
Discards inappropriate predictions as new information is presented	1	2	3	4	(5)
Connects pieces of text into a whole text that makes sense	1	2	3	4	(5)
Offers predictions willingly	1	2	3	4	(5)
Requires prompting	1	2	3	4	(5)

COMMENTS

Analyzing Results

Narrative Retelling Rubric Analysis

Types of Information Gained

By analyzing the narrative rubrics, the teacher can gain valuable information about the child's reading processes. The narrative retelling rubric provides the teacher with the following types of information:

1. ***Level of comprehension:*** The teacher can determine if each passage is at the child's independent, instructional, or frustration reading level by totaling the points in each section of the rubric.
2. ***Knowledge of story structure:*** The teacher can determine the child's knowledge of story structure by analyzing the narrative retelling rubric. The rubrics are designed to identify the characters, setting, plot, and resolution of each story.
3. ***Miscue analysis:*** If the text is read orally, the teacher can discover patterns of errors by completing the miscue analysis sheet. These errors include substitutions and mispronunciations, insertions, omissions, teacher-provided words, and repetitions.
4. ***Inferencing:*** The teacher can analyze a student's ability to infer information beyond the text (for example, a character's motives or emotions).
5. ***Sequencing:*** The teacher can learn how the student uses and understands the sequence of stories by observing the sequence the student uses during the retelling.

Sample Rubric and Discussion

In a previous section of this text, Sample Narrative Retelling, Jessica's retelling of the Form B Third Grade passage was used as an example. This discussion refers to that sample and provides a more detailed look at Jessica's reading of narrative text. For the reader's convenience, the rubric showing Jessica's responses is repeated here.

Leaving Nicodemus

CHARACTERS (2.5 points each)

✓	Willie	✓	Johnny
✓	Little Brother	✓	Daddy

SETTING (3 points each)

✓	On the road from Nicodemus	✓	New house

PLOT (14 points each)

✓ 1. Willie, Little Brother, and Johnny leave Nicodemus.

___ 2. The boys followed the map.

✓ 3. At night they built fires and fired the gun to scare wild animals.

✓ 4. There was a rattlesnake by the fire.

✓ 5. After the fire went out, the rattlesnake left.

RESOLUTION (14 points)

✓ 6. After twenty-two days, they came to their new house and found their father.

Jessica read this passage silently. She did not ask for any assistance during the silent reading. After reading the story, Jessica was asked to retell the story. Here is Jessica's retelling:

> *There are these boys that had to go away . . . these three brothers that went away and they said really we can do that and stuff. They went camping. They said if we keep the fire going and the gun stocked the wild animals won't come get us in the middle of the night. Well, they did . . . then they remembered about wild rattlesnakes like the one and stuff so his brother Willie said not to move and stuff and he was, like, why not? He's, like, look beside you, don't look but there is a rattlesnake beside you. Johnny said so he didn't, and he was trying to think what his Dad was telling him about rattlesnakes and he kept on thinking, 'cause he couldn't breathe or move. He was so scared and his little brother was asleep, but the other two were up and he was telling them that he thought let the fire go out and it will go away, finally the fire went out, and it went away and the wild rattlesnake went into the dark night again and they started back out and went on a deer trail and they took that and they kept on following it and they saw a little house and a man came outside and they thought it was Daddy and so they all ran to him and there was hugs, kisses, laughs, cries and all that they were doing and stuff and that was their journey and that's all I can say.*

Jessica's retelling is very complete. She has put the story into her own words and in the proper sequence. She has provided excellent detail. The only information she has not provided is that the boys followed the map.

Jessica's teacher noted the following observations of Jessica's understanding of this text:

1. Jessica has a good understanding of story structure. She included the characters, setting, plot, and resolution.
2. Jessica has good knowledge of the sequencing of a story.
3. Jessica is able to put the story in her own words and internalizes the story.

Jessica read this text at the independent level based on the scoring of the rubric. This indicates that Jessica would be able to read text at a third grade level without assistance from a teacher. Because this passage is at the independent level, the teacher should continue forward through the passages to determine Jessica's instructional and frustration reading levels.

Expository Retelling Rubric Analysis

Types of Information Gained

As explained in an earlier section of the text, expository and narrative retellings are assessed differently. This allows the teacher to observe different strategies and skills that the student uses when reading. The expository retelling rubric provides the teacher with the following types of information:

1. ***Level of comprehension:*** The teacher can determine if the reading passage is at the child's independent, instructional, or frustration level by figuring the percentage of appropriate prior knowledge and recall responses that the child gives.
2. ***Prior knowledge:*** By examining the child's specific responses to the prompt, "Tell me everything you know about (the topic)," the teacher can judge whether the child has adequate prior knowledge to comprehend the specific passage chosen for the reading. The teacher also can decide if the child's knowledge is accurate.
3. ***Recall:*** The student's responses after reading the text tell the teacher how well the child comprehended what was read. Depending on the responses, the teacher may also get a measure of how the child connects the text information to prior knowledge.
4. ***Inferencing:*** Because the student generates the response rather than simply answering a question, the teacher can assess whether the student is using text information and prior knowledge to make inferences beyond the text.
5. ***Main idea:*** Without asking for the main idea, the teacher can measure the student's ability to recognize the stated

main idea. The teacher also can determine how the student relates the other textual information to that main idea.

6. ***Vocabulary:*** The child often rewords the text by summarizing or using synonyms; this indicates an understanding of the author's word choice and language.
7. ***Miscue analysis:*** If the text is read orally, the teacher may want to complete a miscue analysis sheet and watch for patterns of errors similar to the ones that appeared in the narrative passages.
8. ***Text organization:*** Classroom textbooks for science, social studies, and so on are expository texts. Teachers can assess a student's ability to handle these various text structures by noting any difficulties the student experiences in retrieving information from the expository passages in the CARP.

Sample Rubric and Discussion

In a previous section of this text, Sample Expository Retelling, Kyle's retelling of the Form A Third Grade passage was used as an example. This discussion refers to that sample and provides a more detailed look at Kyle's reading of expository text. For the reader's convenience, the rubric showing Kyle's responses is repeated here.

PRIOR	RECALL	
	✓	1.* Some animals are so huge that it's hard to even picture them in your mind.
✓		2. The tallest animal is the giraffe.
	✓	3. It is as tall as three grown-up people.
	✓	4. It has a very long neck and very long legs.
	✓	5. A giraffe is so tall that it can see things far away.
	✓	6. If it sees something frightening, the giraffe has time to run away.
✓		7. The elephant is the biggest animal on land.
	✓	8. An elephant can weigh as much as sixty grown-up people!
	✓	9. Elephants live in herds.
	✓	10. Some herds have as few as four or five elephants, but others have as many as 1000.
		11. The whale shark is longer than four cars.
		12. It weighs as much as two elephants.
		13. The whale shark is gentle and eats only small plants and fish.
✓		14. The biggest animal that has ever lived on land or sea is the blue whale.
	✓	15. The blue whale weighs more than 1000 grown-up people and is longer than seven cars.

*Stated main idea

Initially, Kyle knew three items of information about big animals that were also stated in the text. These responses indicate Kyle's prior knowledge of the topic. Kyle's responses are more limited than the information provided by the text, and the teacher notes this on the rubric. (See items 2, 7, and 14.) However, Kyle's responses do indicate that he has sufficient knowledge about the topic to construct an understanding of the text.

After Kyle has read the text, the teacher asks him to tell other information that he learned. These items are checked off in the Recall column. Kyle responded to nine items after reading. Simply counting the check marks tells the teacher that Kyle has good comprehension of this text. By closely examining Kyle's exact responses, however, the teacher learns much more about Kyle's ability to understand expository text. Again, here are Kyle's exact responses:

- *"Well, some animals are so big you can't even imagine how big they are."*
- *"A giraffe is tall as three grown-ups."*
- *"It has a really long neck and really long legs."*
- *"The giraffe can see so far away that it can get away before it's killed."*
- *"Elephants weigh as much as 60 grown-ups. They're really big!"*
- *"They live in herds. Sometimes the herds are big and sometimes they're little."*
- *"The blue whale was the biggest animal that ever lived and it weighed like 1000 grown-ups. It was way bigger than an elephant."*
- *"A shark is big too."*

Kyle's teacher noted the following observations of Kyle's understanding of this text:

1. Kyle puts information into his own words, indicating an understanding of the vocabulary and concepts introduced by the author.
2. Kyle makes inferences based on textual information and related to his own prior knowledge of big animals. For instance, he states that a giraffe can see far enough away to get away before getting killed. The killing aspect is not mentioned in the text.
3. Kyle makes evaluative comments on the text such as, *"They're really big!"*
4. Kyle recognizes and restates the main idea, although he does not label it as such.
5. Kyle indicates that he does not always get all of the information. For instance, his comment regarding sharks, *"A shark*

is big too," tells the teacher that Kyle retained a small bit of information about sharks but not all of it.

Because Kyle had some prior knowledge of and/or recalled 85% of the information in this piece of text, this text is at Kyle's instructional reading level. Kyle would be able to read this text in his classroom and have adequate comprehension, but he would also benefit from teacher scaffolding of major concepts and vocabulary. Because Kyle is in the fifth grade, and this passage is written at the third grade reading level, the teacher should also administer the fourth grade passage to determine if it is at Kyle's instructional level. If so, the fifth grade passage should be administered.

Miscue Analysis

What Is a Miscue Analysis?

Goodman (1984) first developed the **miscue analysis** to examine a child's oral reading errors and behaviors within an authentic reading task. Goodman thought it important to compare the graphic similarity between the text word and the child's production to determine which part(s) of the word provided the decoding cues for the child. By looking at all the miscues a child makes on one passage, the teacher can see if a definite pattern of errors exists. The miscue analysis also allows the teacher to analyze how the child uses semantic and syntactic clues to identify words and make sense of the passage. A close examination of these aspects of a child's reading can help the teacher make instructional decisions for appropriate reading strategies that focus on the child's needs.

Many school districts are moving to a more balanced reading program in their schools; they are providing direct instruction in decoding skills within a framework of authentic children's literature. A miscue analysis is particularly helpful for teachers creating a balanced reading program in their classrooms. By analyzing a child's errors made while reading authentic text, the teacher can determine if the child is applying the decoding strategies taught in mini lessons or specialized reading programs.

Through miscue analysis, the teacher gains the following types of information:

1. ***Recognizing beginning, middle, and ending sounds:*** The teacher can determine if there are word recognition errors that primarily occur in the beginning, middle, or end of words. This information can help a teacher design the instructional program for that student.

2. ***Comprehending and monitoring of understanding:*** A teacher can determine if a student is monitoring his or her reading. If a student does not self-correct miscues that do

not make sense, this would indicate that the student is not metacognitively aware.

3. ***Fluency:*** The teacher can examine whether the student attends to punctuation, repeats words or phrases needlessly, or pauses at inappropriate points.
4. ***Vocabulary:*** A teacher can draw conclusions concerning the student's use of and knowledge of vocabulary by examining the types of word substitutions the student makes.

Included in the CARP is a miscue analysis worksheet to facilitate the teacher's examination of a child's reading errors. The teacher should complete the worksheet by first entering the text word in the first column and the child's miscue of that word in the second column. The teacher then compares the two words to determine if they are graphically similar. In the third column, the teacher records a *Y* for yes and an *N* for no under the subheadings for the beginning of the word, the middle of the word, and the ending of the word. The teacher should then decide if the miscue significantly changes the meaning of the text. If the answer is yes, the teacher records a *Y* in the fourth column; if no, an *N*. In the last column, the teacher records whether the child self-corrected the miscue. (See the sample worksheet on page 37.)

Miscue Analysis Worksheet

PASSAGE CARP Narrative STUDENT ____________

FORM A LEVEL 2 DATE ____________

Text Word	Miscue	Is Miscue Graphically Similar? (Y/N) Beg.	Mid.	End.	Is Meaning Changed? (Y/N)	Is Miscue Corrected? (Y/N)
That	What	N	Y	Y	Y	N
Stay	Should	N	N	N	Y	Y

Patterns of Errors

Using the miscue analysis worksheet, the teacher can identify the following patterns of errors.

Graphic Similarities. When evaluating the graphic similarities between text words and child productions, the teacher looks at the beginning graphic cues, the middle cues, and the ending cues. For example, if the text word is "bike" and the child says "hike," the teacher first looks at the beginning of each word to see if they are graphically similar. In this case, the beginning of bike (b) is different from the beginning of hike (h). Further analysis of the graphic similarities reveals that the two words have the same middle and ending graphic representations. In this example, the teacher should look for patterns of similar miscues to develop as the worksheet is completed. If the worksheet reveals that the majority of miscues are different from the text word only at the beginning, the teacher knows that instruction should focus the child's attention on the beginnings of the words. Determining the patterns of a child's miscues provides valuable information about the child's knowledge and use of decoding strategies. The teacher can use this information when developing individual and/or small group lessons.

Meaning Changes. The teacher should also note how often the child's miscues change the meaning of the text. If most of the child's responses change the meaning, the teacher can assume that the child is not reading for meaning and that comprehension of the text will be poor. If the miscues do not significantly change the meaning, the child is comprehending the text beyond the word level.

Self-corrections. Many times a child makes a miscue and then corrects it as more of the text is read. Generally this indicates that the child is a good reader and is making sense of the text. However, if the worksheet indicates a pattern of miscue followed by correction a majority of the time, this may be an indication the child is not reading efficiently. This lack of efficiency slows the reading and makes it a less enjoyable task.

Think-Aloud Rubric Analysis

Types of Information Gained

By analyzing the think-aloud rubric, the teacher can gain information about the processes that the child uses when reading extended text. The think-aloud rubric provides the teacher with the following types of information:

1. ***Predicting events in a story:*** The teacher can analyze the predictions that the child provided to determine if they are logical, if the child changes predictions as new information is gained, and if the child connects each part of the story to the previous sections read.

2. ***Knowledge of story structure:*** The teacher can gain further insight into the child's knowledge of story structure through the think-aloud procedure.

3. ***Type of comprehender:*** The teacher can use Wade's categories to identify which type of reader the student is: a good comprehender, a non–risk taker, a nonintegrator, a schema imposer, or a storyteller.

4. ***Prior knowledge:*** The teacher can determine the child's use of prior knowledge by the predictions the child makes. Children often base their predictions on prior knowledge they have about a topic.

Sample Rubric and Discussion

In a previous section of this text, Sample Think-Aloud, Jessica's retelling of the Third Grade Think-Aloud was used as an example. This discussion refers to that sample and provides a more detailed look at Jessica's think-aloud predictions. For the reader's convenience, Jessica's responses are provided here.

The teacher began the session by saying, **"Read the following paragraph to yourself."** When Jessica had finished the first section, she was asked to make a prediction based on what she had read. Jessica replied, *"I think they will be given a spelling test."* The teacher continued the story and Jessica gave the following predictions:

> *Mrs. Fuller finds a surprise in her desk. I'm not sure what it will be. I think they will try to catch the mouse, probably with a trap. I hope they don't kill it. I think they should keep the mouse.*
>
> *I think they will get Jack one of those big cage things. You know, the one with all those tubes and things. But they will have to send him home with someone for the summer since school is out.*

Finally, the teacher asked Jessica, **"Did you guess what was going to happen? Why or why not?"** Jessica replied, *"I still think they should send the mouse home with someone for the summer. They probably will get a cage for him next year. Otherwise he would just stay in the old classroom."*

The rubric is as follows:

Think-Aloud Protocol

OBSERVATIONS

	Inadequate				Adequate
Uses prior knowledge to establish story line	1	2	3	4	(5)
Makes logical predictions	1	2	3	4	(5)
Discards inappropriate predictions as new information is presented	1	2	3	4	(5)
Connects pieces of text into a whole text that makes sense	1	2	3	4	(5)
Offers predictions willingly	1	2	3	4	(5)
Requires prompting	1	2	3	4	(5)

COMMENTS

Based on Jessica's responses, the teacher makes the following observations:

1. Jessica makes logical predictions and is willing to change them as she receives new information.
2. Jessica uses prior knowledge to make predictions (the reference to the cage with all the tubes).
3. Jessica has good knowledge of story structure and likes to bring a story to closure.

The teacher determines that Jessica has the characteristics of a good comprehender.

References*

Allen, D. D., & Swearingen, R. A. (1991). Informal reading inventories: What are they really asking? Paper presented at the International Reading Association, Las Vegas, NV.

Allen, D. D., & Swearingen, R. A. (1992). Questions asked by and about informal reading inventories. Unpublished manuscript.

Betts, E. (1954). *Foundations of reading instruction.* New York: American Book Company.

Brozo, W. G. (1990). Learning how at-risk readers learn best: A case for interactive assessment. *Journal of Reading,* 33, 522–527.

Caldwell, J. (1985). A new look at the old informal reading inventory. *The Reading Teacher,* 39, 168–173.

Clay, M. M. (1985). *An observation survey of early literacy achievement.* Auckland, New Zealand: Heinemann Publishers.

Collins, M. D., & Cheek, E. H. (1993). *Diagnostic-prescriptive reading instruction: A guide for classroom teachers* (4th ed.). Madison, WI: Brown & Benchmark Publishers.

Cooper, J. D. (1997). *Literacy: Helping children construct meaning* (3rd ed.). Boston: Houghton Mifflin.

D'Angelo, K., & Mahlios, M. (1983). Insertion and omission miscues of good and poor readers. *The Reading Teacher,* 36, 778–782.

Dixon-Krauss, L. (1996). *Vygotsky in the classroom.* White Plains, NY: Longman.

Dufflemeyer, F. A., & Dufflemeyer, B. B. (1987). Main idea questions on informal reading inventories. *The Reading Teacher,* 41, 162–166.

Dufflemeyer, F. A., & Dufflemeyer, B. B. (1989). Are IRI passages suitable for assessing main idea comprehension? *The Reading Teacher,* 42, 358–363.

Ekwall, E. E., & Shanker, J. L. (1993). *Locating and correcting reading difficulties.* New York: Merrill.

Fry, E. (1977). Fry's readability graph: Clarifications, validity, and extension to level 17. *Journal of Reading,* 21, 242–252.

Gillis, M. K., & Olson, M. W. (1986). Informal reading inventories and text type/structure. Paper presented at the Southwest Regional Conference of the International Reading Association, San Antonio, TX.

Goodman, K. (1984). Unity in reading. In A. C. Purves & O. S. Niles (Eds.), *Becoming readers in a complex society. Eighty-third yearbook of the Society for the Study of Education,* pp. 79–114. Chicago: University of Chicago Press.

Helgren-Lempesis, V. A. (1986). An analysis of alternate-form reliability of three commercially prepared informal reading inventories. *Reading Research Quarterly,* 21, 209–215.

Henk, W. A. (1987). Reading assessment of the future: Toward precision diagnosis. *The Reading Teacher,* 40, 860–870.

*Reference section applies to Parts 1, 2, and 3.

Klesius, J. P., & Homan, S. P. (1985). A validity and reliability update on the informal reading inventory with suggestions for improvement. *Journal of Learning Disabilities*, 18, 71–76.

LaBerge, D., & Samuels, S. J. (1974). Toward a theory of automatic information processing in reading. *Cognitive Psychology*, 6, 193–323.

Ogle, D. M. (1986). K-W-L: A teaching model that develops active reading of expository text. *The Reading Teacher*, 39, 564–570.

Pikulski, J. J. (1990). A critical review: Informal reading inventories. *The Reading Teacher*, 43, 514–516.

Readence, J. E., & Martin, M. A. (1988). Comprehension assessment: Alternatives to standardized tests. In S. M. Glazer, L. W. Searfoss, & L. M. Gentile (Eds.), *Reexamining reading diagnosis: New trends and procedures*. Newark, DE: International Reading Association.

Rosenblatt, L. (1983). *Literature as exploration*. New York: Modern Language Association.

Schell, L. M., & Hanna, G. S. (1981). Can informal reading inventories reveal strengths and weaknesses in comprehension subskills? *The Reading Teacher*, 34, 263–267.

Searles, E. F. (1988). What's the value of an IRI? Is it being used? *Reading Horizons*, 28, 92–101.

Smith, G. G., & Keister, D. (1996). Learning about literacy through retelling. In M. D. Collins & B. G. Moss (Eds.), *Literacy assessment for today's schools*, pp. 16–31. Pittsburg, KS: College Reading Association.

Valencia, S., & Pearson, P. D. (1987). Reading assessment: Time for a change. *The Reading Teacher*, 40, 726–732.

Wade, S. E. (1990). Using think-alouds to assess comprehension. *The Reading Teacher*, 43(7), 442–451.

Walker, B. J. (1996). *Diagnostic teaching of reading*. Englewood, NJ: Prentice-Hall.

Warren, T. S. (1985). Informal reading inventories—A new format. Paper presented at the Southeast Regional Conference of the International Reading Association, Nashville, TN.

Winograd, P., Paris, S., & Bridge, C. (1991). Improving the assessment of literacy. *The Reading Teacher*, 45, 108–116.

Using Portfolio Assessment

What Are Portfolios?

Portfolios are collections of artifacts that illustrate a student's academic progress over time. Examples of artifacts from a literacy portfolio might include informal reading assessments, teacher observations, writing samples, student self-assessments, audio recordings of student reading, lists of books read by the student, and results of standardized testing. The materials included in the literacy portfolio are selected by both the student and the teacher. A baseline measure is established at the beginning of a school year so that growth can be documented throughout the year.

The CARP includes checklists to help establish a baseline and to chart progress over time. These checklists include the summary sheet, miscue analysis, observations checklist, reading goals form, and a portfolio analysis form that lists strengths, needs, and strategies to address needs.

Establishing a Baseline

After deciding to use portfolios, the teacher should determine at the beginning of the year (or term or grading period) the reading processes and behaviors that each child uses. Audio recordings of each child reading texts, portions of the CARP, or children's literature demonstrate the child's decoding strategies, fluency, and rate. By completing a miscue analysis, the teacher gathers information about patterns of decoding strategies. Measures of comprehension should include both narrative and expository retellings as well as think-alouds. The teacher might also want to include a sample of the child's writing, lists of books read, observations checklists, and goals for the specified term. A final important document to include would be the teacher's analysis of the accumulated information. All of this information provides the teacher with a baseline by which all other data gathered during the year can be measured. It is important to know where the child begins in order to determine how much progress the child makes.

Measuring Growth over Time

Periodically throughout the year, the teacher and/or the child will add information to the portfolio. This information could include a variety of work samples, reading tapes, think-alouds, and student/teacher evaluations of the work. It should include new examples of audiotaped reading, narrative and expository retellings from the CARP, and analyses of these items. In addition, the teacher may use anecdotal records or narrative notes to make comparisons between baseline data and subsequent data. The teacher may use this information to demonstrate, to both child and parents, the child's reading progress over the grading period. End-of-the-year analyses give a clear picture of the change in reading processes from the beginning of the year and allow for the development of goals for the next year.

Sample Portfolio (Kyle, Fifth Grade)

The sample portfolio that follows represents Kyle's baseline information for the beginning of his fifth grade year. The portfolio includes the narrative retelling and expository retelling sections of the CARP. Kyle's performance on these two sections of the CARP indicate that his instructional reading level is at his grade placement level. The teacher also completed an Observations checklist for oral reading and determined that Kyle has appropriate oral reading skills including decoding, phrasing, fluency, intonation, rate, and text pointing. Kyle's teacher also completed the Portfolio Analysis worksheet by outlining Kyle's strengths, his needs, and strategies to address those needs. With Kyle's assistance the teacher outlined goals for the beginning of the year. Kyle will check off the goals as he meets them and evaluate his own performance. The items included in this portfolio give the teacher information about Kyle's present reading performance and help to plan instruction. Additional administrations of the CARP or other reading tasks can be compared to this baseline data to help Kyle monitor his progress throughout the year.

CARP Summary Sheet

STUDENT Kyle GRADE 5 GENDER M AGE 10

SCHOOL Mercer TEACHER Jones

CARP GIVEN BY Jones DATE OF ADMINISTRATION 9-6-99

NARRATIVE RETELLING				EXPOSITORY RETELLING			
FORM A PASSAGES				FORM A PASSAGES			
Silent ___ Oral ___	Ind.	Inst.	Frust.	Silent ___ Oral ___	Ind.	Inst.	Frust.
GRADE ONE				GRADE ONE			
GRADE TWO	✓			GRADE TWO			
GRADE THREE	✓			GRADE THREE		✓	
GRADE FOUR		✓		GRADE FOUR		✓	
GRADE FIVE				GRADE FIVE		✓	
GRADE SIX				GRADE SIX			
GRADE SEVEN				GRADE SEVEN			
GRADE EIGHT				GRADE EIGHT			
GRADE NINE				GRADE NINE			

NARRATIVE RETELLING				EXPOSITORY RETELLING			
FORM B PASSAGES				FORM B PASSAGES			
Silent ___ Oral ___	Ind.	Inst.	Frust.	Silent ___ Oral ___	Ind.	Inst.	Frust.
GRADE ONE				GRADE ONE			
GRADE TWO				GRADE TWO			
GRADE THREE				GRADE THREE			
GRADE FOUR				GRADE FOUR			
GRADE FIVE		✓		GRADE FIVE			
GRADE SIX				GRADE SIX			
GRADE SEVEN				GRADE SEVEN			
GRADE EIGHT				GRADE EIGHT			
GRADE NINE				GRADE NINE			

WORD LIST SCORING SHEET

Kyle
9-99

GRADE 1		GRADE 2		GRADE 3	
____	1. birthday	✓	1. puppy	✓	1. sports
____	2. she	✓	2. apartment	✓	2. supper
____	3. car	✓	3. pound	✓	3. important
____	4. bike	✓	4. remember	✓	4. sign
____	5. blue	✓	5. around	–	5. thought
____	6. mother	✓	6. cricket	✓	6. other
____	7. friend	✓	7. suddenly	✓	7. should
____	8. bus	✓	8. animal	✓	8. problem
____	9. girl	✓	9. danger	✓	9. started
____	10. school	✓	10. curious	✓	10. report
____	11. dog	✓	11. enough	✓	11. thumb
____	12. coat	✓	12. choose	✓	12. stolen
____	13. book	✓	13. napkin	✓	13. rescue
____	14. it	–	14. warning	✓	14. collar
____	15. name	✓	15. quiet	✓	15. patch
____	16. ten	✓	16. speak	✓	16. ache
____	17. what	✓	17. raise	✓	17. accident
____	18. milk	✓	18. tooth	–	18. nephew
____	19. home	✓	19. skunk	–	19. pelican
____	20. have	✓	20. young	✓	20. throat
			IND		INST

18–20 correct	Independent
14–17 correct	Instructional
Fewer than 14 correct	Frustration

WORD LIST SCORING SHEET *(continued)*

Given 1st

Kyle 9-99

GRADE 4		GRADE 5		GRADE 6	
✓	1. neighbor	______	1. concert	______	1. decimal
✓	2. stroller	______	2. quickly	______	2. lemonade
–	3. sprinkler	______	3. famous	______	3. curtains
✓	4. offered	______	4. audience	______	4. kindergarten
✓	5. really	______	5. bowed	______	5. honorable
✓	6. railing	______	6. breathe	______	6. extraordinary
✓	7. ambulance	______	7. swept	______	7. observation
✓	8. wheelchair	______	8. sonata	______	8. neighbor
✓	9. hospital	______	9. continue	______	9. horizon
✓	10. knew	______	10. bravo	______	10. officially
✓	11. canyon	______	11. bodyguard	______	11. abrupt
–	12. erupting	______	12. epic	______	12. chaos
✓	13. gleeful	______	13. frantic	______	13. critical
✓	14. jeered	______	14. gorge	______	14. kerosene
✓	15. maze	______	15. illusion	______	15. lava
–	16. numb	______	16. jerky	______	16. marble
–	17. orphan	______	17. knolls	______	17. topaz
✓	18. quail	______	18. nuisance	______	18. unreasonable
✓	19. racket	______	19. ravine	______	19. woefully
✓	20. whine	______	20. tonsils	______	20. frothy

INST

18–20 correct	Independent
14–17 correct	Instructional
Fewer than 14 correct	Frustration

Second Grade

NARRATIVE

(294 words)

Form A—

Teacher's Copy

Kyle
9-99

1st Story

Ray's Best Friend

Ray's family was moving. They had lived in the same apartment building for as long as Ray could remember. They were moving to a house in the country.

"I don't want to go. I will miss my friends," said Ray.

"You will make new friends," said Ray's mother.

The day came for the move. Ray said goodbye to all of his friends. Ray would miss his best friend, Elliott, most of all.

The new house was bigger than the apartment. It had a big yard with a fence around it. Ray didn't have any friends at the new house, though. He was very lonely.

"I have an idea," his mother said one day. "Now that we have a big yard with a fence, would you like to get a puppy?"

"Oh, yes," said Ray. He had always wanted a puppy, but he could not have one in the apartment.

Ray and his mother went to the pound to find a puppy. There were lots of dogs and puppies at the pound. There were big dogs and little dogs. Ray walked around and looked in each of the cages. It was very difficult to pick just the right dog. In the very last cage, though, in the puppy room was a little brown puppy. It had short brown fur and was the smallest puppy in the pound. His eyes were big and his ears flopped down almost into his eyes.

"I want that one," said Ray, pointing to the smallest puppy.

When they got home, Ray's mother said, "Your puppy needs a name. What do you want its name to be?"

"Since he will be my best friend, I think I will name him Elliott," said Ray, remembering his best friend in the apartment building.

No word errors

Second Grade

NARRATIVE

Kyle's Retelling

9-99

This kid, Ray, is moving. Ray didn't want to go because he would miss his friends. When the day came, Ray said goodbye to everybody. Ray didn't like his new house because there were no kids to play with. Then Mother said, "Would you like a puppy?" They went to the dog pound to get one. He picked the littlest one there. He named him Elliott.

Retelling Protocol

Purpose-Setting Statement: Ray finds a new best friend when he moves to the country. Read this story to find out who is Ray's new best friend.

Ray's Best Friend

CHARACTERS (4 points each)

✓ Ray ✓ Mother ✓ Puppy (Elliott) ✓ Boy (Elliott)

SETTING (6 points each)

____ House in the country ✓ Pound

PLOT (12 points each)

✓ 1. Ray did not want to move because he would miss his friends.

✓ 2. Ray said goodbye to all of his friends.

✓ 3. Ray was lonely in his new home.

✓ 4. Mother took Ray to the pound to get a puppy.

✓ 5. Ray selected the smallest puppy in the pound.

RESOLUTION (12 points)

✓ 6. Ray named his new puppy Elliott.

		READING LEVELS	
Character Total	16	(Independent)	(Above 85 Points)
Setting Total	6	Instructional	70–84 Points
Plot Total	60	Frustration	Below 70 Points
Resolution Total	12		
TOTAL POINTS	94		

OBSERVATIONS

	Inappropriate				Appropriate
Includes detail	1	2	3	4	(5)
Uses prior knowledge to establish story line	1	2	3	(4)	5
Infers beyond text	1	2	(3)	4	5
	Out of Sequence				**In Sequence**
Tells story in correct sequence	1	2	3	4	(5)
	Verbatim				**In Own Words**
Restates story verbatim	1	2	3	(4)	5

Third Grade

NARRATIVE

(494 words)

Form A—

Teacher's Copy

Kyle
9-99
2nd Story

Sports Day

Liza

"We are having Sports Day at school," Lisa said to her dad. "I have to do a report about a sport. I can't decide what to tell about." "I'll help you think of something after supper," said Dad. "Now I have a surprise for you. You know that the Bears have an important game today. Well, we are going to that game." "Oh, great!" shouted Lisa. Then she said, "I know! I can be a reporter and tell about this game on Sports Day." Then Lisa went to get the sign that she took to every game. It was for the player she liked best, Henry Wills. If the Bears could win today's game, they would be in first place. This was a very important ball game. Lisa thought the Bears could win. She said to her dad, "They played a great game the other day. If they can play like that today, they should win."

At the game, Lisa and her dad sat in back of the Bears. They would have no problem seeing the game. At last the ball game started. Lisa held up her sign and shouted, "Go, Henry, go!" The other players, the Owls, were up at bat first. They made one home run. Then the Bears were up at bat. The first player made a home run! Lisa took pictures of the ball game. She didn't want to forget a thing. Soon it was the last time for the Owls to be up at bat. They had five runs, and so did the Bears. But the Owls couldn't get a hit. Now the Bears were going to bat. They needed to hit one home run. Henry Wills was the first one up. The ball raced at Henry. He hit a home run! The Bears were now in first place! "Lisa!" said Dad. "We should talk to Henry Wills."

Before going down to the players, Lisa wanted to show her sign again. She started to put up her sign, but somehow she let go of it. The sign fell down on Henry Wills! Henry read the sign and laughed. He looked up and saw Lisa. He held up the sign and asked, "Is this your sign?" "Yes," said Lisa. "Thank you for getting it." Then she said, "I'm doing a report about this game. May I talk with you?" "Yes," said Henry.

The first thing Lisa asked was, "How did you get to be the best?" "I have worked at it," said Henry. "Sometimes it was all work. But many times it is fun, too. Today was one of the fun times!" Lisa talked some more with Henry. Then she said, "I should let you go. Thanks, Mr. Wills." "Wait!" said Henry. He got a ball and signed it. "This is for you," he said. "Thanks, Mr. Wills!" said Lisa. Then Dad took the best picture of the game. It was a picture of Lisa and Henry Wills.

Third Grade

NARRATIVE

Kyle's Retelling

9-99

Lisa has to make a report about a sport for school. Her dad tells her he's taking her to a Bears baseball game. Then she gets this idea that she can write her report about the game. Her favorite player is a guy named Wills; she made a sign for him. Well, they went to the game, and the score was tied. Of course, Wills hits a home run and saves the day. Lisa meets Wills and he gave her an autographed ball. They have their picture made and Lisa gets a great report that she probably made an A on.

Retelling Protocol

Purpose-Setting Statement: Lisa and her father go to a Bears baseball game. Read this story to find out what happens to Lisa.

Sports Day

CHARACTERS (3 points each)

✓ Lisa ✓ Lisa's dad ✓ Henry Wills

SETTING (6 points)

✓ Bears game (stadium)

PLOT (14 points each)

✓ 1. Lisa's school is having Sports Day and she must report about a sport.
✓ 2. Lisa's father takes her to a Bears baseball game.
✓ 3. Lisa takes a sign for her favorite player.
✓ 4. Wills hits a home run, which wins the game.
____ 5. Lisa drops the sign on Henry Wills.

RESOLUTION (15 points)

✓ 6. Lisa gets to interview Henry Wills for her report and has her picture taken with him.

		READING LEVELS	
Character Total	9	(Independent)	(Above 85 Points)
Setting Total	6	Instructional	70–84 Points
Plot Total	56	Frustration	Below 70 Points
Resolution Total	15		
TOTAL POINTS	86		

OBSERVATIONS

	Inappropriate				Appropriate
Includes detail	1	2	3	4	(5)
Uses prior knowledge to establish story line	1	2	3	4	(5)
Infers beyond text *Infers about the grade*	1	2	3	(4)	5
	Out of Sequence				**In Sequence**
Tells story in correct sequence	1	2	3	4	(5)
	Verbatim				**In Own Words**
Restates story verbatim	1	2	3	4	(5)

Fourth Grade

NARRATIVE

(296 words)

Form A—

Teacher's Copy

Kyle
9-99
3rd Story

A Special Trade

TP
Bartholomew is Nelly's neighbor. When Nelly was very small, he would take her for a walk every day in her stroller to Mrs. Pringle's vegetable garden.

Bartholomew never pushed too fast. When they were coming to a bump, Bartholomew always told Nelly:

"Hang on, Nelly!" he would always say. "Here's a bump!"

Nelly would shout "BUMP!" as she rode over it.

If they saw a nice dog they'd stop and pet it, but if it was mean Bartholomew would shoo it away. scoot

When Mrs. Pringle's sprinkler was on, he would say, "Get ready, get set, CHARRRRGE!" Prinkles

Nelly would shout "Wheeeee!" as he pushed her through it.

When Nelly began to walk, Bartholomew took her by the hand. "No–No!" she cried, pulling her hand back. Nelly didn't want any help, so Bartholomew offered his hand only when she really needed it. He knew that Nelly was getting older. putting

Bartholomew was getting older, too. He needed a walking stick now, so they both walked very slowly. When they walked up stairs, they both held on to the railing.

The neighbors called them "ham and eggs" because they were always together. Even on Halloween they were together . . . and on the coldest day of winter when everyone was inside.

One day Bartholomew went out alone and fell down the stairs. An ambulance came to take him to the hospital, and then he was gone for a long time.

When Bartholomew came home, he was in a wheelchair. The smile was gone from his eyes.

"I guess our walks are over," he said. "No they aren't," said Nelly. "I can take you for walks now." She knew just how to do it, too. Nice and easy, not too fast.

Fourth Grade

NARRATIVE

Kyle's Retelling

9-99

Nelly's neighbor, Bart something, takes her for walks when she's little and holds her hand so she doesn't fall. Then the guy gets older and he walks slower, so Nelly helps him to walk like he helped her. Then one day the guy falls down, and they have to call an ambulance. When he comes home he's in a wheelchair, and he's worried that he can't walk with Nelly anymore. But Nelly takes him for walks in his wheelchair.

Retelling Protocol

Purpose-Setting Statement: This is the story of a special relationship between Nelly and Bartholomew. Read this story to find out what happens as Nelly and Bartholomew grow older.

A Special Trade

CHARACTERS (5 points each)

✓ Nelly ✓ Bartholomew

SETTING (2 points each)

___ Mrs. Pringle's vegetable garden ___ Stairs ___ Various seasons

PLOT (14 points each)

___ 1. Bartholomew takes Nelly for walks in her stroller.
✓ 2. Bartholomew holds Nelly's hand during walks as Nelly grows older.
✓ 3. Bartholomew needs a walking stick and walks slower.
✓ 4. Bartholomew falls down stairs and is taken to the hospital.
✓ 5. Bartholomew returns in a wheelchair.

RESOLUTION (14 points)

✓ 6. Nelly takes Bartholomew for nice and easy walks.

Character Total	10
Setting Total	0
Plot Total	56
Resolution Total	14
TOTAL POINTS	80

READING LEVELS

Independent	Above 85 Points
Instructional (circled)	70–84 Points
Frustration	Below 70 Points

OBSERVATIONS

	Inappropriate				Appropriate
Includes detail	1	2	3	(4)	5
Uses prior knowledge to establish story line	1	2	3	(4)	5
Infers beyond text	1	2	(3)	4	5
	Out of Sequence				**In Sequence**
Tells story in correct sequence	1	2	3	(4)	5
	Verbatim				**In Own Words**
Restates story verbatim	1	2	3	(4)	5

Fifth Grade

NARRATIVE

(317 words)

Form B—

Teacher's Copy

Kyle
9-99
4th Story

Making French Toast

Bernie was teaching Bonnie how to make French toast. Bonnie was in a hurry, she was hungry.

"First, you need a mixing bowl, a fork, and a frying pan," Bernie said slowly.

"Done," said Bonnie.

"Now, to make eight slices of French toast, you need two eggs, a dash of cinnamon and sugar, half a teaspoon of salt, and two thirds of a cup of milk," said Bernie.

"Okay, but don't I need bread? It's French toast, you know," Bonnie pointed out.

"Don't rush me," Bernie complained. "I was going to say eight slices of bread next, also two tablespoons of butter."

"Sorry," said Bonnie.

"Now put the eggs, milk, cinnamon, sugar, and salt into the bowl. Use the fork to beat them until they're foamy. Melt the butter in the frying pan over a medium flame. Then dip a slice of bread in the egg mixture, and brown the slice on each side in the frying pan . . . Hey!" Bernie yelped.

Bonnie had stuck a plain piece of bread in the buttered frying pan and was pouring the egg mixture over it. "I figured this way was faster," she said. "I'm so hungry!"

"But that's wrong!" cried Bernie. He looked at the mess in the frying pan. "I was hungry too," he moaned. "Now I've lost my appetite."

Bonnie nodded sadly. "Me too," she said.

Fifth Grade

NARRATIVE

Kyle's Retelling

9-99

There were these two friends, Bernie and Bonnie, and they were going to make French toast. Bernie was going to show Bonnie. Bernie told Bonnie all the cooking stuff she would need and all the food. So Bonnie puts the bread in the pan and throws the egg stuff all over it. Bernie told her that's not the way to do it, but she didn't listen.

Retelling Protocol

Purpose-Setting Statement: This story tells about two children who are making French toast. Find out what happens to Bonnie's French toast.

Making French Toast

CHARACTERS (4 points each)

__✓__ Bernie __✓__ Bonnie

SETTING (10 points)

__✓__ Kitchen

PLOT (14 points each)

__✓__ 1. Bernie teaches Bonnie to make French toast.

__✓__ 2. Bernie tells Bonnie that she needs a bowl, fork, and frying pan.

__✓__ 3. Bernie tells Bonnie what ingredients she needs.

______ 4. Bonnie is in a hurry because she is hungry.

__✓__ 5. Bonnie puts the bread in the pan and puts the egg mixture over it.

RESOLUTION (12 points)

______ 6. Bonnie and Bernie lose their appetites.

Character Total	8
Setting Total	10
Plot Total	56
Resolution Total	0
TOTAL POINTS	74

READING LEVELS

Independent	Above 85 Points
Instructional (circled)	70–84 Points
Frustration	Below 70 Points

OBSERVATIONS

	Inappropriate				Appropriate
Includes detail	1	2	(3)	4	5
Uses prior knowledge to establish story line	1	2	(3)	4	5
Infers beyond text	1	2	(3)	4	5
	Out of Sequence				**In Sequence**
Tells story in correct sequence	1	2	(3)	4	5
	Verbatim				**In Own Words**
Restates story verbatim	1	2	3	4	(5)

Miscue Analysis Worksheet

PASSAGE CARP Narrative STUDENT Kyle

FORM B LEVEL 5 DATE 9-6-99

Text Word	Miscue	Is Miscue Graphically Similar? (Y/N) Beg.	Mid.	End.	Is Meaning Changed? (Y/N)	Is Miscue Corrected? (Y/N)
cinnamon	cimamon	Y	N	Y	N	N
foamy	floating	Y	N	Y	Y	N
yelped	yelled	Y	Y	N	N	N
appetite	apart	Y	N	Y	Y	N

How Big Is Big? (Level 3.0)

TOPIC: Big Animals

PRIOR	RECALL	
	✓	**1.*** Some animals are so huge that it's hard to even picture them in your mind.
✓		**2.** The tallest animal is the giraffe.
	✓	**3.** It is as tall as three grown-up people.
	✓	**4.** It has a very long neck and very long legs.
	✓	**5.** A giraffe is so tall that it can see things far away.
	✓	**6.** If it sees something frightening, the giraffe has time to run away.
✓		**7.** The elephant is the biggest animal on land.
	✓	**8.** An elephant can weigh as much as sixty grown-up people!
	✓	**9.** Elephants live in herds.
	✓	**10.** Some herds have as few as four or five elephants, but others have as many as a thousand.
		11. The whale shark is longer than four cars.
		12. It weighs as much as two elephants.
		13. The whale shark is gentle and eats only small plants and fish.
✓		**14.** The biggest animal that has ever lived on land or sea is the blue whale.
	✓	**15.** The blue whale weighs more than one thousand grown-up people and is longer than seven cars.

*Stated main idea

OBSERVATIONS

	Inadequate				Adequate
Has prior knowledge	1	2	(3)	4	5
Recalls information	1	2	3	(4)	5
Uses prior knowledge to infer	1	2	(3)	4	5
Recognizes stated main idea	1	2	3	4	(5)

	Verbatim				In Own Words
Restates text verbatim	1	2	3	(4)	5

OTHER FACTUAL INFORMATION GIVEN BY THE STUDENT

Third Grade
EXPOSITORY

Kyle's
Retelling

9-99

PRIOR RESPONSES

- The tallest animal is the giraffe. (#2)
- The elephant is the biggest animal on land. (#7)
- The biggest animal that has ever lived on land or sea is the blue whale. (#14)

RECALL RESPONSES

- Well, some animals are so big you can't even imagine how big they are. (#1)
- A giraffe is as tall as three grown-ups. (#3)
- It has a really long neck and really long legs. (#4)
- The giraffe can see so far away that it can get away before it's killed. (#5, #6)
- Elephants weigh as much as sixty grown-ups. They're really big! (#8)
- They live in herds. Sometimes the herds are big and sometimes they're little. (#9, #10)
- The blue whale was the biggest animal that ever lived and it weighed like 1000 grown-ups. It was way bigger than an elephant. (#15)
- A shark is big too.

Antarctica (Level 4.0)

TOPIC: Antarctica

PRIOR	RECALL	
✓		**1.** Surrounding the South Pole is the continent of Antarctica.
✓		**2.*** Antarctica is the coldest place on Earth.
	✓	**3.** In summer the average temperature is below freezing.
	✓	**4.** In summer there are long periods of daylight.
	✓	**5.** The ice cap is a mile thick in some places.
	✓	**6.** Huge sheets of ice are called glaciers.
	✓	**7.** When chunks of ice break off from glaciers, they form icebergs.
	✓	**8.** The continent is divided by a large mountain range with some peaks over 14,000 feet.
		9. There is no life in the interior of the continent.
	✓	**10.** In the surrounding waters and along the coasts are fish, birds, whales, and six kinds of seals.
	✓	**11.** One type of seal is the leopard seal, which preys on penguins and other seals.
	✓	**12.** The most common Antarctica seal is the crabeater, which eats krill.
		13. Two Antarctica flying birds are the blue-eyed shag and the southern giant fulmar.
✓		**14.** The most familiar Antarctica bird is the penguin.
	✓	**15.** Penguins' bodies are protected from the cold by a thick layer of fat.

*Stated main idea

OBSERVATIONS

	Inadequate				Adequate
Has prior knowledge	1	2	(3)	4	5
Recalls information	1	2	3	(4)	5
Uses prior knowledge to infer	1	2	3	(4)	5
Recognizes stated main idea	1	2	3	4	(5)

	Verbatim				In Own Words
Restates text verbatim	1	2	3	(4)	5

OTHER FACTUAL INFORMATION GIVEN BY THE STUDENT

Fourth Grade

EXPOSITORY

Kyle's Retelling

9-99

PRIOR RESPONSES

- It's about the coldest place there is. (#2)
- The South Pole is there. (#1)
- Penguins live there. (#14)

RECALL RESPONSES

- Let's see. It gets below freezing in the summer and they have really long days. (#3, #4)
- It's covered by an ice cap that's one mile thick. (#5)
- It has big pieces of ice called glaciers, and they make icebergs if they fall off and float in the ocean. You know, those can be really dangerous to ships and boats. (#6, #7)
- There's some big mountains in the middle of Antarctica. (#8)
- They have lots of fish, birds, and seals and whales. (#10)
- Two kinds of seals are leopards and crabeaters. (#11, #12)
- The penguins have fat to keep them warm when it's really cold. (#15)

How the Electric Eel Makes Electricity (Level 5.0)

TOPIC: Electric Eels

PRIOR	RECALL	
	✓	**1.** Unlike other fish, the electric eel has a fin along its stomach, which helps the eel move in a wavy motion.
	✓	**2.** The electric eel moves only to come to the top for air.
	✓	**3.** The eel must come to the top for air every fifteen minutes.
	✓	**4.*** Some of the electric eel's muscles have developed to make more electricity than normal muscles.
	✓	**5.** The eel has three electric organs: the main, the Sachs, and the Hunters.
	✓	**6.** The main organ sends out a strong charge.
		7. The Sachs organ sends out a weak charge.
		8. The Hunters organ helps the other two organs.
	✓	**9.** The electric eel is a blind, toothless, slow-moving fish.
		10. The Sachs organ sends a weak electric charge out the tail and back to receptor pits in the eel's head to create an electric field around the eel.
	✓	**11.** When some object comes into this field, the eel can tell what it is and how far away it is.
	✓	**12.** If the object is something the eel wants to eat, it sends out a huge electric charge.

*Stated main idea

OBSERVATIONS

	Inadequate				Adequate
Has prior knowledge	1	(2)	3	4	5
Recalls information	1	2	(3)	4	5
Uses prior knowledge to infer	1	2	(3)	4	5
Recognizes stated main idea	1	2	3	4	(5)

	Verbatim				In Own Words
Restates text verbatim	1	2	3	(4)	5

OTHER FACTUAL INFORMATION GIVEN BY THE STUDENT

The eel stings people with electricity

It looks like a snake

Fifth Grade

EXPOSITORY

Kyle's Retelling

9-99

PRIOR RESPONSES

- The eel stings people with electricity.
- It looks like a snake.

RECALL RESPONSES

- The eel moves in a wavy way like a snake because it has a fin on its stomach. (#1)
- It comes to the top of the water every fifteen minutes to get air. (#2, #3)
- It has some special muscles that make its electricity. (#4)
- It has three things that send out charges: the main, the Sachs, and the Hunter. Only the main one has a strong shock. (#5, #6)
- The eel is blind, and it don't have teeth. (#9)
- It can tell when something like a fish is close. If it wants to eat the fish, it just shocks it. (#11, #12)

Observations Checklist—Oral Reading

STUDENT Kyle **TEXT** CARP—5th Expository

	Appropriate	Needs Work
Automatic Decoding	✓	
Phrasing	✓	
Fluency	✓	
Intonation	✓	
Rate	120 wpm oral 150 wpm silent	
Text Pointing	✓	

Portfolio Analysis

STUDENT Kyle DATE 9-6-99

MATERIALS Narrative & expository retellings—CARP—Baseline

1. STRENGTHS

- instructional level for both narrative and expository at grade level
- can decode most words
- uses prior knowledge
- fluent
- makes inferences some of the time

2. NEEDS

- begin reading more challenging materials
- make better connections between prior knowledge and text materials for better inferencing
- continue reading wide variety of books

3. STRATEGIES TO ADDRESS NEEDS

- complete a think-aloud from CARP to gain better picture of comprehension processes
- keep reading list of books that are easy, on level, and challenging

Reading Goals

STUDENT Kyle

Goals	Completed	How Did I Do?
Read 5 challenging books		
Practice think-aloud		
Read book repeatedly to improve rate—record		
Make new recording of read-aloud—CARP		

The Assessment Tool

Classroom Assessment of Reading Processes Assessment Materials

This section contains the assessment material for the CARP. Included are the teacher and student materials for narrative and expository retelling passages, as well as teacher scripts and student passages for the think-alouds.

Word Lists

WORD LIST 1

birthday	dog
she	coat
car	book
bike	it
blue	name
mother	ten
friend	what
bus	milk
girl	home
school	have

WORD LIST 2

puppy

apartment

pound

remember

around

cricket

suddenly

animal

danger

curious

enough

choose

napkin

warning

quiet

speak

raise

tooth

skunk

young

WORD LIST 3

sports
supper
important
sign
thought
other
should
problem
started
report
thumb
stolen
rescue
collar
patch
ache
accident
nephew
pelican
throat

WORD LIST 4

neighbor

stroller

sprinkler

offered

really

railing

ambulance

wheelchair

hospital

knew

canyon

erupting

gleeful

jeered

maze

numb

orphan

quail

racket

whine

WORD LIST 5

concert	bodyguard
quickly	epic
famous	frantic
audience	gorge
bowed	illusion
breathe	jerky
swept	knolls
sonata	nuisance
continue	ravine
bravo	tonsils

WORD LIST 6

decimal

lemonade

curtains

kindergarten

honorable

extraordinary

observation

neighbor

horizon

officially

abrupt

chaos

critical

kerosene

lava

marble

topaz

unreasonable

woefully

frothy

WORD LIST 7

patio

lizard

character

vacation

schedule

political

revolution

immense

recognize

tsunami

continent

enormous

compressed

shallow

preceding

trough

civilization

colossal

accurate

volcanic

WORD LIST 8

situation

devastation

unbeknownst

disgruntled

bedraggled

opportunity

debris

biopsy

malignant

terrified

obstructing

forlorn

serious

imagine

havoc

momentous

amiable

horrifying

comprehend

gratified

WORD LIST 9

reverie

astonished

metallic

apparently

transfixed

consultation

specimen

extinct

existence

threatening

encountered

acknowledge

visibility

eternity

semester

university

flabbergasted

suspected

gesturing

encounter

WORD LIST SCORING SHEET

GRADE 1		GRADE 2		GRADE 3	
________	1. birthday	________	1. puppy	________	1. sports
________	2. she	________	2. apartment	________	2. supper
________	3. car	________	3. pound	________	3. important
________	4. bike	________	4. remember	________	4. sign
________	5. blue	________	5. around	________	5. thought
________	6. mother	________	6. cricket	________	6. other
________	7. friend	________	7. suddenly	________	7. should
________	8. bus	________	8. animal	________	8. problem
________	9. girl	________	9. danger	________	9. started
________	10. school	________	10. curious	________	10. report
________	11. dog	________	11. enough	________	11. thumb
________	12. coat	________	12. choose	________	12. stolen
________	13. book	________	13. napkin	________	13. rescue
________	14. it	________	14. warning	________	14. collar
________	15. name	________	15. quiet	________	15. patch
________	16. ten	________	16. speak	________	16. ache
________	17. what	________	17. raise	________	17. accident
________	18. milk	________	18. tooth	________	18. nephew
________	19. home	________	19. skunk	________	19. pelican
________	20. have	________	20. young	________	20. throat

18–20 correct	Independent
14–17 correct	Instructional
Fewer than 14 correct	Frustration

WORD LIST SCORING SHEET *(continued)*

GRADE 4		GRADE 5		GRADE 6	
______	1. neighbor	______	1. concert	______	1. decimal
______	2. stroller	______	2. quickly	______	2. lemonade
______	3. sprinkler	______	3. famous	______	3. curtains
______	4. offered	______	4. audience	______	4. kindergarten
______	5. really	______	5. bowed	______	5. honorable
______	6. railing	______	6. breathe	______	6. extraordinary
______	7. ambulance	______	7. swept	______	7. observation
______	8. wheelchair	______	8. sonata	______	8. neighbor
______	9. hospital	______	9. continue	______	9. horizon
______	10. knew	______	10. bravo	______	10. officially
______	11. canyon	______	11. bodyguard	______	11. abrupt
______	12. erupting	______	12. epic	______	12. chaos
______	13. gleeful	______	13. frantic	______	13. critical
______	14. jeered	______	14. gorge	______	14. kerosene
______	15. maze	______	15. illusion	______	15. lava
______	16. numb	______	16. jerky	______	16. marble
______	17. orphan	______	17. knolls	______	17. topaz
______	18. quail	______	18. nuisance	______	18. unreasonable
______	19. racket	______	19. ravine	______	19. woefully
______	20. whine	______	20. tonsils	______	20. frothy

18–20 correct	Independent
14–17 correct	Instructional
Fewer than 14 correct	Frustration

WORD LIST SCORING SHEET *(continued)*

GRADE 7

________	1. patio
________	2. lizard
________	3. character
________	4. vacation
________	5. schedule
________	6. political
________	7. revolution
________	8. immense
________	9. recognize
________	10. tsunami
________	11. continent
________	12. enormous
________	13. compressed
________	14. shallow
________	15. preceding
________	16. trough
________	17. civilization
________	18. colossal
________	19. accurate
________	20. volcanic

GRADE 8

________	1. situation
________	2. devastation
________	3. unbeknownst
________	4. disgruntled
________	5. bedraggled
________	6. opportunity
________	7. debris
________	8. biopsy
________	9. malignant
________	10. terrified
________	11. obstructing
________	12. forlorn
________	13. serious
________	14. imagine
________	15. havoc
________	16. momentous
________	17. amiable
________	18. horrifying
________	19. comprehend
________	20. gratified

GRADE 9

________	1. reverie
________	2. astonished
________	3. metallic
________	4. apparently
________	5. transfixed
________	6. consultation
________	7. specimen
________	8. extinct
________	9. existence
________	10. threatening
________	11. encountered
________	12. acknowledge
________	13. visibility
________	14. eternity
________	15. semester
________	16. university
________	17. flabbergasted
________	18. suspected
________	19. gesturing
________	20. occurrence

18–20 correct	Independent
14–17 correct	Instructional
Fewer than 14 correct	Frustration

Narrative Retelling

Brief Directions for Administering Retelling Passages

Step One. Administer the word lists before the narrative text to determine the appropriate entry level retelling passage. Select a word list that is one year below the student's grade placement, and ask the student to read each word orally. Proceed through the word lists until an instructional level has been reached. Select a retelling passage that corresponds to the highest *independent* level reached on the word lists.

Step Two. Two forms of retelling passages are provided. You may want to use one form as oral reading passages and one as silent reading passages. Tell the student that he or she will be reading a story orally or silently and will be asked to retell the story when he or she is finished. Read the purpose-setting statement for the chosen story.

Step Three. Ask the student to read the story orally. As the student reads, mark any deviations from the printed text. The following marking system is suggested:

TYPE OF STUDENT ERROR	TEACHER'S MARKING
Substitutions/mispronunciations	Write the student's response above the text word.
Insertions	Write the added word(s) above the text line and indicate the location of the insertion using the symbol ^ .
Omissions	Circle the omitted word(s).
Teacher provided	Write "TP" above any word that is pronounced or provided for the student.

The following miscues are considered metacognitive attempts of the student to make sense of the reading and should not be counted as errors. The teacher may choose to mark these miscues because they do provide valuable information for understanding the student's processing of text.

TYPE OF MISCUE	TEACHER'S MARKING
Repetitions	Draw a straight line above all words and phrases that are repeated.
Self-corrections	When the student corrects any error, mark the correction by writing a "C" over the miscue.
Synonyms	When the student provides a synonym for a printed word, write the substituted word above the text and draw a line through the printed word.

Step Four. After the student completes the oral reading of the text, remove or turn over the text. Ask the student to retell the story by saying, **"Tell this story as if you were telling it to a friend who has not heard it before."** Mark student responses on the protocol sheet.

At the end of the retelling, the teacher may want to prompt or ask questions about any area the student has neglected to include. These prompted responses should not be included in the scoring, but they may provide additional important information.

Step Five. Score the retelling using the scoring matrix at the bottom of the protocol page. If the student's performance falls in the independent level, have the student repeat the process with the next higher level of text. The student should continue reading and retelling texts until the frustration level has been reached. If the first text is at the instructional level, have the student read the next lower level passage and continue backward to find the independent level before continuing higher to find the frustration level. If the first text is at the frustration level, proceed backward until instructional and independent levels of reading have been reached.

Narrative Passages and Rubrics: Form A

First Grade

NARRATIVE

(231 words)

Form A—

Teacher's Copy

Penny Gets Wheels

It was Penny's birthday. She got ten one dollar bills. "I am rich, and I am older now," she said to her mom. "I don't need to walk anymore. I will go on wheels."

"Wheels?" asked her mom.

"Yes," said Penny. "I would like a car, but I know I'm not rich enough or old enough. I think I will buy a bike."

"You'll need a lot of money to buy a bike," said her mom.

"Ten dollars is a lot of money," Penny said.

Then she ran outside and down the street to the sports shop on the corner.

"Today is my birthday," she said to the salesperson. "I would like to buy that blue racing bike. How much does it cost?"

"This bike costs one hundred dollars," he said.

Penny pointed to another bike. "How much is that one?"

"Ninety-one dollars," said the salesperson.

"I'm not that rich," Penny said.

Penny looked at many things. But she didn't want to buy anything she saw. Then she saw some roller skates. They cost nine dollars. She picked up a skate and spun its wheels.

"I guess these are all I have enough to buy," she said.

Penny paid for the skates. She went outside, put them on, and started to skate home. She still wished she were old enough to have a car or rich enough to own a bike.

Retelling Protocol

Purpose-Setting Statement: It is Penny's birthday. Read this story to find out what Penny gets for her birthday.

Penny Gets Wheels

CHARACTERS (2 points each)

_____ Penny _____ Mother _____ Salesperson

SETTING (5 points each)

_____ Penny's house _____ Sports shop

PLOT (14 points each)

_____ 1. Penny got ten dollars for her birthday.

_____ 2. Penny feels rich.

_____ 3. Penny would like to buy a car but decides she is not old enough or rich enough.

_____ 4. She goes to the sports shop to buy a bike.

_____ 5. Penny does not have enough money for a bike.

RESOLUTION (14 points)

_____ 6. She decides to buy roller skates.

Character Total	_____
Setting Total	_____
Plot Total	_____
Resolution Total	_____
TOTAL POINTS	_____

READING LEVELS	
Independent	Above 85 Points
Instructional	70–84 Points
Frustration	Below 70 Points

NARRATIVE RETELLING FORM A

OBSERVATIONS

	Inappropriate				**Appropriate**
Includes detail	1	2	3	4	5
Uses prior knowledge to establish story line	1	2	3	4	5
Infers beyond text	1	2	3	4	5
	Out of Sequence				**In Sequence**
Tells story in correct sequence	1	2	3	4	5
	Verbatim				**In Own Words**
Restates story verbatim	1	2	3	4	5

Second Grade

NARRATIVE

(294 words)

Form A—

Teacher's Copy

Ray's Best Friend

Ray's family was moving. They had lived in the same apartment building for as long as Ray could remember. They were moving to a house in the country.

"I don't want to go. I will miss my friends," said Ray.

"You will make new friends," said Ray's mother.

The day came for the move. Ray said goodbye to all of his friends. Ray would miss his best friend, Elliott, most of all.

The new house was bigger than the apartment. It had a big yard with a fence around it. Ray didn't have any friends at the new house, though. He was very lonely.

"I have an idea," his mother said one day. "Now that we have a big yard with a fence, would you like to get a puppy?"

"Oh, yes," said Ray. He had always wanted a puppy, but he could not have one in the apartment.

Ray and his mother went to the pound to find a puppy. There were lots of dogs and puppies at the pound. There were big dogs and little dogs. Ray walked around and looked in each of the cages. It was very difficult to pick just the right dog. In the very last cage, though, in the puppy room was a little brown puppy. It had short brown fur and was the smallest puppy in the pound. His eyes were big and his ears flopped down almost into his eyes.

"I want that one," said Ray, pointing to the smallest puppy.

When they got home, Ray's mother said, "Your puppy needs a name. What do you want its name to be?"

"Since he will be my best friend, I think I will name him Elliott," said Ray, remembering his best friend in the apartment building.

Retelling Protocol

Purpose-Setting Statement: Ray finds a new best friend when he moves to the country. Read this story to find out who is Ray's new best friend.

Ray's Best Friend

CHARACTERS (4 points each)

_____ Ray _____ Mother _____ Puppy (Elliott) _____ Boy (Elliott)

SETTING (6 points each)

_____ House in the country _____ Pound

PLOT (12 points each)

_____ 1. Ray did not want to move because he would miss his friends.

_____ 2. Ray said goodbye to all of his friends.

_____ 3. Ray was lonely in his new home.

_____ 4. Mother took Ray to the pound to get a puppy.

_____ 5. Ray selected the smallest puppy in the pound.

RESOLUTION (12 points)

_____ 6. Ray named his new puppy Elliott.

Character Total	_____
Setting Total	_____
Plot Total	_____
Resolution Total	_____
TOTAL POINTS	_____

READING LEVELS	
Independent	Above 85 Points
Instructional	70–84 Points
Frustration	Below 70 Points

OBSERVATIONS

	Inappropriate				Appropriate
Includes detail	1	2	3	4	5
Uses prior knowledge to establish story line	1	2	3	4	5
Infers beyond text	1	2	3	4	5
	Out of Sequence				**In Sequence**
Tells story in correct sequence	1	2	3	4	5
	Verbatim				**In Own Words**
Restates story verbatim	1	2	3	4	5

Third Grade

NARRATIVE

(494 words)

Form A—

Teacher's Copy

Sports Day

"We are having Sports Day at school," Lisa said to her dad. "I have to do a report about a sport. I can't decide what to tell about." "I'll help you think of something after supper," said Dad. "Now I have a surprise for you. You know that the Bears have an important game today. Well, we are going to that game." "Oh, great!" shouted Lisa. Then she said, "I know! I can be a reporter and tell about this game on Sports Day." Then Lisa went to get the sign that she took to every game. It was for the player she liked best, Henry Wills. If the Bears could win today's game, they would be in first place. This was a very important ball game. Lisa thought the Bears could win. She said to her dad, "They played a great game the other day. If they can play like that today, they should win."

At the game, Lisa and her dad sat in back of the Bears. They would have no problem seeing the game. At last the ball game started. Lisa held up her sign and shouted, "Go, Henry, go!" The other players, the Owls, were up at bat first. They made one home run. Then the Bears were up at bat. The first player made a home run! Lisa took pictures of the ball game. She didn't want to forget a thing. Soon it was the last time for the Owls to be up at bat. They had five runs, and so did the Bears. But the Owls couldn't get a hit. Now the Bears were going to bat. They needed to hit one home run. Henry Wills was the first one up. The ball raced at Henry. He hit a home run! The Bears were now in first place! "Lisa!" said Dad. "We should talk to Henry Wills."

Before going down to the players, Lisa wanted to show her sign again. She started to put up her sign, but somehow she let go of it. The sign fell down on Henry Wills! Henry read the sign and laughed. He looked up and saw Lisa. He held up the sign and asked, "Is this your sign?" "Yes," said Lisa. "Thank you for getting it." Then she said, "I'm doing a report about this game. May I talk with you?" "Yes," said Henry.

The first thing Lisa asked was, "How did you get to be the best?" "I have worked at it," said Henry. "Sometimes it was all work. But many times it is fun, too. Today was one of the fun times!" Lisa talked some more with Henry. Then she said, "I should let you go. Thanks, Mr. Wills." "Wait!" said Henry. He got a ball and signed it. "This is for you," he said. "Thanks, Mr. Wills!" said Lisa. Then Dad took the best picture of the game. It was a picture of Lisa and Henry Wills.

Retelling Protocol

Purpose-Setting Statement: Lisa and her father go to a Bears baseball game. Read this story to find out what happens to Lisa.

Sports Day

CHARACTERS (3 points each)

_____ Lisa _____ Lisa's dad _____ Henry Wills

SETTING (6 points)

_____ Bears game (stadium)

PLOT (14 points each)

_____ 1. Lisa's school is having Sports Day and she must report about a sport.

_____ 2. Lisa's father takes her to a Bears baseball game.

_____ 3. Lisa takes a sign for her favorite player.

_____ 4. Wills hits a home run, which wins the game.

_____ 5. Lisa drops the sign on Henry Wills.

RESOLUTION (15 points)

_____ 6. Lisa gets to interview Henry Wills for her report and has her picture taken with him.

Character Total	_____
Setting Total	_____
Plot Total	_____
Resolution Total	_____
TOTAL POINTS	_____

READING LEVELS

Independent	Above 85 Points
Instructional	70–84 Points
Frustration	Below 70 Points

OBSERVATIONS

	Inappropriate				Appropriate
Includes detail	1	2	3	4	5
Uses prior knowledge to establish story line	1	2	3	4	5
Infers beyond text	1	2	3	4	5
	Out of Sequence				**In Sequence**
Tells story in correct sequence	1	2	3	4	5
	Verbatim				**In Own Words**
Restates story verbatim	1	2	3	4	5

Fourth Grade

NARRATIVE

(296 words)

Form A—

Teacher's Copy

A Special Trade

Bartholomew is Nelly's neighbor. When Nelly was very small, he would take her for a walk every day in her stroller to Mrs. Pringle's vegetable garden.

Bartholomew never pushed too fast. When they were coming to a bump, Bartholomew always told Nelly:

"Hang on, Nelly!" he would always say. "Here's a bump!"

Nelly would shout "BUMP!" as she rode over it.

If they saw a nice dog they'd stop and pet it, but if it was mean Bartholomew would shoo it away.

When Mrs. Pringle's sprinkler was on, he would say, "Get ready, get set, CHARRRRGE!"

Nelly would shout "Wheeeee!" as he pushed her through it.

When Nelly began to walk, Bartholomew took her by the hand. "No–No!" she cried, pulling her hand back. Nelly didn't want any help, so Bartholomew offered his hand only when she really needed it. He knew that Nelly was getting older.

Bartholomew was getting older, too. He needed a walking stick now, so they both walked very slowly. When they walked up stairs, they both held on to the railing.

The neighbors called them "ham and eggs" because they were always together. Even on Halloween they were together . . . and on the coldest day of winter when everyone was inside.

One day Bartholomew went out alone and fell down the stairs. An ambulance came to take him to the hospital, and then he was gone for a long time.

When Bartholomew came home, he was in a wheelchair. The smile was gone from his eyes.

"I guess our walks are over," he said. "No they aren't," said Nelly. "I can take you for walks now." She knew just how to do it, too. Nice and easy, not too fast.

Retelling Protocol

Purpose-Setting Statement: This is the story of a special relationship between Nelly and Bartholomew. Read this story to find out what happens as Nelly and Bartholomew grow older.

A Special Trade

CHARACTERS (5 points each)

_____ Nelly _____ Bartholomew

SETTING (2 points each)

_____ Mrs. Pringle's vegetable garden _____ Stairs _____ Various seasons

PLOT (14 points each)

_____ 1. Bartholomew takes Nelly for walks in her stroller.

_____ 2. Bartholomew holds Nelly's hand during walks as Nelly grows older.

_____ 3. Bartholomew needs a walking stick and walks slower.

_____ 4. Bartholomew falls down stairs and is taken to the hospital.

_____ 5. Bartholomew returns in a wheelchair.

RESOLUTION (14 points)

_____ 6. Nelly takes Bartholomew for nice and easy walks.

			READING LEVELS	
Character Total	_____		Independent	Above 85 Points
Setting Total	_____		Instructional	70–84 Points
Plot Total	_____		Frustration	Below 70 Points
Resolution Total	_____			
TOTAL POINTS	_____			

OBSERVATIONS

	Inappropriate				**Appropriate**
Includes detail	1	2	3	4	5
Uses prior knowledge to establish story line	1	2	3	4	5
Infers beyond text	1	2	3	4	5
	Out of Sequence				**In Sequence**
Tells story in correct sequence	1	2	3	4	5
	Verbatim				**In Own Words**
Restates story verbatim	1	2	3	4	5

Fifth Grade

NARRATIVE

(307 words)

Form A—

Teacher's Copy

The Tortoise Who Talked Too Much

The tortoise used to live in a pond near the foot of the Himalayas. Two wild young geese, flying far from their home in search of food, landed on the pond. There they met the tortoise, and a friendship got started. By and by, the three creatures became the best of friends.

The day came when the two geese felt ready to fly back home. Not wanting to leave their friend, they said, "We have a lovely home on Mount Cittakuta in a cave of gold. Will you come home with us, friend?"

"Gladly," the tortoise said. "But how shall I ever get there? If I follow you, it will take forever."

"Oh, it will be no problem to take you there. You just have to keep your mouth shut and not say a word on the way."

"That is easy enough," the tortoise said. "Take me with you."

So the two geese gave the tortoise a stick to hold between his teeth. Each goose took hold of one end of the stick and rose into the air, flying for home. The tortoise held fast, his teeth fastened tightly on the stick.

As they flew above the town, some village children looked up and saw this strange sight in the air. They pointed, laughed, and jeered, saying, "Look at that, will you! Two geese carrying a tortoise on a stick."

Just as the geese were flying over the palace of the king, the tortoise felt he had to answer the children. He was about to say, "Well, and what of it? If my friends carry me through the air, what is that to you?" But the moment he opened his mouth to speak, the tortoise fell into the king's open courtyard and died.

The moral is: Whoever cannot keep from talking will come to trouble, sooner or later.

Retelling Protocol

Purpose-Setting Statement: Two geese and a tortoise become friends. Read this story to find out what happens when the two geese take the tortoise to a new home.

The Tortoise Who Talked Too Much

CHARACTERS (4 points each)

_____ Two geese _____ Tortoise _____ Village children

SETTING (4 points each)

_____ A pond _____ In the air

PLOT (8 points each)

_____ 1. Two geese and a tortoise become friends.
_____ 2. The two geese must fly home.
_____ 3. The geese invite the tortoise to their home.
_____ 4. The tortoise says he cannot follow, because it would take too long.
_____ 5. The geese say they will take the tortoise, but he must keep his mouth closed.
_____ 6. The tortoise holds a stick in his mouth and the two geese take the ends of the stick in their mouths and take off.
_____ 7. The village children taunt the tortoise.
_____ 8. The tortoise opens his mouth to respond.
_____ 9. The tortoise falls to his death.
_____10. The moral is: Whoever cannot keep from talking will come to trouble, sooner or later.

Character Total _____
Setting Total _____
Plot Total _____
TOTAL POINTS _____

READING LEVELS

Independent	Above 85 Points
Instructional	70–84 Points
Frustration	Below 70 Points

OBSERVATIONS

	Inappropriate				Appropriate
Includes detail	1	2	3	4	5
Uses prior knowledge to establish story line	1	2	3	4	5
Infers beyond text	1	2	3	4	5
	Out of Sequence				**In Sequence**
Tells story in correct sequence	1	2	3	4	5
	Verbatim				**In Own Words**
Restates story verbatim	1	2	3	4	5

Sixth Grade

NARRATIVE

(419 words)

Form A—

Teacher's Copy

A Name for a Kitten

No one knows whether the King's kitten was white, black, or striped; but history says His Majesty was so fond of his pet that he asked the royal council to choose a name for it.

"I want a very strong, powerful, and honorable name for my dearest kitten," he said. "So I propose to call it 'Sky,' because the sky is above everything and anyone on earth."

"That is a most noble name, indeed!" said his Prime Mandarin. "But though the sky is above the clouds, the clouds sometimes dare to hide its blue beauty."

"A very interesting observation!" praised the King. "Clouds, though lower than the sky, can be more powerful. I want my pet to have an extraordinarily strong name. I will call it 'Cloud.'"

"What a lovely name!" said the Chief Magician. "But is it really strong? The wind scatters the clouds, and sometimes even pushes them across the sea and beyond the horizon."

"True, very true," mused the King. "And since the wind is more powerful than the clouds which, though lower than the sky, dare to hide its blue beauty, I'll call my darling 'Wind.'"

"A most fitting name for a prancing, running kitten," said the King's General. "But is wind as powerful as the Magician suggests? A high solid wall can bar the wind."

"A wall? I didn't think of that, but now that you mention it—of course you're right, General! A wall stops the wind which scatters the clouds which hide the sky. 'Wall!' That's a fine, strong name."

"Is it really?" wondered the King's Steward. "Only yesterday the thick eastern wall of Your Majesty's garden tumbled down."

"How horrible!" said the King. "Happily the name 'Wall' wasn't yet officially proclaimed! And what made it tumble down?"

"Mice," said the Steward.

"Mice? I didn't realize they were more powerful than the wall which stops the wind which scatters the clouds which hide the sky. I'll call my dearest pet 'Mouse,'" said the King.

"But any cat just eats mice!" exclaimed the little servant girl, who was preparing tea for the royal council.

"How strange! How wonderful! And who eats cats?" said the King.

"Why—nobody, Sir!" laughed the little girl.

"In that case, the extraordinarily strong and powerful name we wanted for the Royal Kitten has been found!" declared the King. "Gentlemen, I hereby most solemnly and officially name it 'CAT'!"

And that's how kittens came to have the extraordinary name of "cat" right up to this present day!

"A Name for a Kitten: A Folk Tale from Vietnam," translated by Beatrice Tanaka. *Cricket*, Vol. 1, No. 2, Oct. 1973. Permission granted by Beatrice Tanaka.

Retelling Protocol

Purpose-Setting Statement: This story is about a king who is trying to find a good name for his kitten. Read this story to find out what name he chooses and why.

A Name for a Kitten

CHARACTERS (2 points each)

_____ King	_____ Chief Magician	_____ King's Steward	_____ King's kitten
_____ Prime Mandarin	_____ King's General	_____ Servant girl	

SETTING (6 points)

_____ King's council chamber or palace (accept any reasonable answer)

PLOT (10 points each)

_____ 1. King wants a name for his kitten.

_____ 2. King suggests "Sky."

_____ 3. Prime Mandarin points out that the clouds hide the sky, so he suggests "Cloud."

_____ 4. Chief Magician points out that wind blows away clouds, so he suggests "Wind."

_____ 5. King's General points out that a wall blocks the wind, so he suggests "Wall."

_____ 6. King's Steward points out that mice make walls tumble down, so he suggests "Mouse."

_____ 7. Little servant girl points out that cats eat mice.

RESOLUTION (10 points)

_____ 8. King names kitten "Cat."

Character Total	_____
Setting Total	_____
Plot Total	_____
Resolution Total	_____
TOTAL POINTS	_____

READING LEVELS

Independent	Above 85 Points
Instructional	70–84 Points
Frustration	Below 70 Points

OBSERVATIONS

	Inappropriate				Appropriate
Includes detail	1	2	3	4	5
Uses prior knowledge to establish story line	1	2	3	4	5
Infers beyond text	1	2	3	4	5
	Out of Sequence				**In Sequence**
Tells story in correct sequence	1	2	3	4	5
	Verbatim				**In Own Words**
Restates story verbatim	1	2	3	4	5

Seventh Grade

NARRATIVE

(539 words)

Form A—

Teacher's Copy

Maria and the Coquis

The worst day of my life then was the day Felicia and I found the coqui.

A coqui is a little frog, so tiny it is no bigger than the end of a grown-up's finger. My father says coquis live only on Puerto Rico. People who visit here sometimes think that the loud chirping song they hear so often is from birds, but it is not. It is coquis calling to one another—"Co-KEEE! Co-KEEE! Co-KEEE!"—over and over again in the night and in the rain. Parts of El Yunque's rain forest are so dark that coquis sing there all day long.

On that bad day when we found the coqui, Felicia and her mother, father, and nine brothers, and my mother, father, four brothers, and I all went up El Yunque to have a picnic. There is a place where you can cook, with little open-sided huts with tin roofs for getting out of the rain.

Felicia and I went to see a waterfall that is not far from the cooking-place while my mother and her mother made the food and the boys and men played ball.

We made a game of flower-hunting as we walked past the waterfall and over its rough bridge. We went under the umbrella like branches of the Sierra palms and past thick hanging ropes of vines. There was soft, bright green moss beside us, with tiny plants pushing through, making little rain-forest worlds all by themselves. There were round, silent tree snails, bumps on tree trunks—and always the coquis, singing, singing, singing. It is said that they call the name of an Indian god, so he will never be forgotten.

Suddenly, in a very dark place on the other side of the bridge, when the sun disappeared and the rain suddenly poured down as if someone in the sky had emptied a bucket—suddenly a tiny, almost white coqui jumped into the path. He sat there staring at us with his big dark eyes.

We got on our knees and watched him in the rain and he watched us back.

Then—I do not like to remember this part—then Felicia said—oh, very softly—she said, "Coqui, you must be Maria's friend now; for I do not know how to tell her that I am going away."

And then, while the coqui sat there, still staring, and the rain stopped, Felicia told me that she was going to Boston, Massachusetts, far away, where there would be snow and that I, Maria, would stay here with only rain to change the weather.

And so I ran, not looking at Felicia or at the coqui that she had asked to be my friend. I ran down the path, seeing nothing. I hid from Felicia and far from where our two families were, until my father came and found me.

Soon after that, Felicia left and it rained every day, and El Yunque wore dark angry clouds like a hat. I sat on our patio after school and watched lizards playing on Felicia's patio. I did not go up El Yunque anymore, not even a little way, and I did not look for the coqui.

Retelling Protocol

Purpose-Setting Statement: A beautiful day in the rain forest turns sad for Maria. Read this story to find out why.

Maria and the Coquis

CHARACTERS (4 points each)

_____ Maria   _____ Felicia   _____ their families

SETTING (4 points)

_____ Puerto Rico   _____ El Yunque

PLOT (10 points each)

_____ 1. Maria, Felicia, and their families picnic at El Yunque.

_____ 2. Maria and Felicia make a game of flower-hunting in the rain forest.

_____ 3. A tiny white coqui jumps into their path.

_____ 4. Felicia asks the coqui to be Maria's friend.

_____ 5. Felicia reveals that she is moving to Boston, Massachusetts.

_____ 6. Maria runs away.

_____ 7. Maria's father comes to her.

RESOLUTION (10 points)

_____ 8. Felicia moves away.

Character Total	_____
Setting Total	_____
Plot Total	_____
Resolution Total	_____
TOTAL POINTS	_____

READING LEVELS

Independent	Above 85 Points
Instructional	70–84 Points
Frustration	Below 70 Points

OBSERVATIONS

	Inappropriate				Appropriate
Includes detail	1	2	3	4	5
Uses prior knowledge to establish story line	1	2	3	4	5
Infers beyond text	1	2	3	4	5
	Out of Sequence				**In Sequence**
Tells story in correct sequence	1	2	3	4	5
	Verbatim				**In Own Words**
Restates story verbatim	1	2	3	4	5

Eighth Grade

NARRATIVE

(491 words)

Form A—

Teacher's Copy

Matt's Gift

Matt had always enjoyed assisting other people. When he was younger, Matt would look for lost animals or rake leaves for neighbors who could not. One time he even raised enough money to provide Thanksgiving dinner for a family after their home had burned. However, this situation was different. Matt's neighbor, Mrs. Ramirez, had always been like another grandmother to Matt. His mother could call Mrs. Ramirez anytime night or day to come take care of Matt when her job as a police officer called her away.

Mrs. Ramirez had not been feeling well for weeks before Matt's mother convinced her to go to the doctor for a biopsy. Matt did not comprehend how serious the situation was until his mother sat him down one night and explained.

"Mrs. Ramirez has a malignant tumor and will only live for about six more months. It is important that we help make this last six months the best we can," his mother said.

Matt was stunned by the news. He could not imagine life without having Mrs. Ramirez next door. He knew that he wanted to do something that would show Mrs. Ramirez how much she meant to him.

Mrs. Ramirez was born in Venezuela in 1919. She had moved to the United States in 1942 with her husband who had worked for an export company until his death in 1980. She had never returned to Venezuela, although she still had a brother living there. When her sister had died in 1994, Mrs. Ramirez was devastated because she had not been able to see her sister before her death. So, Matt reasoned, what better gift could he give Mrs. Ramirez than a trip to Venezuela to visit the family she had left behind so long ago.

The first thing Matt thought to do was to get a part-time job. However, he knew he would not raise enough money within the six months. So, Matt decided to organize a neighborhood-wide benefit talent show. He convinced the minister of the church down the street to allow him to use the activities hall for the show. Neighbors volunteered to provide not only the talent but also refreshments and other support. One of Matt's neighbors, a local news anchor, featured Mrs. Ramirez's plight and Matt's goal in a Dare to Care spot. Unbeknownst to Matt, Mrs. Ramirez, or the news anchor, the president of the export company for which Mr. Ramirez had worked was watching the news that evening. He recognized Mrs. Ramirez and remembered the many years of hard work Mr. Ramirez had provided to his company. He was also impressed by Matt's desire to give Mrs. Ramirez her final wish. The president contacted the local news station and offered to provide the additional money needed to make the trip to Venezuela possible. Although Matt was sad about Mrs. Ramirez's cancer, he was gratified that Mrs. Ramirez would have the opportunity to see her family again.

Retelling Protocol

Purpose-Setting Statement: Matt wants to help Mrs. Ramirez, who is dying of cancer. Read this story to find out about his plan.

Matt's Gift

CHARACTERS (4 points each)

_____ Matt _____ Mrs. Ramirez

_____ News anchor _____ President of export company

SETTING (4 points)

_____ Matt's neighborhood

PLOT (10 points each)

_____ 1. Matt found out that Mrs. Ramirez is very ill and will live for only six more months.

_____ 2. Matt wanted to do something to show Mrs. Ramirez how much he cared.

_____ 3. Mrs. Ramirez had never returned to visit her family in Venezuela.

_____ 4. Matt decided to give Mrs. Ramirez a trip to Venezuela.

_____ 5. Matt organized a neighborhood talent show.

_____ 6. The local television station featured the story on the news.

_____ 7. The president of the export company for which Mr. Ramirez had worked saw the news story.

RESOLUTION (10 points)

_____ 8. The president of the export company provided the money Matt needed to pay for Mrs. Ramirez's trip.

		READING LEVELS	
Character Total	_____	Independent	Above 85 Points
Setting Total	_____	Instructional	70–84 Points
Plot Total	_____	Frustration	Below 70 Points
Resolution Total	_____		
TOTAL POINTS	_____		

OBSERVATIONS

	Inappropriate				**Appropriate**
Includes detail	1	2	3	4	5
Uses prior knowledge to establish story line	1	2	3	4	5
Infers beyond text	1	2	3	4	5
	Out of Sequence				**In Sequence**
Tells story in correct sequence	1	2	3	4	5
	Verbatim				**In Own Words**
Restates story verbatim	1	2	3	4	5

Ninth Grade

NARRATIVE

(566 words)

Form A—

Teacher's Copy

Roberto's Encounter in the Field

That day had begun pretty much as any other day in Roberto's life and it would probably have continued the same way if it had not been for the spaceship that landed in his father's field. Roberto's father had asked him to check on the fence lines for the fields where he kept his cattle. He was sure he had fewer cows in those fields and he suspected a break in the fence lines.

As Roberto began walking the fence line he was thinking about how unfair it was that he could not go into town to the city swimming pool like all his other friends. He always had to work in the fields, helping his father run the small farm that had been in his family for over a hundred years.

Suddenly Roberto was brought out of his reverie by a bright flash of light in the field on his right. He turned toward the light and was astonished by the sight before him. There was a bright metallic object in the field that seemed to have Christmas lights strung all around it that were much brighter than any lights he had ever seen before and seemed unusually bright even on this sunny day.

As he stood in dumbfounded amazement, a door opened in the side of the craft and out stepped two apparently human beings, a man and a woman. They looked like any people you would meet on the street; the only difference being the clothes they wore which were made out of some sort of metallic material that seemed to change colors as they moved. The two walked toward the fence line where Roberto stood transfixed by the sight. At first they did not see him, but the man stopped suddenly, gesturing to his companion to stop as well and pointing to where Roberto stood. After a brief consultation, the two approached Roberto and spoke to him in perfectly plain if slightly altered English.

"We are truly sorry that you saw us. We had planned on stopping in this field only for a few minutes and did not wish to be seen by anyone," the man said.

"Who are you?" asked Roberto, slightly perplexed.

"We know you will not believe this, but we are time-travelers. We have returned to the Earth from the year 2579 to gather specimens of Earth creatures that have become extinct. We took two of your cows back to our time where they have produced several calves and we are now returning them to where they came from," the woman explained to Roberto.

"Yeah, right," thought Roberto to himself, but he said to the time-travelers, "What will you do after you return the cows, erase my memory or something so I won't tell anyone what I saw so my knowledge of your existence won't change the future as it now exists?"

"No," the woman responded. "We will simply return to our ship and our time because we know and you know that no one would believe you if you told them you had seen time-travelers from the future."

Roberto realized they were right and watched quietly as the two time-travelers completed their work, returned to their ship, took off, and disappeared from sight. Even though Roberto never told anyone about this encounter, he was never quite the same after his experience with the time-travelers.

Retelling Protocol

Purpose-Setting Statement: Roberto has an experience he can share with no one. Read this story to find out about that experience.

Roberto's Encounter in the Field

CHARACTERS (4 points each)

_____ Roberto   _____ Time-travelers

SETTING (4 points)

_____ Field

PLOT (8 points each)

_____ 1. Roberto checked for breaks in the fence line because his father said some cows were missing.
_____ 2. Roberto was startled by a bright light in the field.
_____ 3. A bright metallic object was in the field.
_____ 4. Two beings walked out of a door in the side of the craft.
_____ 5. The two approached Roberto.
_____ 6. They identified themselves as time-travelers from 2579.
_____ 7. They have come back in time to gather specimens of Earth creatures that have become extinct.
_____ 8. The time-travelers returned two cows to the field.
_____ 9. Roberto asked if they were going to erase his memory.
_____ 10. The time-travelers replied that erasing Roberto's memory would not be necessary because no one would believe him anyway.

RESOLUTION (8 points)

_____ 11. Roberto never told anyone of this experience.

Character Total	_____
Setting Total	_____
Plot Total	_____
Resolution Total	_____
TOTAL POINTS	_____

READING LEVELS

Independent	Above 85 Points
Instructional	70–84 Points
Frustration	Below 70 Points

OBSERVATIONS

	Inappropriate				Appropriate
Includes detail	1	2	3	4	5
Uses prior knowledge to establish story line	1	2	3	4	5
Infers beyond text	1	2	3	4	5
	Out of Sequence				**In Sequence**
Tells story in correct sequence	1	2	3	4	5
	Verbatim				**In Own Words**
Restates story verbatim	1	2	3	4	5

Penny Gets Wheels

It was Penny's birthday. She got ten one dollar bills. "I am rich, and I am older now," she said to her mom. "I don't need to walk anymore. I will go on wheels."

"Wheels?" asked her mom.

"Yes," said Penny. "I would like a car, but I know I'm not rich enough or old enough. I think I will buy a bike."

"You'll need a lot of money to buy a bike," said her mom.

"Ten dollars is a lot of money," Penny said.

Then she ran outside and down the street to the sports shop on the corner.

"Today is my birthday," she said to the salesperson. "I would like to buy that blue racing bike. How much does it cost?"

"This bike costs one hundred dollars," he said.

Penny pointed to another bike. "How much is that one?"

"Ninety-one dollars," said the salesperson.

"I'm not that rich," Penny said.

Penny looked at many things. But she didn't want to buy anything she saw.

Then she saw some roller skates. They cost nine dollars. She picked up a skate and spun its wheels.

"I guess these are all I have enough to buy," she said.

Penny paid for the skates. She went outside, put them on, and started to skate home. She still wished she were old enough to have a car or rich enough to own a bike.

Ray's Best Friend

Ray's family was moving. They had lived in the same apartment building for as long as Ray could remember. They were moving to a house in the country.

"I don't want to go. I will miss my friends," said Ray.

"You will make new friends," said Ray's mother.

The day came for the move. Ray said goodbye to all of his friends. Ray would miss his best friend, Elliott, most of all.

The new house was bigger than the apartment. It had a big yard with a fence around it. Ray didn't have any friends at the new house, though. He was very lonely.

"I have an idea," his mother said one day. "Now that we have a big yard with a fence, would you like to get a puppy?"

"Oh, yes," said Ray. He had always wanted a puppy, but he could not have one in the apartment.

Ray and his mother went to the pound to find a puppy. There were lots of dogs and puppies at the pound. There were big dogs and little dogs. Ray walked around and looked in each of the cages. It was very difficult to pick just the right dog. In the very last cage, though, in the puppy room was a little brown puppy. It had short brown fur and was the smallest puppy in the pound. His eyes were big and his ears flopped down almost into his eyes.

"I want that one," said Ray, pointing to the smallest puppy.

When they got home, Ray's mother said, "Your puppy needs a name. What do you want its name to be?"

"Since he will be my best friend, I think I will name him Elliott," said Ray, remembering his best friend in the apartment building.

Sports Day

"We are having Sports Day at school," Lisa said to her dad. "I have to do a report about a sport. I can't decide what to tell about." "I'll help you think of something after supper," said Dad. "Now I have a surprise for you. You know that the Bears have an important game today. Well, we are going to that game." "Oh, great!" shouted Lisa. Then she said, "I know! I can be a reporter and tell about this game on Sports Day." Then Lisa went to get the sign that she took to every game. It was for the player she liked best, Henry Wills. If the Bears could win today's game, they would be in first place. This was a very important ball game. Lisa thought the Bears could win. She said to her dad, "They played a great game the other day. If they can play like that today, they should win."

At the game, Lisa and her dad sat in back of the Bears. They would have no problem seeing the game. At last the ball game started. Lisa held up her sign and shouted, "Go, Henry, go!" The other players, the Owls, were up at bat first. They made one home run. Then the Bears were up at bat. The first player made a home run! Lisa took pictures of the ball game. She didn't want to forget a thing. Soon it was the last time for the Owls to be up at bat. They had five runs, and so did the Bears. But the Owls couldn't get a hit. Now the Bears were going to bat. They needed to hit one home run. Henry Wills was the first one up. The ball raced at Henry. He hit a home run! The Bears were now in first place! "Lisa!" said Dad. "We should talk to Henry Wills."

Before going down to the players, Lisa wanted to show her sign again. She started to put up her sign, but somehow she let go of it. The sign fell down on Henry Wills! Henry read the sign and laughed. He looked up and saw Lisa. He held up the sign and asked, "Is this your sign?" "Yes," said Lisa. "Thank you for getting it." Then she said, "I'm doing a report about this game. May I talk with you?" "Yes," said Henry.

The first thing Lisa asked was, "How did you get to be the best?" "I have worked at it," said Henry. "Sometimes it was all work. But many times it is fun, too. Today was one of the fun times!" Lisa talked some more with Henry. Then she said, "I should let you go. Thanks, Mr. Wills." "Wait!" said Henry. He got a ball and signed it. "This is for you," he said. "Thanks, Mr. Wills!" said Lisa. Then Dad took the best picture of the game. It was a picture of Lisa and Henry Wills.

A Special Trade

Bartholomew is Nelly's neighbor. When Nelly was very small, he would take her for a walk every day in her stroller to Mrs. Pringle's vegetable garden.

Bartholomew never pushed too fast. When they were coming to a bump, Bartholomew always told Nelly:

"Hang on, Nelly!" he would always say. "Here's a bump!"

Nelly would shout "BUMP!" as she rode over it.

If they saw a nice dog they'd stop and pet it, but if it was mean Bartholomew would shoo it away.

When Mrs. Pringle's sprinkler was on, he would say, "Get ready, get set, CHARRRRGE!"

Nelly would shout "Wheeeee!" as he pushed her through it.

When Nelly began to walk, Bartholomew took her by the hand. "No–No!" she cried, pulling her hand back. Nelly didn't want any help, so Bartholomew offered his hand only when she really needed it. He knew that Nelly was getting older.

Bartholomew was getting older, too. He needed a walking stick now, so they both walked very slowly. When they walked up stairs, they both held on to the railing.

The neighbors called them "ham and eggs" because they were always together. Even on Halloween they were together . . . and on the coldest day of winter when everyone was inside.

One day Bartholomew went out alone and fell down the stairs. An ambulance came to take him to the hospital, and then he was gone for a long time.

When Bartholomew came home, he was in a wheelchair. The smile was gone from his eyes.

"I guess our walks are over," he said. "No they aren't," said Nelly. "I can take you for walks now." She knew just how to do it, too. Nice and easy, not too fast.

The Tortoise Who Talked Too Much

The tortoise used to live in a pond near the foot of the Himalayas. Two wild young geese, flying far from their home in search of food, landed on the pond. There they met the tortoise, and a friendship got started. By and by, the three creatures became the best of friends.

The day came when the two geese felt ready to fly back home. Not wanting to leave their friend, they said, "We have a lovely home on Mount Cittakuta in a cave of gold. Will you come home with us, friend?"

"Gladly," the tortoise said. "But how shall I ever get there? If I follow you, it will take forever."

"Oh, it will be no problem to take you there. You just have to keep your mouth shut and not say a word on the way."

"That is easy enough," the tortoise said. "Take me with you."

So the two geese gave the tortoise a stick to hold between his teeth. Each goose took hold of one end of the stick and rose into the air, flying for home. The tortoise held fast, his teeth fastened tightly on the stick.

As they flew above the town, some village children looked up and saw this strange sight in the air. They pointed, laughed, and jeered, saying, "Look at that, will you! Two geese carrying a tortoise on a stick."

Just as the geese were flying over the palace of the king, the tortoise felt he had to answer the children. He was about to say, "Well, and what of it? If my friends carry me through the air, what is that to you?" But the moment he opened his mouth to speak, the tortoise fell into the king's open courtyard and died.

The moral is: Whoever cannot keep from talking will come to trouble, sooner or later.

A Name for a Kitten

No one knows whether the King's kitten was white, black, or striped; but history says His Majesty was so fond of his pet that he asked the royal council to choose a name for it.

"I want a very strong, powerful, and honorable name for my dearest kitten," he said. "So I propose to call it 'Sky,' because the sky is above everything and anyone on earth."

"That is a most noble name, indeed!" said his Prime Mandarin. "But though the sky is above the clouds, the clouds sometimes dare to hide its blue beauty."

"A very interesting observation!" praised the King. "Clouds, though lower than the sky, can be more powerful. I want my pet to have an extraordinarily strong name. I will call it 'Cloud.'"

"What a lovely name!" said the Chief Magician. "But is it really strong? The wind scatters the clouds, and sometimes even pushes them across the sea and beyond the horizon."

"True, very true," mused the King. "And since the wind is more powerful than the clouds which, though lower than the sky, dare to hide its blue beauty, I'll call my darling 'Wind.'"

"A most fitting name for a prancing, running kitten," said the King's General. "But is wind as powerful as the Magician suggests? A high solid wall can bar the wind."

"A wall? I didn't think of that, but now that you mention it—of course you're right, General! A wall stops the wind which scatters the clouds which hide the sky. 'Wall!' That's a fine, strong name."

"Is it really?" wondered the King's Steward. "Only yesterday the thick eastern wall of Your Majesty's garden tumbled down."

"How horrible!" said the King. "Happily the name 'Wall' wasn't yet officially proclaimed! And what made it tumble down?"

"Mice," said the Steward.

"Mice? I didn't realize they were more powerful than the wall which stops the wind which scatters the clouds which hide the sky. I'll call my dearest pet 'Mouse,'" said the King.

"But any cat just eats mice!" exclaimed the little servant girl, who was preparing tea for the royal council.

"How strange! How wonderful! And who eats cats?" said the King.

"Why—nobody, Sir!" laughed the little girl.

"In that case, the extraordinarily strong and powerful name we wanted for the Royal Kitten has been found!" declared the King. "Gentlemen, I hereby most solemnly and officially name it 'CAT'!"

And that's how kittens came to have the extraordinary name of "cat" right up to this present day!

Maria and the Coquis

The worst day of my life then was the day Felicia and I found the coqui.

A coqui is a little frog, so tiny it is no bigger than the end of a grown-up's finger. My father says coquis live only on Puerto Rico. People who visit here sometimes think that the loud chirping song they hear so often is from birds, but it is not. It is coquis calling to one another—"Co-KEEE! Co-KEEE! Co-KEEE!"—over and over again in the night and in the rain. Parts of El Yunque's rain forest are so dark that coquis sing there all day long.

On that bad day when we found the coqui, Felicia and her mother, father, and nine brothers, and my mother, father, four brothers, and I all went up El Yunque to have a picnic. There is a place where you can cook, with little open-sided huts with tin roofs for getting out of the rain.

Felicia and I went to see a waterfall that is not far from the cooking-place while my mother and her mother made the food and the boys and men played ball.

We made a game of flower-hunting as we walked past the waterfall and over its rough bridge. We went under the umbrella like branches of the Sierra palms and past thick hanging ropes of vines. There was soft, bright green moss beside us, with tiny plants pushing through, making little rain-forest worlds all by themselves. There were round, silent tree snails, bumps on tree trunks—and always the coquis, singing, singing, singing. It is said that they call the name of an Indian god, so he will never be forgotten.

Suddenly, in a very dark place on the other side of the bridge, when the sun disappeared and the rain suddenly poured down as if someone in the sky had emptied a bucket—suddenly a tiny, almost white coqui jumped into the path. He sat there staring at us with his big dark eyes.

We got on our knees and watched him in the rain and he watched us back.

Then—I do not like to remember this part—then Felicia said—oh, very softly—she said, "Coqui, you must be Maria's friend now; for I do not know how to tell her that I am going away."

And then, while the coqui sat there, still staring, and the rain stopped, Felicia told me that she was going to Boston, Massachusetts, far away, where there would be snow and that I, Maria, would stay here with only rain to change the weather.

And so I ran, not looking at Felicia or at the coqui that she had asked to be my friend. I ran down the path, seeing nothing. I hid from Felicia and far from where our two families were, until my father came and found me.

Soon after that, Felicia left and it rained every day, and El Yunque wore dark angry clouds like a hat. I sat on our patio after school and watched lizards playing on Felicia's patio. I did not go up El Yunque anymore, not even a little way, and I did not look for the coqui.

Matt's Gift

Matt had always enjoyed assisting other people. When he was younger, Matt would look for lost animals or rake leaves for neighbors who could not. One time he even raised enough money to provide Thanksgiving dinner for a family after their home had burned. However, this situation was different. Matt's neighbor, Mrs. Ramirez, had always been like another grandmother to Matt. His mother could call Mrs. Ramirez anytime night or day to come take care of Matt when her job as a police officer called her away.

Mrs. Ramirez had not been feeling well for weeks before Matt's mother convinced her to go to the doctor for a biopsy. Matt did not comprehend how serious the situation was until his mother sat him down one night and explained.

"Mrs. Ramirez has a malignant tumor and will only live for about six more months. It is important that we help make this last six months the best we can," his mother said.

Matt was stunned by the news. He could not imagine life without having Mrs. Ramirez next door. He knew that he wanted to do something that would show Mrs. Ramirez how much she meant to him.

Mrs. Ramirez was born in Venezuela in 1919. She had moved to the United States in 1942 with her husband who had worked for an export company until his death in 1980. She had never returned to Venezuela, although she still had a brother living there. When her sister had died in 1994, Mrs. Ramirez was devastated because she had not been able to see her sister before her death. So, Matt reasoned, what better gift could he give Mrs. Ramirez than a trip to Venezuela to visit the family she had left behind so long ago.

The first thing Matt thought to do was to get a part-time job. However, he knew he would not raise enough money within the six months. So, Matt decided to organize a neighborhood-wide benefit talent show. He convinced the minister of the church down the street to allow him to use the activities hall for the show. Neighbors volunteered to provide not only the talent but also refreshments and other support. One of Matt's neighbors, a local news anchor, featured Mrs. Ramirez's plight and Matt's goal in a Dare to Care spot. Unbeknownst to Matt, Mrs. Ramirez, or the news anchor, the president of the export company for which Mr. Ramirez had worked was watching the news that evening. He recognized Mrs. Ramirez and remembered the many years of hard work Mr. Ramirez had provided to his company. He was also impressed by Matt's desire to give Mrs. Ramirez her final wish. The president contacted the local news station and offered to provide the additional money needed to make the trip to Venezuela possible. Although Matt was sad about Mrs. Ramirez's cancer, he was gratified that Mrs. Ramirez would have the opportunity to see her family again.

Roberto's Encounter in the Field

That day had begun pretty much as any other day in Roberto's life and it would probably have continued the same way if it had not been for the spaceship that landed in his father's field. Roberto's father had asked him to check on the fence lines for the fields where he kept his cattle. He was sure he had fewer cows in those fields and he suspected a break in the fence lines.

As Roberto began walking the fence line he was thinking about how unfair it was that he could not go into town to the city swimming pool like all his other friends. He always had to work in the fields, helping his father run the small farm that had been in his family for over a hundred years.

Suddenly Roberto was brought out of his reverie by a bright flash of light in the field on his right. He turned toward the light and was astonished by the sight before him. There was a bright metallic object in the field that seemed to have Christmas lights strung all around it that were much brighter than any lights he had ever seen before and seemed unusually bright even on this sunny day.

As he stood in dumbfounded amazement, a door opened in the side of the craft and out stepped two apparently human beings, a man and a woman. They looked like any people you would meet on the street; the only difference being the clothes they wore which were made out of some sort of metallic material that seemed to change colors as they moved. The two walked toward the fence line where Roberto stood transfixed by the sight. At first they did not see him, but the man stopped suddenly, gesturing to his companion to stop as well and pointing to where Roberto stood. After a brief consultation, the two approached Roberto and spoke to him in perfectly plain if slightly altered English.

"We are truly sorry that you saw us. We had planned on stopping in this field only for a few minutes and did not wish to be seen by anyone," the man said.

"Who are you?" asked Roberto, slightly perplexed.

"We know you will not believe this, but we are time-travelers. We have returned to the Earth from the year 2579 to gather specimens of Earth creatures that have become extinct. We took two of your cows back to our time where they have produced several calves and we are now returning them to where they came from," the woman explained to Roberto.

"Yeah, right," thought Roberto to himself, but he said to the time-travelers, "What will you do after you return the cows, erase my memory or something so I won't tell anyone what I saw so my knowledge of your existence won't change the future as it now exists?"

"No," the woman responded. "We will simply return to our ship and our time because we know and you know that no one would believe you if you told them you had seen time-travelers from the future."

Roberto realized they were right and watched quietly as the two time-travelers completed their work, returned to their ship, took off, and disappeared from sight. Even though Roberto never told anyone about this encounter, he was never quite the same after his experience with the time-travelers.

Narrative Passages and Rubrics: Form B

First Grade

NARRATIVE

(340 words)

Form B—

Teacher's Copy

Walter and the Mall

One day Pam and Walter went to the mall with Mother. Pam and Walter like it there. It wasn't a big mall, but there were many things to see.

Mother said, "Pam, I have many things to do. Why don't you take Walter for a little walk? You have come here many times, so you can find your way. Then come back and meet me here."

"OK, Mother," said Pam, and she went for a walk with Walter.

Pam liked the big fountain in the mall, so she and Walter went to look at it.

Then they went to look at some fish.

"Fish! Fish!" said Walter.

Walter couldn't say very many words, but *fish* was one word he could say.

Last of all, they stopped to look at some little cats.

Pam and Walter went to look at some more things. Pam stopped to look at some skates.

"Maybe I could get some skates someday," she thought.

Then Pam said to Walter, "Now we'll go meet Mother."

But Walter wasn't there!

"Walter! Walter!" shouted Pam.

But Walter was nowhere to be found.

"Maybe he went back to see the cats," thought Pam.

She ran over to the cats, but Walter wasn't there.

Then Pam thought, "He liked the fish best."

So she ran over to the fish. No Walter.

Pam decided to go back and get Mother.

"Maybe she can find Walter," thought Pam.

On her way back, Pam saw the big fountain. There were many boys and girls there. They were all laughing. Pam looked to see what was so funny.

"Walter!" shouted Pam. "What are you doing in there?"

And Walter said, "I a fish! I a fish!"

Pam helped Walter get out of the fountain. Then she took him to meet Mother.

"You are back just in time," said Mother. "Thank you for taking Walter for a—WALTER!"

"I a fish," said Walter.

Then Pam told Mother everything. Mother laughed. Pam and Walter laughed, too.

Then Mother said, "It's time to go home, little fish."

Retelling Protocol

Purpose-Setting Statement: Pam's mother asks her to watch her brother, Walter, at the mall. Read the story to find out what happens to Walter when Pam looks away for just a second.

Walter and the Mall

CHARACTERS (5 points each)

_____ Pam _____ Walter _____ Mother

SETTING (5 points)

_____ Mall

PLOT (10 points each)

_____ 1. Mother, Pam, and Walter went to the mall.

_____ 2. Pam took Walter for a quick walk.

_____ 3. They looked at the fountain, some fish, and some cats.

_____ 4. Pam stopped to look at some skates.

_____ 5. When Pam turned back around, Walter was gone.

_____ 6. Pam looked for Walter at the places they had stopped.

_____ 7. Pam decided to get Mother's help.

RESOLUTION (10 points)

_____ 8. Pam found Walter pretending he was a fish in the fountain.

Character Total	_____	**READING LEVELS**	
Setting Total	_____	Independent	Above 85 Points
Plot Total	_____	Instructional	70–84 Points
Resolution Total	_____	Frustration	Below 70 Points
TOTAL POINTS	_____		

OBSERVATIONS

	Inappropriate				Appropriate
Includes detail	1	2	3	4	5
Uses prior knowledge to establish story line	1	2	3	4	5
Infers beyond text	1	2	3	4	5
	Out of Sequence				**In Sequence**
Tells story in correct sequence	1	2	3	4	5
	Verbatim				**In Own Words**
Restates story verbatim	1	2	3	4	5

Second Grade

NARRATIVE

(317 words)

Form B—

Teacher's Copy

Skunk Baby

At the pond, Skunk Baby put his paw on top of a curious-looking toad. In a sudden jump, the toad leaped high and hopped away. The skunk tried to follow, but the toad was soon out of sight.

Then a fox came out of the woods. He stood quietly—listening. He sniffed the warm night air. He sniffed again. He smelled something nearby.

Slowly the fox crept toward the pond. Skunk Baby had stopped to watch the hard-working beaver. The happy chirping of a cricket sounded near.

The fox was almost at the pond.

Suddenly, he saw the skunk. The fox crouched close to the ground. He had never seen a skunk before. The little fat, furry animal looked as though he would make a tasty supper.

Slowly the fox crept closer.

Closer . . . closer . . .

Now he was close enough. He crouched lower—ready to spring.

The frogs stopped their singing.

The cricket was still.

The pond grew quiet.

Slap! The beaver's tail hit the water in warning.

Skunk Baby jumped! His instinct told him that danger was near.

He saw the fox's yellow eyes and sharp pointed teeth. He heard a low growl.

For the first time in his life, Skunk Baby was afraid. He squeaked in fright. By instinct, he stamped the ground with his front feet. Then, half turning, he raised his tail high. He sprayed a strong-smelling liquid at the fox.

Suddenly his mother was beside him. She, too, sprayed the enemy, catching the fox full in the face with the liquid. Her smell was even more powerful.

The fox pawed at his burning eyes. Rolling over and over on the ground, he tried to rid himself of the smell. He ran to the pond and leaped into the water.

Tonight the young fox had learned an important lesson. And so had the little skunk.

Retelling Protocol

Purpose-Setting Statement: This passage tells about a meeting between a baby skunk and a fox. Read the story to find out what happens.

Skunk Baby

CHARACTERS (5 points each)

_____ Skunk Baby _____ Fox

SETTING (10 points)

_____ At the pond

PLOT (10 points each)

_____ 1. Skunk Baby follows a toad.

_____ 2. A fox comes out of the woods.

_____ 3. Skunk Baby watches a beaver.

_____ 4. Fox thinks Skunk Baby will make a tasty meal.

_____ 5. The fox creeps closer to Skunk Baby.

_____ 6. The beaver slaps his tail.

_____ 7. Skunk Baby sprays the fox and the fox runs away.

RESOLUTION (10 points)

_____ 8. Skunk Baby and the fox both learn important lessons.

Character Total	_____
Setting Total	_____
Plot Total	_____
Resolution Total	_____
TOTAL POINTS	_____

READING LEVELS	
Independent	Above 85 Points
Instructional	70–84 Points
Frustration	Below 70 Points

OBSERVATIONS

	Inappropriate				Appropriate
Includes detail	1	2	3	4	5
Uses prior knowledge to establish story line	1	2	3	4	5
Infers beyond text	1	2	3	4	5
	Out of Sequence				**In Sequence**
Tells story in correct sequence	1	2	3	4	5
	Verbatim				**In Own Words**
Restates story verbatim	1	2	3	4	5

Third Grade

NARRATIVE

(344 words)

Form B—

Teacher's Copy

Leaving Nicodemus

All of Nicodemus came out to say good-by. "Poor babies," they said, "going a hundred fifty miles all by themselves." But we knew we could do it. Because our Daddy had told us so.

We went to the river, and we followed the map. We walked all day, and when Little Brother got tired, I carried him. At night we stopped and made a fire. "We'll take turns," I said to Willie. "First, I'll watch the fire and you'll sleep. We'll fire the gun sometimes. It will scare the wild animals away." There were plenty of wild animals on the prairie—wolves, panthers, coyotes. Each night our fire and the sound of the gun kept them away.

But one night I heard Willie call to me. "Johnny," he said, "wake up but don't move." I opened my eyes and there on the ground next to me was a big prairie rattlesnake warming itself by the fire. I didn't move, I didn't breathe, for fear it would bite me.

"What shall we do?" Willie whispered. I tried to think of what Daddy would do and then I remembered something. Daddy once told me that snakes like warm places.

I said to Willie, "Let the fire go out." It seemed like we were there for hours staying so still. At last the fire went out. The night air got chilly, and the snake moved away into the darkness.

For twenty-two days we followed the river. Then one day we came to a deer trail. It led away from the river, just as the map showed. "This way," I said to my brothers. We walked along the trail. Then, on the side of the hill, we saw a little house with a garden in front. Corn was growing. A man came out of the house, and when he saw us, he began to run toward us.

"Daddy!"

"Willie! Johnny! Little Brother!"

Then there was such hugging and kissing and talking and crying and laughing and singing that I'll bet they heard us all the way back to Nicodemus.

Retelling Protocol

Purpose-Setting Statement: This story tells about three young boys who are on a trip on their own from one home to another. Read this story to find out what happens to them on the trip.

Leaving Nicodemus

CHARACTERS (2.5 points each)

_____ Willie _____ Little Brother _____ Johnny _____ Daddy

SETTING (3 points each)

_____ On the road from Nicodemus _____ New house

PLOT (14 points each)

_____ 1. Willie, Little Brother, and Johnny leave Nicodemus.

_____ 2. The boys follow the map.

_____ 3. At night they build fires and fire the gun to scare wild animals.

_____ 4. There is a rattlesnake by the fire.

_____ 5. After the fire goes out, the rattlesnake leaves.

RESOLUTION (14 points)

_____ 6. After twenty-two days, they come to their new house and find their father.

Character Total	_____
Setting Total	_____
Plot Total	_____
Resolution Total	_____
TOTAL POINTS	_____

READING LEVELS	
Independent	Above 85 Points
Instructional	70–84 Points
Frustration	Below 70 Points

OBSERVATIONS

	Inappropriate				Appropriate
Includes detail	1	2	3	4	5
Uses prior knowledge to establish story line	1	2	3	4	5
Infers beyond text	1	2	3	4	5
	Out of Sequence				**In Sequence**
Tells story in correct sequence	1	2	3	4	5
	Verbatim				**In Own Words**
Restates story verbatim	1	2	3	4	5

Fourth Grade

NARRATIVE

(354 words)

Form B—

Teacher's Copy

Mighty Mini

Mini was a young whale shark—the largest kind of fish in the world. Most of the time, she swam peacefully in the open sea. Now she was upset by her strange surroundings.

Mini had swum into the lagoon, or big bay, of a South Seas island. High tides had swept her over a coral reef in the bay. Now she was lost in a maze of channels, with walls of coral all around.

A week later, Mini was still there. She swam a regular route around the pond, but she always steered clear of the coral reef. People began to worry. How could such a big fish find enough to eat in such a small space? They didn't want Mini to die, so they decided to send for help.

The scientific team studied Mini for several weeks. They watched what she ate and how she acted. They even clipped a metal tag to her dorsal fin so they would be able to keep track of her in the open sea. However, getting her to go back to the sea was still a problem. Not even food could lure her back through the passage in the reef to freedom.

Then the island people had an idea. They tied many nets together to form one great big net three hundred feet long. Then they stretched it across the pond. Mini was cornered in the end nearest the reef.

Splash! Into the water went many of Mini's would-be rescuers. She fled to the other end of the pond. Soon she was swimming her old route once more, quiet as a goldfish.

For four days the island people tried to free the shark, and for four days they failed. Finally everybody gave up. They were worn out. When they returned a day later, Mini was gone. She had finally taken the path to freedom.

Reprinted from the September 1981 issue of *Ranger Rick* magazine, with the permission of the publisher, the National Wildlife Federation. Copyright 1981 by the National Wildlife Federation.

Retelling Protocol

Purpose-Setting Statement: This story tells about a whale shark who swims into a lagoon. Read the story to find out what happens to Mini.

Mighty Mini

CHARACTERS

_____ Mini, a young shark (4 points)

_____ The scientific team (3 points)

_____ The island people (3 points)

SETTING (6 points)

_____ Lagoon

PLOT (14 points each)

_____ 1. Mini swims into the lagoon and becomes lost.

_____ 2. People become worried and decide to help.

_____ 3. A scientific team studies Mini.

_____ 4. The island people corner Mini, but she escapes.

_____ 5. The island people try to free Mini, but they finally give up.

RESOLUTION (14 points)

_____ 6. Mini finally leaves on her own.

Character Total	_____
Setting Total	_____
Plot Total	_____
Resolution Total	_____
TOTAL POINTS	_____

READING LEVELS

Independent	Above 85 Points
Instructional	70–84 Points
Frustration	Below 70 Points

OBSERVATIONS

	Inappropriate				Appropriate
Includes detail	1	2	3	4	5
Uses prior knowledge to establish story line	1	2	3	4	5
Infers beyond text	1	2	3	4	5
	Out of Sequence				**In Sequence**
Tells story in correct sequence	1	2	3	4	5
	Verbatim				**In Own Words**
Restates story verbatim	1	2	3	4	5

Fifth Grade

NARRATIVE

(317 words)

Form B—

Teacher's Copy

Making French Toast

Bernie was teaching Bonnie how to make French toast. Bonnie was in a hurry, she was hungry.

"First, you need a mixing bowl, a fork, and a frying pan," Bernie said slowly.

"Done," said Bonnie.

"Now, to make eight slices of French toast, you need two eggs, a dash of cinnamon and sugar, half a teaspoon of salt, and two thirds of a cup of milk," said Bernie.

"Okay, but don't I need bread? It's French toast, you know," Bonnie pointed out.

"Don't rush me," Bernie complained. "I was going to say eight slices of bread next, also two tablespoons of butter."

"Sorry," said Bonnie.

"Now put the eggs, milk, cinnamon, sugar, and salt into the bowl. Use the fork to beat them until they're foamy. Melt the butter in the frying pan over a medium flame. Then dip a slice of bread in the egg mixture, and brown the slice on each side in the frying pan . . . Hey!" Bernie yelped.

Bonnie had stuck a plain piece of bread in the buttered frying pan and was pouring the egg mixture over it. "I figured this way was faster," she said. "I'm so hungry!"

"But that's wrong!" cried Bernie. He looked at the mess in the frying pan. "I was hungry too," he moaned. "Now I've lost my appetite."

Bonnie nodded sadly. "Me too," she said.

Retelling Protocol

Purpose-Setting Statement: This story tells about two children who are making French toast. Find out what happens to Bonnie's French toast.

Making French Toast

CHARACTERS (4 points each)

_____ Bernie _____ Bonnie

SETTING (10 points)

_____ Kitchen

PLOT (14 points each)

_____ 1. Bernie teaches Bonnie to make French toast.

_____ 2. Bernie tells Bonnie that she needs a bowl, fork, and frying pan.

_____ 3. Bernie tells Bonnie what ingredients she needs.

_____ 4. Bonnie is in a hurry because she is hungry.

_____ 5. Bonnie puts the bread in the pan and puts the egg mixture over it.

RESOLUTION (12 points)

_____ 6. Bonnie and Bernie lose their appetites.

		READING LEVELS	
Character Total	_____	Independent	Above 85 Points
Setting Total	_____	Instructional	70–84 Points
Plot Total	_____	Frustration	Below 70 Points
Resolution Total	_____		
TOTAL POINTS	_____		

OBSERVATIONS

	Inappropriate				**Appropriate**
Includes detail	1	2	3	4	5
Uses prior knowledge to establish story line	1	2	3	4	5
Infers beyond text	1	2	3	4	5
	Out of Sequence				**In Sequence**
Tells story in correct sequence	1	2	3	4	5
	Verbatim				**In Own Words**
Restates story verbatim	1	2	3	4	5

Sixth Grade

NARRATIVE

(503 words)

Form B—

Teacher's Copy

Amelia and the Lemonade Stand

Amelia lived in a small brick house on J Street with her mother, her father, and her three-year-old sister, Caroline. Amelia was six.

Amelia and Caroline liked to have lemonade stands on hot, sticky summer days when there was nothing else to do. Mother would pull out the old game table and set it up behind the leafy curtains of the willow tree in their front yard. Then she would pull out three old lawn chairs and set them up behind the table.

Whenever someone would walk by, he would ask, "How much for a glass of lemonade?" and Mother would say, "Fifty cents."

When they were all done, Mother would divide up all the money and give half to Caroline and half to Amelia. Caroline always spent hers on candy, but Amelia liked to save her money in her shiny, pink piggy bank.

One Sunday afternoon, Amelia and Caroline wanted to have a lemonade stand, but Mother was very busy. She had to bake a cake for Amelia's kindergarten bake sale, which was on Monday night. Then, Mother had an idea.

She brought out the table and two chairs and set them in the shade outside the kitchen window. "This way I can keep an eye on you while I bake the cake," Mother said.

Then Amelia and Caroline went inside and made the lemonade. Suddenly, Amelia had a bright idea. In her kindergarten class they had just learned how to write dollars and cents. So Amelia made a sign that said what she thought stood for fifty cents.

Amelia and Caroline sat outside for nearly an hour. Every time someone would walk by, Amelia would hold the sign up high, but the person would take one look at it and keep on walking.

Then Caroline started to cry. Their neighbor, Mrs. Fields, came rushing out to see what the matter was. "Whatever is the matter, Caroline?" Mrs. Fields asked.

"We can't sell any lemonade," Amelia chimed in. "People take one look at our sign and just keep on walking."

"Let me see your sign," replied Mrs. Fields. "Oh dear!" she exclaimed as she looked at the sign.

"What's the matter?" asked a worried Amelia.

"It seems that you have gotten the decimal in the wrong place."

"What's a decimal?" asked Amelia.

"It's that dot. You see, you have written fifty *dollars,* which is quite a lot of money. You have to put the dot in front of the five to make it say fifty cents."

Mrs. Fields changed the sign with a pen from her purse and gave it back to Amelia. Then, Mrs. Fields bought a glass of lemonade. And more and more people kept coming to buy lemonade. Amelia and Caroline had to go make third and fourth batches of lemonade.

From that day on, Amelia and Caroline never needed Mother to be outside with them when they had a lemonade stand, and Amelia always made a sign and never, ever got the decimal in the wrong place again.

By Julie Shaddox, copyright © 1999. Used by permission of the author.

Retelling Protocol

Purpose-Setting Statement: Caroline and Amelia set up a lemonade stand and learn an important lesson about math. Read to find out how.

Amelia and the Lemonade Stand

CHARACTERS (3 points each)

_____ Amelia _____ Caroline _____ Mother _____ Mrs. Fields

SETTING (8 points)

_____ Lemonade stand

PLOT (8 points each)

_____ 1. Amelia and Caroline set up a lemonade stand.

_____ 2. Mother helps with the lemonade stand.

_____ 3. Mother divides up the money.

_____ 4. Amelia and Caroline want to set up the stand, but Mother cannot help.

_____ 5. Amelia makes a sign she thinks stands for fifty cents.

_____ 6. No one buys the lemonade and Caroline starts to cry.

_____ 7. Mrs. Fields comes to find out what the problem is.

_____ 8. Mrs. Fields looks at the sign and notices a problem.

_____ 9. Mrs. Fields changes the sign.

RESOLUTION (8 points)

_____ 10. Caroline and Amelia learn a lesson about decimal points.

Character Total	_____
Setting Total	_____
Plot Total	_____
Resolution Total	_____
TOTAL POINTS	_____

READING LEVELS

Independent	Above 85 Points
Instructional	70–84 Points
Frustration	Below 70 Points

OBSERVATIONS

	Inappropriate				Appropriate
Includes detail	1	2	3	4	5
Uses prior knowledge to establish story line	1	2	3	4	5
Infers beyond text	1	2	3	4	5
	Out of Sequence				**In Sequence**
Tells story in correct sequence	1	2	3	4	5
	Verbatim				**In Own Words**
Restates story verbatim	1	2	3	4	5

Seventh Grade

NARRATIVE

(449 words)

Form B—

Teacher's Copy

Samantha and the Envelope

It was the Friday of a three-day weekend and as Samantha walked home from school that day she was thinking about how she would spend the long weekend. As she turned the corner at Park Street, Samantha noticed an envelope lying on the ground that seemed to be full of some sort of paper. Samantha picked up the envelope absent-mindedly.

As Samantha started to look at the envelope, her friend, Jeremy, ran up to her.

"I'm having some friends over tomorrow to watch the game on TV," said Jeremy. "You want to come?"

Samantha was surprised by the invitation because she was new to the neighborhood and had never really gotten to know Jeremy and his friends.

"Sure, I'd like to come," replied Samantha as she put the envelope in her backpack. Jeremy ran off as Samantha continued on her way home. Opening the front door of her house, Samantha dropped the backpack on the table in the front hall, forgetting completely about the envelope.

On Saturday, Samantha arrived at Jeremy's house just as the game was about to begin. Several other friends of Jeremy's got to his house at the same time and everyone was busy talking and laughing. Jeremy's mother brought in some popcorn and soft drinks for the kids and then went back into her office. Samantha knew that Jeremy's mother was the chairperson of a local charity and that they were in the middle of a money-raising campaign. Everyone liked Jeremy's mom, she was always friendly to the kids in the neighborhood and several of the kids asked Jeremy if his mother would watch the game with them.

"No, she's not in a very good mood," said Jeremy. "She's been really busy with the campaign and a terrible thing happened yesterday."

"What happened?" asked several of the kids.

"One of the people who is working with Mom was taking some money to deposit it in the bank. She doesn't know exactly how it happened, but the envelope with the money got lost. Mom feels just terrible."

"Oh," Samantha gasped, jumping out of her chair and running out of the door.

Samantha ran all of the way home and grabbed her backpack. Opening it up, she grabbed the envelope and looked inside. There Samantha found checks and cash along with a bank deposit form for the charity's bank account. Samantha ran back to Jeremy's house and asked to see his mother.

As Samantha handed Jeremy's mother the envelope, his mother said, "I'm so excited. We are having a banquet for the volunteers of the charity next week. I think you should come as our guest of honor. Now, who does everyone think will win this game?"

Retelling Protocol

Purpose-Setting Statement: Samantha finds an envelope on the ground on her way home from school. Read this story to find out what happens with the envelope.

Samantha and the Envelope

CHARACTERS (4 points each)

_____ Samantha _____ Jeremy _____ Jeremy's Mother

SETTING (4 points each)

_____ On the way home from school _____ Jeremy's house

PLOT (8 points each)

_____ 1. Samantha finds an envelope on the ground.
_____ 2. Jeremy invites Samantha to his house.
_____ 3. Samantha is surprised by the invitation.
_____ 4. Samantha put the envelope in her backpack.
_____ 5. Samantha drops her backpack on the table in the front hall.
_____ 6. On Saturday, Samantha goes to Jeremy's house.
_____ 7. Several of the kids ask about Jeremy's mother.
_____ 8. Jeremy tells about her charity losing the envelope of money and checks.
_____ 9. Samantha runs home and looks in the envelope.

RESOLUTION (8 points)

_____ 10. Samantha gives Jeremy's mother the envelope of money and checks.

			READING LEVELS	
Character Total	_____		Independent	Above 85 Points
Setting Total	_____		Instructional	70–84 Points
Plot Total	_____		Frustration	Below 70 Points
Resolution Total	_____			
TOTAL POINTS	_____			

OBSERVATIONS

	Inappropriate				Appropriate
Includes detail	1	2	3	4	5
Uses prior knowledge to establish story line	1	2	3	4	5
Infers beyond text	1	2	3	4	5
	Out of Sequence				**In Sequence**
Tells story in correct sequence	1	2	3	4	5
	Verbatim				**In Own Words**
Restates story verbatim	1	2	3	4	5

Eighth Grade

NARRATIVE

(470 words)

Form B—

Teacher's Copy

Annie's Fourteenth Birthday

Nothing had prepared Annie for the events of that momentous Saturday in June of 1995. It was her fourteenth birthday and Annie had been planning to have friends over for a cookout to celebrate. The day had been beautiful with temperatures in the nineties, but early in the afternoon the storm clouds began moving in. By 3:00 P.M., it looked like it was going to be a major storm. The National Weather Service had been issuing thunderstorm warnings since noon, but at about 3:30 a tornado watch was issued.

Annie was watching the clouds swirling around overhead and worrying that her cookout was going to be a complete washout when the tornado sirens sounded. As usual when the sirens sounded, Annie's father called to her to go down to the storm cellar. They always went to the cellar when the sirens sounded, even though a tornado had never actually hit their town. Her family usually spent the time playing an amiable game of hearts. This time, however, Annie could tell her parents were worried.

Annie looked across the cellar at her mother who was holding the small family dog, Scrappy. That was when Annie realized that her cat, Boomer, was not in the cellar. She started up the stairs, but her father called her back down just as a sound similar to a freight train was heard.

Annie had always heard that tornadoes sounded like a train. Could it be that there actually was going to be a tornado this time? Annie looked at her parents and realized that they had gone from worried to terrified. Annie realized that this was not just another alert, this was actually a tornado! Upstairs, it sounded like everything was being torn apart. It lasted for several minutes, during which time they could hear the sounds of destruction upstairs; it was followed by an equally horrifying silence.

Annie's father went up the cellar stairs slowly, seeming almost afraid to open the cellar door and see the tornado's results. It took him several minutes to force the cellar door open because of the debris obstructing the door. Her father gasped when he saw the havoc upstairs. Annie followed her father upstairs and stood stunned as she saw what remained of her house.

Looking about her it seemed that the only thing left standing was the bed in the central bedroom, looking forlorn and out of place under the still cloudy skies. Annie felt like she had been hit in the chest when she thought about Boomer and realized that nothing could have survived in the devastation before her. But then Annie heard the sound of a cat meowing and out from under the bed came a disgruntled Boomer, wet and bedraggled, but alive. Annie guessed it was true, cats really do have nine lives.

Retelling Protocol

Purpose-Setting Statement: Annie experiences an unusual event on her fourteenth birthday. Read this story to learn the outcome of Annie's day.

Annie's Fourteenth Birthday

CHARACTERS (4 points each)

_____ Annie _____ Mother _____ Father

SETTING (4 points each)

_____ Annie's house _____ Storm cellar

PLOT (8 points each)

_____ 1. Annie was planning a cookout for her fourteenth birthday.

_____ 2. Tornado sirens sounded.

_____ 3. Annie, her parents, and her dog, Scrappy, went to the storm cellar.

_____ 4. Annie realized that her cat, Boomer, was not in the cellar.

_____ 5. Just as Annie started up the stairs to find Boomer she heard a sound similar to a freight train.

_____ 6. Annie and her parents could hear the destruction of everything above ground.

_____ 7. Annie's father had difficulty opening the door of the cellar because debris was obstructing the door.

_____ 8. The only thing left standing was the bed in the central bedroom.

_____ 9. Annie knew Boomer could not have survived the storm.

RESOLUTION (8 points)

_____ 10. Boomer crawled out from under the bed.

		READING LEVELS	
Character Total	_____	Independent	Above 85 Points
Setting Total	_____	Instructional	70–84 Points
Plot Total	_____	Frustration	Below 70 Points
Resolution Total	_____		
TOTAL POINTS	_____		

OBSERVATIONS

	Inappropriate				Appropriate
Includes detail	1	2	3	4	5
Uses prior knowledge to establish story line	1	2	3	4	5
Infers beyond text	1	2	3	4	5
	Out of Sequence				**In Sequence**
Tells story in correct sequence	1	2	3	4	5
	Verbatim				**In Own Words**
Restates story verbatim	1	2	3	4	5

Ninth Grade

NARRATIVE

(559 words)

Form B—

Teacher's Copy

The Trip Home

Terry and Thomas had just finished their first semester at the university and could not wait to get home for their semester break. In order to save on airfare, they had decided to drive their own car back home for the break from the large university in New York to their parents' home in Texas. The weather reports were not looking promising because a major snowstorm was heading across the northern plain states and the Midwest. Terry and Thomas decided that the earlier they started, the greater the chance of missing the snow.

The first snow they encountered was just outside of Buffalo, New York, but it didn't seem too threatening.

"Hey, this is a piece of cake. If this is the worst Mother Nature has to throw at us we should make it home in record time," Thomas said to his twin, Terry.

Terry woke up from a light doze just long enough to look outside, acknowledge his brother's comment, and readjust the pillow he had cradling his head. He awoke an hour later expecting Thomas to have made great progress, but was flabbergasted to see that they had only traveled another thirty miles.

"Come on, Thomas, speed it up—we'll never make it home at this rate!" Terry complained and then noticed that his brother's hands were gripping the steering wheel in a death grip, a white-knuckled sort of grip. Looking out, Terry noticed that the snow had worsened, with visibility down to just a few hundred feet and snow drifting across the highway and rising in soft mounds in the low spots. "Wow, I definitely don't like the look of this, maybe we should stop and let this pass."

"It's not going to just pass, Terry. In fact, I think if we stop it will just get worse and we won't be able to make it home at all this weekend." Thomas leaned forward in the seat, straining to see the road in front of him, afraid that with all this drifting snow he would just drive off the shoulder of the road.

As they passed through Erie, Pennsylvania, the snow seemed to lighten up some, which in turn lightened the hearts of both young men. They increased their speed slightly and were just beginning to relax when the second wave of the storm hit them with a force neither brother had ever experienced, with driving snow and north winds that exceeded forty miles per hour. Thomas strained to see in front of him, but the heavy snow and bitter winds resulted in white-outs, dropping visibility to mere feet in front of the car. Thomas slowed down to what seemed like a crawl, trying to see the road in front of him. Twice he felt the wheels of the car leave the road and grip the rough surface of the shoulder, but after what seemed an eternity, the storm passed with a suddenness that left the young men breathless. As they entered Cleveland, Ohio, the skies cleared and the moon and stars brightened the evening sky.

"Let's stop here, and call Mom and Dad. I bet they are worried sick about us," said Thomas as relief from the strain flooded him, awakening his brother from another light doze.

"Yeah, I could really use a break after all this driving," said Terry as his brother glared at him in disgust.

Retelling Protocol

Purpose-Setting Statement: Getting home for semester break is not easy for Thomas and Terry. Read this story to find out about their drive home.

The Trip Home

CHARACTERS (5 points each)

_____ Thomas _____ Terry

SETTING (5 points each)

_____ In the car between New York and Texas _____ Snowstorm

PLOT (8 points each)

_____ 1. Thomas and Terry decided to drive home to Texas for their semester break from the university.

_____ 2. The weather reports indicated they would be driving through a snowstorm.

_____ 3. They first encountered snow in Buffalo, but it was not too bad.

_____ 4. Terry dozed while Thomas slowly drove the next thirty miles.

_____ 5. Terry suggested they stop to let the storm pass, but Thomas was afraid they would get snowed in.

_____ 6. The snow let up in Erie, Pennsylvania.

_____ 7. The second wave of the storm hit them with driving snows and winds exceeding forty miles per hour.

_____ 8. Twice the wheels of the car left the road.

RESOLUTION (8 points each)

_____ 9. The storm passed suddenly as the boys entered Cleveland, Ohio.

_____ 10. The boys stopped to call their parents.

Character Total	_____
Setting Total	_____
Plot Total	_____
Resolution Total	_____
TOTAL POINTS	_____

READING LEVELS	
Independent	Above 85 Points
Instructional	70–84 Points
Frustration	Below 70 Points

OBSERVATIONS

	Inappropriate				Appropriate
Includes detail	1	2	3	4	5
Uses prior knowledge to establish story line	1	2	3	4	5
Infers beyond text	1	2	3	4	5
	Out of Sequence				**In Sequence**
Tells story in correct sequence	1	2	3	4	5
	Verbatim				**In Own Words**
Restates story verbatim	1	2	3	4	5

Walter and the Mall

One day Pam and Walter went to the mall with Mother. Pam and Walter like it there. It wasn't a big mall, but there were many things to see.

Mother said, "Pam, I have many things to do. Why don't you take Walter for a little walk? You have come here many times, so you can find your way. Then come back and meet me here."

"OK, Mother," said Pam, and she went for a walk with Walter.

Pam liked the big fountain in the mall, so she and Walter went to look at it.

Then they went to look at some fish.

"Fish! Fish!" said Walter.

Walter couldn't say very many words, but *fish* was one word he could say.

Last of all, they stopped to look at some little cats.

Pam and Walter went to look at some more things. Pam stopped to look at some skates.

"Maybe I could get some skates someday," she thought.

Then Pam said to Walter, "Now we'll go meet Mother."

But Walter wasn't there!

"Walter! Walter!" shouted Pam.

But Walter was nowhere to be found.

"Maybe he went back to see the cats," thought Pam.

She ran over to the cats, but Walter wasn't there.

Then Pam thought, "He liked the fish best."

So she ran over to the fish. No Walter.

Pam decided to go back and get Mother.

"Maybe she can find Walter," thought Pam.

On her way back, Pam saw the big fountain. There were many boys and girls there. They were all laughing. Pam looked to see what was so funny.

"Walter!" shouted Pam. "What are you doing in there?"

And Walter said, "I a fish! I a fish!"

Pam helped Walter get out of the fountain. Then she took him to meet Mother.

"You are back just in time," said Mother. "Thank you for taking Walter for a—WALTER!"

"I a fish," said Walter.

Then Pam told Mother everything. Mother laughed. Pam and Walter laughed, too.

Then Mother said, "It's time to go home, little fish."

Skunk Baby

At the pond, Skunk Baby put his paw on top of a curious-looking toad. In a sudden jump, the toad leaped high and hopped away. The skunk tried to follow, but the toad was soon out of sight.

Then a fox came out of the woods. He stood quietly—listening. He sniffed the warm night air. He sniffed again. He smelled something nearby.

Slowly the fox crept toward the pond. Skunk Baby had stopped to watch the hard-working beaver. The happy chirping of a cricket sounded near.

The fox was almost at the pond.

Suddenly, he saw the skunk. The fox crouched close to the ground. He had never seen a skunk before. The little fat, furry animal looked as though he would make a tasty supper.

Slowly the fox crept closer.

Closer . . . closer . . .

Now he was close enough. He crouched lower—ready to spring.

The frogs stopped their singing.

The cricket was still.

The pond grew quiet.

Slap! The beaver's tail hit the water in warning.

Skunk Baby jumped! His instinct told him that danger was near.

He saw the fox's yellow eyes and sharp pointed teeth. He heard a low growl.

For the first time in his life, Skunk Baby was afraid. He squeaked in fright. By instinct, he stamped the ground with his front feet. Then, half turning, he raised his tail high. He sprayed a strong-smelling liquid at the fox.

Suddenly his mother was beside him. She, too, sprayed the enemy, catching the fox full in the face with the liquid. Her smell was even more powerful.

The fox pawed at his burning eyes. Rolling over and over on the ground, he tried to rid himself of the smell. He ran to the pond and leaped into the water.

Tonight the young fox had learned an important lesson. And so had the little skunk.

Leaving Nicodemus

All of Nicodemus came out to say good-by. "Poor babies," they said, "going a hundred fifty miles all by themselves." But we knew we could do it. Because our Daddy had told us so.

We went to the river, and we followed the map. We walked all day, and when Little Brother got tired, I carried him. At night we stopped and made a fire. "We'll take turns," I said to Willie. "First, I'll watch the fire and you'll sleep. We'll fire the gun sometimes. It will scare the wild animals away." There were plenty of wild animals on the prairie—wolves, panthers, coyotes. Each night our fire and the sound of the gun kept them away.

But one night I heard Willie call to me. "Johnny," he said, "wake up but don't move." I opened my eyes and there on the ground next to me was a big prairie rattlesnake warming itself by the fire. I didn't move, I didn't breathe, for fear it would bite me.

"What shall we do?" Willie whispered. I tried to think of what Daddy would do and then I remembered something. Daddy once told me that snakes like warm places.

I said to Willie, "Let the fire go out." It seemed like we were there for hours staying so still. At last the fire went out. The night air got chilly, and the snake moved away into the darkness.

For twenty-two days we followed the river. Then one day we came to a deer trail. It led away from the river, just as the map showed. "This way," I said to my brothers. We walked along the trail. Then, on the side of the hill, we saw a little house with a garden in front. Corn was growing. A man came out of the house, and when he saw us, he began to run toward us.

"Daddy!"

"Willie! Johnny! Little Brother!"

Then there was such hugging and kissing and talking and crying and laughing and singing that I'll bet they heard us all the way back to Nicodemus.

Mighty Mini

Mini was a young whale shark—the largest kind of fish in the world. Most of the time, she swam peacefully in the open sea. Now she was upset by her strange surroundings.

Mini had swum into the lagoon, or big bay, of a South Seas island. High tides had swept her over a coral reef in the bay. Now she was lost in a maze of channels, with walls of coral all around.

A week later, Mini was still there. She swam a regular route around the pond, but she always steered clear of the coral reef. People began to worry. How could such a big fish find enough to eat in such a small space? They didn't want Mini to die, so they decided to send for help.

The scientific team studied Mini for several weeks. They watched what she ate and how she acted. They even clipped a metal tag to her dorsal fin so they would be able to keep track of her in the open sea. However, getting her to go back to the sea was still a problem. Not even food could lure her back through the passage in the reef to freedom.

Then the island people had an idea. They tied many nets together to form one great big net three hundred feet long. Then they stretched it across the pond. Mini was cornered in the end nearest the reef.

Splash! Into the water went many of Mini's would-be rescuers. She fled to the other end of the pond. Soon she was swimming her old route once more, quiet as a goldfish.

For four days the island people tried to free the shark, and for four days they failed. Finally everybody gave up. They were worn out. When they returned a day later, Mini was gone. She had finally taken the path to freedom.

Making French Toast

Bernie was teaching Bonnie how to make French toast. Bonnie was in a hurry, she was hungry.

"First, you need a mixing bowl, a fork, and a frying pan," Bernie said slowly.

"Done," said Bonnie.

"Now, to make eight slices of French toast, you need two eggs, a dash of cinnamon and sugar, half a teaspoon of salt, and two thirds of a cup of milk," said Bernie.

"Okay, but don't I need bread? It's French toast, you know," Bonnie pointed out.

"Don't rush me," Bernie complained. "I was going to say eight slices of bread next, also two tablespoons of butter."

"Sorry," said Bonnie.

"Now put the eggs, milk, cinnamon, sugar, and salt into the bowl. Use the fork to beat them until they're foamy. Melt the butter in the frying pan over a medium flame. Then dip a slice of bread in the egg mixture, and brown the slice on each side in the frying pan . . . Hey!" Bernie yelped.

Bonnie had stuck a plain piece of bread in the buttered frying pan and was pouring the egg mixture over it. "I figured this way was faster," she said. "I'm so hungry!"

"But that's wrong!" cried Bernie. He looked at the mess in the frying pan. "I was hungry too," he moaned. "Now I've lost my appetite."

Bonnie nodded sadly. "Me too," she said.

Amelia and the Lemonade Stand

Amelia lived in a small brick house on J Street with her mother, her father, and her three-year-old sister, Caroline. Amelia was six.

Amelia and Caroline liked to have lemonade stands on hot, sticky summer days when there was nothing else to do. Mother would pull out the old game table and set it up behind the leafy curtains of the willow tree in their front yard. Then she would pull out three old lawn chairs and set them up behind the table.

Whenever someone would walk by, he would ask, "How much for a glass of lemonade?" and Mother would say, "Fifty cents."

When they were all done, Mother would divide up all the money and give half to Caroline and half to Amelia. Caroline always spent hers on candy, but Amelia liked to save her money in her shiny, pink piggy bank.

One Sunday afternoon, Amelia and Caroline wanted to have a lemonade stand, but Mother was very busy. She had to bake a cake for Amelia's kindergarten bake sale, which was on Monday night. Then, Mother had an idea.

She brought out the table and two chairs and set them in the shade outside the kitchen window. "This way I can keep an eye on you while I bake the cake," Mother said.

Then Amelia and Caroline went inside and made the lemonade. Suddenly, Amelia had a bright idea. In her kindergarten class they had just learned how to write dollars and cents. So Amelia made a sign that said what she thought stood for fifty cents.

Amelia and Caroline sat outside for nearly an hour. Every time someone would walk by, Amelia would hold the sign up high, but the person would take one look at it and keep on walking.

Then Caroline started to cry. Their neighbor, Mrs. Fields, came rushing out to see what the matter was. "Whatever is the matter, Caroline?" Mrs. Fields asked.

"We can't sell any lemonade," Amelia chimed in. "People take one look at our sign and just keep on walking."

"Let me see your sign," replied Mrs. Fields. "Oh dear!" she exclaimed as she looked at the sign.

"What's the matter?" asked a worried Amelia.

"It seems that you have gotten the decimal in the wrong place."

"What's a decimal?" asked Amelia.

"It's that dot. You see, you have written fifty *dollars,* which is quite a lot of money. You have to put the dot in front of the five to make it say fifty cents."

Mrs. Fields changed the sign with a pen from her purse and gave it back to Amelia. Then, Mrs. Fields bought a glass of lemonade. And more and more people kept coming to buy lemonade. Amelia and Caroline had to go make third and fourth batches of lemonade.

From that day on, Amelia and Caroline never needed Mother to be outside with them when they had a lemonade stand, and Amelia always made a sign and never, ever got the decimal in the wrong place again.

Samantha and the Envelope

It was the Friday of a three-day weekend and as Samantha walked home from school that day she was thinking about how she would spend the long weekend. As she turned the corner at Park Street, Samantha noticed an envelope lying on the ground that seemed to be full of some sort of paper. Samantha picked up the envelope absent-mindedly.

As Samantha started to look at the envelope, her friend, Jeremy, ran up to her.

"I'm having some friends over tomorrow to watch the game on TV," said Jeremy. "You want to come?"

Samantha was surprised by the invitation because she was new to the neighborhood and had never really gotten to know Jeremy and his friends.

"Sure, I'd like to come," replied Samantha as she put the envelope in her backpack. Jeremy ran off as Samantha continued on her way home. Opening the front door of her house, Samantha dropped the backpack on the table in the front hall, forgetting completely about the envelope.

On Saturday, Samantha arrived at Jeremy's house just as the game was about to begin. Several other friends of Jeremy's got to his house at the same time and everyone was busy talking and laughing. Jeremy's mother brought in some popcorn and soft drinks for the kids and then went back into her office. Samantha knew that Jeremy's mother was the chairperson of a local charity and that they were in the middle of a money-raising campaign. Everyone liked Jeremy's mom, she was always friendly to the kids in the neighborhood and several of the kids asked Jeremy if his mother would watch the game with them.

"No, she's not in a very good mood," said Jeremy. "She's been really busy with the campaign and a terrible thing happened yesterday."

"What happened?" asked several of the kids.

"One of the people who is working with Mom was taking some money to deposit it in the bank. She doesn't know exactly how it happened, but the envelope with the money got lost. Mom feels just terrible."

“Oh,” Samantha gasped, jumping out of her chair and running out of the door.

Samantha ran all of the way home and grabbed her backpack. Opening it up, she grabbed the envelope and looked inside. There Samantha found checks and cash along with a bank deposit form for the charity’s bank account. Samantha ran back to Jeremy’s house and asked to see his mother.

As Samantha handed Jeremy’s mother the envelope, his mother said, “I’m so excited. We are having a banquet for the volunteers of the charity next week. I think you should come as our guest of honor. Now, who does everyone think will win this game?”

Annie's Fourteenth Birthday

Nothing had prepared Annie for the events of that momentous Saturday in June of 1995. It was her fourteenth birthday and Annie had been planning to have friends over for a cookout to celebrate. The day had been beautiful with temperatures in the nineties, but early in the afternoon the storm clouds began moving in. By 3:00 P.M., it looked like it was going to be a major storm.

The National Weather Service had been issuing thunderstorm warnings since noon, but at about 3:30 a tornado watch was issued.

Annie was watching the clouds swirling around overhead and worrying that her cookout was going to be a complete washout when the tornado sirens sounded. As usual when the sirens sounded, Annie's father called to her to go down to the storm cellar. They always went to the cellar when the sirens sounded, even though a tornado had never actually hit their town. Her family usually spent the time playing an amiable game of hearts. This time, however, Annie could tell her parents were worried.

Annie looked across the cellar at her mother who was holding the small family dog, Scrappy. That was when Annie realized that her cat, Boomer, was not in the cellar. She started up the stairs, but her father called her back down just as a sound similar to a freight train was heard.

Annie had always heard that tornadoes sounded like a train. Could it be that there actually was going to be a tornado this time? Annie looked at her parents and realized that they had gone from worried to terrified. Annie realized that this was not just another alert, this was actually a tornado! Upstairs, it sounded like everything was being torn apart. It lasted for several minutes, during which time they could hear the sounds of destruction upstairs; it was followed by an equally horrifying silence.

Annie's father went up the cellar stairs slowly, seeming almost afraid to open the cellar door and see the tornado's results. It took him several minutes to force the cellar door open because of the debris obstructing the door. Her father gasped when he saw the havoc upstairs. Annie followed her father upstairs and stood stunned as she saw what remained of her house.

Looking about her it seemed that the only thing left standing was the bed in the central bedroom, looking forlorn and out of place under the still cloudy skies. Annie felt like she had been hit in the chest when she thought about Boomer and realized that nothing could have survived in the devastation before her. But then Annie heard the sound of a cat meowing and out from under the bed came a disgruntled Boomer, wet and bedraggled, but alive. Annie guessed it was true, cats really do have nine lives.

The Trip Home

Terry and Thomas had just finished their first semester at the university and could not wait to get home for their semester break. In order to save on airfare, they had decided to drive their own car back home for the break from the large university in New York to their parents' home in Texas. The weather reports were not looking promising because a major snowstorm was heading across the northern plain states and the Midwest. Terry and Thomas decided that the earlier they started, the greater the chance of missing the snow.

The first snow they encountered was just outside of Buffalo, New York, but it didn't seem too threatening.

"Hey, this is a piece of cake. If this is the worst Mother Nature has to throw at us we should make it home in record time," Thomas said to his twin, Terry.

Terry woke up from a light doze just long enough to look outside, acknowledge his brother's comment, and readjust the pillow he had cradling his head. He awoke an hour later expecting Thomas to have made great progress, but was flabbergasted to see that they had only traveled another thirty miles.

"Come on, Thomas, speed it up—we'll never make it home at this rate!" Terry complained and then noticed that his brother's hands were gripping the steering wheel in a death grip, a white-knuckled sort of grip. Looking out, Terry noticed that the snow had worsened, with visibility down to just a few hundred feet and snow drifting across the highway and rising in soft mounds in the low spots. "Wow, I definitely don't like the look of this, maybe we should stop and let this pass."

"It's not going to just pass, Terry. In fact, I think if we stop it will just get worse and we won't be able to make it home at all this weekend." Thomas leaned forward in the seat, straining to see the road in front of him, afraid that with all this drifting snow he would just drive off the shoulder of the road.

As they passed through Erie, Pennsylvania, the snow seemed to lighten up some, which in turn lightened the hearts of both young men. They increased their speed slightly and were just beginning to relax when the second wave of the storm hit them with a force neither brother had ever experienced, with driving snow and north winds that exceeded forty miles per hour. Thomas strained to see in front of him, but the heavy snow and bitter winds resulted in whiteouts, dropping visibility to mere feet in front of the car. Thomas slowed down to what seemed like a crawl, trying to see the road in front of him. Twice he felt the wheels of the car leave the road and grip the rough surface of the shoulder, but after what seemed an eternity, the storm passed with a suddenness that left the young men breathless. As they entered Cleveland, Ohio, the skies cleared and the moon and stars brightened the evening sky.

"Let's stop here, and call Mom and Dad. I bet they are worried sick about us," said Thomas as relief from the strain flooded him, awakening his brother from another light doze.

"Yeah, I could really use a break after all this driving," said Terry as his brother glared at him in disgust.

Expository Retelling

Brief Directions for Administering Expository Passages

Step One. Select the beginning point for the expository passages in either of two ways: (1) use the highest *independent* level achieved with the retelling passages, or (2) use a level that is at least one grade level below the student's grade placement.

Step Two. Introduce the reading by saying, **"Tell me everything you know about (the topic)."** Record the student's responses in the Prior column if this information appears in the passage. Record any other information in the section in the middle of the protocol page. If the student gives 90% of the passage information, choose another passage.

Step Three. Ask the student to read the passage *silently.*

Step Four. After the student finishes reading the passage, ask, **"What information about (the topic) did you learn from reading this passage?"** Record the student responses in the Recall column on the protocol page. Complete the Observations checklist at the bottom of the protocol page.

If the student provides 90% or more of the information in the Prior and Recall columns combined, the passage can be considered at the student's independent level. If the student provides between 75% and 90% of the information, the passage is at the instructional level for the student. If the student knows or recalls less than 75% of the information, the passage is too difficult, and the teacher should select and administer an easier passage.

Expository Passages and Rubrics: Form A

First Grade

EXPOSITORY

(117 words)

Form A—

Teacher's Copy

Who Helps Bear Cubs?

New bear cubs are so little. They can't see well. They can't get things to eat. But they are cute! When cubs are so little, they do not go out. The mother bear gives her cubs all that they need. Soon the cubs are not so little. They go out with their mother. Everything is new to the cubs! They want to see everything. The cubs have a good time jumping, rolling, and playing.

The mother bear is with her cubs all the time. She helps them find things to eat. She helps them know all about the things bears do. Someday, when the cubs are big, their mother will not need to help them.

Retelling Protocol: Who Helps Bear Cubs? (Level 1.0)

TOPIC: Bear Cubs

PRIOR	RECALL	
		1. Bear cubs are so little.
		2. Bear cubs can't see well.
		3. Bear cubs can't get things to eat.
		4.* Mother bear gives her cubs all that they need.
		5. Soon bear cubs go out with their mother.
		6. Bear cubs want to see everything.
		7. Bear cubs jump, roll, and play.
		8. Mother bear helps the cubs find things to eat.
		9. Mother bear helps the cubs know all the things that bears do.
		10. Someday the Mother bear will not help the cubs.

*Stated main idea

OBSERVATIONS					
	Inadequate				**Adequate**
Has prior knowledge	1	2	3	4	5
Recalls information	1	2	3	4	5
Uses prior knowledge to infer	1	2	3	4	5
Recognizes stated main idea	1	2	3	4	5
	Verbatim				**In Own Words**
Restates text verbatim	1	2	3	4	5

OTHER FACTUAL INFORMATION GIVEN BY THE STUDENT

Second Grade

EXPOSITORY

(172 words)

Form A—

Teacher's Copy

Trees and Animals Need Each Other

Soil and trees are not the only things that depend on each other. Forest plants and animals need each other, too. The forest gives food and shelter to many animals. Squirrels and birds make their homes in tree branches. Raccoons live in holes in tree trunks. Insects live in tree bark. Many animals eat the seeds and nuts that grow on trees. Deer eat bark. Insects eat leaves, wood, and roots.

In return, the animals help more trees and plants to grow. How? Trees and plants grow from seeds and nuts. Birds scatter seeds that allow new plants to grow. Have you ever seen a squirrel bury an acorn? Squirrels bury more nuts than they can eat. Each nut they bury has a chance to become a new tree.

So forest animals and plants depend on each other in many ways. If whole forests are cut down, animals may lose their homes and die. If we learn how living things depend on each other, we can help forest life continue.

Retelling Protocol: Trees and Animals Need Each Other (Level 2.0)

TOPIC: Trees and Animals

PRIOR	RECALL	
		1.* Forest plants and animals need each other.
		2. Squirrels and birds make their homes in trees.
		3. Raccoons live in holes in trees.
		4. Animals eat the seeds and nuts of trees.
		5. Deer eat bark.
		6. Insects eat various parts of trees.
		7. Trees and plants grow from seeds and nuts.
		8. Birds scatter seeds.
		9. Squirrels bury more nuts than they can eat.
		10. Some of the nuts become trees.
		11. If forests are cut down, animals will lose their homes.
		12. If we learn how living things depend on each other, we can help the forest to continue.

*Stated main idea

OBSERVATIONS

	Inadequate				Adequate
Has prior knowledge	1	2	3	4	5
Recalls information	1	2	3	4	5
Uses prior knowledge to infer	1	2	3	4	5
Recognizes stated main idea	1	2	3	4	5

	Verbatim				In Own Words
Restates text verbatim	1	2	3	4	5

OTHER FACTUAL INFORMATION GIVEN BY THE STUDENT

Third Grade

EXPOSITORY

(326 words)

Form A—

Teacher's Copy

How Big Is Big?

Animals live in all parts of the world. They come in many sizes. Some animals are so tiny that you can't see them. Some are so huge that it's hard to even picture them in your mind. Find out just how big some animals are. Do you know which animal is the tallest of all? It is the giraffe. A giraffe is taller than any other animal on land. It is about as tall as three grown-up people. The giraffe has a very long neck and very long legs.

A giraffe is so tall that it can see things that are a long way off. If it sees something frightening, the giraffe has time to run away. The giraffe's long legs help it run very fast.

The giraffe is the tallest animal on land, but the elephant is the biggest. An elephant can weigh as much as sixty grown-up people!

Elephants live in herds. A herd is a group of animals that live together. They care for each other and look for food together. In some herds there are only four or five elephants, but in other herds there may be up to a thousand elephants!

Not all big animals live on land. Some live in the water. The whale shark is a very big fish. It is longer than four cars. It weighs as much as two elephants. Many people are afraid of sharks, but no one needs to be afraid of the whale shark. The whale shark is quite gentle and eats only small plants and fish.

The biggest animal that has ever lived on land or sea is the blue whale. The blue whale is huge. It weighs more than one thousand grown-up people. It is longer than seven cars.

Retelling Protocol: How Big Is Big? (Level 3.0)

TOPIC: Big Animals

PRIOR	RECALL	
		1.* Some animals are so huge that it's hard to even picture them in your mind.
		2. The tallest animal is the giraffe.
		3. It is as tall as three grown-up people.
		4. It has a very long neck and very long legs.
		5. A giraffe is so tall that it can see things far away.
		6. If it sees something frightening, the giraffe has time to run away.
		7. The elephant is the biggest animal on land.
		8. An elephant can weigh as much as sixty grown-up people!
		9. Elephants live in herds.
		10. Some herds have as few as four or five elephants, but others have as many as a thousand.
		11. The whale shark is longer than four cars.
		12. It weighs as much as two elephants.
		13. The whale shark is gentle and eats only small plants and fish.
		14. The biggest animal that has ever lived on land or sea is the blue whale.
		15. The blue whale weighs more than one thousand grown-up people and is longer than seven cars.

*Stated main idea

OBSERVATIONS	Inadequate				Adequate
Has prior knowledge	1	2	3	4	5
Recalls information	1	2	3	4	5
Uses prior knowledge to infer	1	2	3	4	5
Recognizes stated main idea	1	2	3	4	5
	Verbatim				**In Own Words**
Restates text verbatim	1	2	3	4	5

OTHER FACTUAL INFORMATION GIVEN BY THE STUDENT

Fourth Grade

EXPOSITORY

(234 words)

Form A—

Teacher's Copy

Antarctica

Surrounding the South Pole is the continent of Antarctica. It is the coldest place on Earth. Even in summer, the average temperature is below freezing. However, in summer there are long periods of daylight.

Antarctica is covered with a solid ice cap. In some places it is a mile thick. Huge sheets of ice are called glaciers. They creep slowly down the mountains to the sea. When chunks of ice break off from glaciers, they form icebergs.

A large mountain range divides the continent in two. Some of these mountains rise over fourteen thousand feet. Some are completely buried in the ice cap. There is almost no life in the interior of the continent. In the surrounding waters and along the coasts, however, are fish, birds, whales, and six kinds of seals.

The leopard seal has strong jaws and sharp teeth. It sometimes preys on penguins and other seals. A more peaceful creature is the Weddell seal. The most common Antarctica seal is the crabeater. It does not eat crabs at all, but small sea animals called krill.

The birds that make Antarctica their home depend on the sea for food. Even those that fly, such as the blue-eyed shags and the southern giant fulmar, rarely venture far inland.

The most familiar Antarctica birds are penguins. They don't fly at all. A thick layer of fat protects penguins' bodies from the harsh Antarctic climate.

Retelling Protocol: Antarctica (Level 4.0)

TOPIC: Antarctica

PRIOR	RECALL	
		1. Surrounding the South Pole is the continent of Antarctica.
		2.* Antarctica is the coldest place on Earth.
		3. In summer, the average temperature is below freezing.
		4. In summer, there are long periods of daylight.
		5. The ice cap is a mile thick in some places.
		6. Huge sheets of ice are called glaciers.
		7. When chunks of ice break off from glaciers, they form icebergs.
		8. The continent is divided by a large mountain range with some peaks over 14,000 feet.
		9. There is no life in the interior of the continent.
		10. In the surrounding waters and along the coasts are fish, birds, whales, and six kinds of seals.
		11. One type of seal is the leopard seal, which preys on penguins and other seals.
		12. The most common Antarctica seal is the crabeater, which eats krill.
		13. Two Antarctica flying birds are the blue-eyed shag and the southern giant fulmar.
		14. The most familiar Antarctica bird is the penguin.
		15. Penguins' bodies are protected from the cold by a thick layer of fat.

*Stated main idea

OBSERVATIONS					
	Inadequate				**Adequate**
Has prior knowledge	1	2	3	4	5
Recalls information	1	2	3	4	5
Uses prior knowledge to infer	1	2	3	4	5
Recognizes stated main idea	1	2	3	4	5
	Verbatim				**In Own Words**
Restates text verbatim	1	2	3	4	5

OTHER FACTUAL INFORMATION GIVEN BY THE STUDENT

Fifth Grade

EXPOSITORY

(322 words)

Form A—

Teacher's Copy

How the Electric Eel Makes Electricity

The electric eel does not have a fin along its back like most fish. It has a fin along its stomach. This "swimming" fin helps the eel move in a wavy motion. The eel also has smaller fins that help it steer. The electric eel spends much of its time lying quietly in the water. It moves only to come to the top for a breath of air. It would drown if it did not come up for air about every fifteen minutes.

All living things—including people—make electricity. This electricity is made in the nerves, glands, and muscles. Over millions of years, some of the electric eel's muscles have developed to make more electricity than normal muscles.

The muscles that produce electricity are known as electric organs. There are three electric organs: the main, the Sachs, and the Hunters. The main organ sends out a strong charge. The Sachs organ sends out a weak one. The Hunters organ seems to help the other two.

The electric eel is a blind, toothless, slow-moving fish. Without its electricity, it would have a hard time defending itself or catching its food.

The electric eel uses an electric field like a pilot uses radar. The Sachs organ sends a weak electric charge out the tail and back to receptor pits in the eel's head. This sets up a weak electric field around the eel. When something touches this field, the regular pattern is distorted. This change in the field tells the eel something is there. The eel can tell what is in its field and how far away it is.

If an object in its field is something the eel would like to eat, its main electric organ sends out a huge electric charge. Small fish and frogs are stunned or killed by the shock. The eel can catch them easily. Larger fish and animals are stunned or scared away.

Retelling Protocol: How the Electric Eel Makes Electricity (Level 5.0)

TOPIC: Electric Eels

PRIOR	RECALL	
		1. Unlike other fish, the electric eel has a fin along its stomach, which helps the eel move in a wavy motion.
		2. The electric eel moves only to come to the top for air.
		3. The eel must come to the top for air every fifteen minutes.
		4.* Some of the electric eel's muscles have developed to make more electricity than normal muscles.
		5. The eel has three electric organs: the main, the Sachs, and the Hunters.
		6. The main organ sends out a strong charge.
		7. The Sachs sends out a weak charge.
		8. The Hunters organ helps the other two organs.
		9. The electric eel is a blind, toothless, slow-moving fish.
		10. The Sachs organ sends a weak electric charge out the tail and back to receptor pits in the eel's head to create an electric field around the eel.
		11. When some object comes into this field, the eel can tell what it is and how far away it is.
		12. If the object is something the eel wants to eat, it sends out a huge electric charge.

*Stated main idea

OBSERVATIONS

	Inadequate				Adequate
Has prior knowledge	1	2	3	4	5
Recalls information	1	2	3	4	5
Uses prior knowledge to infer	1	2	3	4	5
Recognizes stated main idea	1	2	3	4	5
	Verbatim				**In Own Words**
Restates text verbatim	1	2	3	4	5

OTHER FACTUAL INFORMATION GIVEN BY THE STUDENT

Sixth Grade

EXPOSITORY

(215 words)

Form A—

Teacher's Copy

Rice

Rice is the major food for at least half of the people in the world. Millions of farm families spend their lives growing this important food crop.

Rice is grown where there is plenty of water and a long, warm growing season. Over 90 percent of the world's rice is grown in Asia. The People's Republic of China grows the most rice. It is followed by India and Japan. In the United States, rice is grown mostly in Texas, California, Louisiana, and Arkansas. In Europe, Italy is where the most rice is grown. In Africa, it is grown mostly along the Nile River in Egypt.

There are two major kinds of rice. They are upland rice and lowland rice. Upland rice is grown in places where there is plenty of rain. Lowland rice is grown in fields that have been flooded with water. Most farmers grow this second kind of rice.

First, rice is planted in a muddy field. After about four weeks the young rice plants are ready to be moved to a plowed and flooded field. This field is called the rice paddy. When the leaves on the plants begin to turn from green to yellow, the field is drained. The rice becomes ripe in the sun. Then the rice is harvested.

Retelling Protocol: Rice (Level 6.0)

TOPIC: Rice

PRIOR	RECALL	
		1.* Rice is the major food for at least half of the people in the world.
		2. Rice needs plenty of water and a long, warm growing season.
		3. Over 90 percent of the world's rice is grown in Asia.
		4. The People's Republic of China grows the most rice.
		5. India and Japan follow China in the production of rice.
		6. Texas, California, Louisiana, and Arkansas are the leading rice-producing states in the United States.
		7. In Europe, Italy is where the most rice is grown.
		8. In Africa, it is grown mostly along the Nile River in Egypt.
		9. There are two major kinds of rice: upland and lowland.
		10. Upland rice is grown where there is plenty of rain.
		11. Lowland rice is grown in fields that have been flooded with water.
		12. First, rice is planted in a muddy field.
		13. After about four weeks, the young plants are moved to a rice paddy, a plowed and flooded field.
		14. When the leaves on the plants begin to turn from green to yellow, the field is drained.
		15. The rice becomes ripe in the sun and is soon harvested.

*Stated main idea

OBSERVATIONS

	Inadequate				Adequate
Has prior knowledge	1	2	3	4	5
Recalls information	1	2	3	4	5
Uses prior knowledge to infer	1	2	3	4	5
Recognizes stated main idea	1	2	3	4	5

	Verbatim				In Own Words
Restates text verbatim	1	2	3	4	5

OTHER FACTUAL INFORMATION GIVEN BY THE STUDENT

Seventh Grade

EXPOSITORY

(528 words)

Form A—

Teacher's Copy

A Mom with a Mission

To us, insects may not seem like the best parents. After mating, the female usually lays her eggs, then either leaves or dies. Without protection, many of the eggs and newly hatched young are eaten by predators. Other insects starve after hatching because they can't find enough food to eat. But moms of the treehopper species *Umbonia ataliba* give their young a better start in life.

Treehoppers are small insects that survive by sucking juices from living plants. Treehoppers are also called "thorn bugs," but they are not true bugs. Because of their body structure, they belong to the order *Homoptera* and are therefore related to cicadas, aphids, whiteflies, and scale insects. Although treehoppers are found all over the world, they are especially common in the warm tropics. This species lives along the edges of tropical forests in Central America.

One thing that makes treehoppers different from most other insects is that they often care for their eggs and young. After mating, a treehopper mom lays about ninety eggs near the tip of a tender branch. Then she sits silently below the eggs, guarding them against predators. If a hungry lizard, bird, or grasshopper comes along, the treehopper does her best to keep it away, standing in front of or over her eggs to protect them. Sometimes she'll even kick at the predator or spread her wings to startle the intruder and drive it off.

After the eggs hatch, the female treehopper continues her guard duty. But now she has other responsibilities as well. The young treehoppers, called nymphs, must feed on plant juices if they are to survive. Mom uses her sharp, beaklike mouth to drill feeding holes through the bark of the branch. The nymphs move to these feeding holes and start sucking juices.

The nymphs don't look anything like their brightly patterned mom. They are brown or yellow and blend in with the bark of their branch. This camouflage helps them hide from predators. As they grow, the young treehoppers molt four times. Each time they shed their skin, they look more like adult treehoppers. However, they still need their mom to guard against predators and drill feeding holes for them. If something happens to her before the nymphs reach adulthood, they usually die.

It takes *Umbonia* nymphs about six weeks to grow up. When they molt for the fourth time, the young treehoppers are finally adults. Now they can drill their own feeding holes. They also have a useful appendage called the pronotum, which projects like a crest above the treehopper's body—making the insect look like a thorn on a twig. The pronotum is hard and sharp and helps to keep the treehoppers from becoming a meal for a lizard or other animal.

As adults, the treehoppers are also ready to begin mating, and soon the females fly through the forest to lay their own eggs. Mom's mission is now accomplished. An *Umbonia* female only raises one clutch of young in her life, and then she dies. However, by giving her young a head start, Mom has helped make sure that the forest will be filled with treehoppers for generations to come.

Retelling Protocol: A Mom with a Mission (Level 7.0)

TOPIC: Treehoppers

PRIOR	RECALL	
		1. Unlike other insects, treehoppers do not abandon their eggs or young.
		2. Treehoppers are small insects that survive by sucking juices from living plants.
		3. Treehoppers are sometimes called "thorn bugs," but they are not bugs.
		4. They belong to the order *Homoptera* and are related to cicadas, aphids, whiteflies, and scale insects.
		5. They are most commonly found in warm tropical regions like the tropical forests of Central America.
		6. A treehopper mom lays about ninety eggs on a branch, which she guards against predators.
		7. The treehopper mom drills feeding holes in branches for her young.
		8. The young treehoppers molt four times before they look like the adult treehoppers.
		9. The young treehoppers need their mother's protection and assistance with food until they reach adulthood.
		10. It takes about six weeks for the nymphs to grow up.
		11. The adult treehopper has a thorn-like appendage called the pronotum, which the treehopper uses for protection.
		12. A treehopper mom raises only one clutch of young in her life, and then she dies.

OBSERVATIONS	Inadequate				Adequate
Has prior knowledge	1	2	3	4	5
Recalls information	1	2	3	4	5
Uses prior knowledge to infer	1	2	3	4	5
Recognizes stated main idea	1	2	3	4	5
	Verbatim				**In Own Words**
Restates text verbatim	1	2	3	4	5

OTHER FACTUAL INFORMATION GIVEN BY THE STUDENT

Eighth Grade

EXPOSITORY

(365 words)

Form A—

Teacher's Copy

The How and Why of Fingerprints

A young woman wandered into the police station in a small town in Maine. She told police that she did not know who she was or where she had come from. The woman was suffering from amnesia, a loss of memory.

The chief of police took a set of the woman's fingerprints. The prints were sent to the Federal Bureau of Investigation (FBI) fingerprint file in Washington, D.C., where they were matched with a set taken when the woman applied for a job with the government twenty years earlier. The woman's family was called, and they came to take her home.

Fingerprints are a sure, no-fail way of finding out who someone is. You can change your name, move to another country, get a new job, change your hairstyle, or put on or take off weight, but there is no way to change your fingerprints.

In earlier times, other means were used to make sure of someone's identity. For example, people might be branded for life to show that they had once committed crimes. In ancient Rome, soldiers who deserted the army were marked with a tattoo when they were found.

In later times, law officers depended on their memory or used photographs to identify criminals. But memories fail, and people's looks change.

Around 1870, a French scientist named Alphonse Bertillon found a way to measure and record the sizes of certain bones in the body. This method of identification was used for about thirty years. Then, around the beginning of the twentieth century, two men were found to have the same Bertillon measurements! This proved that the system was not foolproof.

During the 1900s, police began to accept fingerprints as the best method of identification. Police departments set up their own files of fingerprints. In 1924, the FBI formed a national fingerprint file, which now holds copies of the fingerprints of 200 million people. The fingerprints on file are not only of people who have been involved in crimes. For example, men and women applying for the armed services and for certain jobs are asked for their fingerprints. That is why the police in Maine were able to identify the woman with amnesia.

Retelling Protocol: The How and Why of Fingerprints (Level 8.0)

TOPIC: Ways to Identify Individuals

PRIOR	RECALL	
		1.* Fingerprints are a sure, no-fail way of finding out who someone is.
		2. In earlier times, criminals were branded.
		3. In ancient Rome, soldiers who deserted were marked with a tattoo.
		4. Law officers have depended on memory or used photographs.
		5. Alphonse Bertillon found a way to measure and record the sizes of certain bones in the body.
		6. The Bertillon system was not foolproof because some people have the same Bertillon measurements as others.
		7. During the 1900s, police began to accept fingerprints as the best method of identification.
		8. In 1924, the FBI formed a national fingerprint file.
		9. The national fingerprint file now has fingerprints of 200 million people.

*Stated main idea

OBSERVATIONS					
	Inadequate				**Adequate**
Has prior knowledge	1	2	3	4	5
Recalls information	1	2	3	4	5
Uses prior knowledge to infer	1	2	3	4	5
Recognizes stated main idea	1	2	3	4	5
	Verbatim				**In Own Words**
Restates text verbatim	1	2	3	4	5

OTHER FACTUAL INFORMATION GIVEN BY THE STUDENT

Ninth Grade

EXPOSITORY

(522 words)

Form A—

Teacher's Copy

The Decision That Led to Civil War

Four years before the Civil War began, the first shots were fired—not on a battlefield, but in the Supreme Court. This occurred in 1857, when the Court considered a crucial question: Should a slave living in a free state be considered free?

The Court's answer to this question was no, and it sent shock waves through every state, slave and free alike. According to the ruling, which became known as the Dred Scott decision, a slave would always be regarded as property, no matter where he or she happened to be.

When the case began, Virginia-born Dred Scott had spent all of his fifty-one years in slavery. He had been owned by a St. Louis family, which had sold him to a local army surgeon. The doctor then took Scott from the slave state of Missouri to the free state of Illinois and later to the free territory of Wisconsin. Scott was then taken back to Missouri by his owner, who died there.

Automatically, the surgeon's widow inherited Scott. But when his former St. Louis owners learned what had happened, they launched a legal battle to have Scott and slaves like him declared free. They argued that he had spent so much time in free territory that he should now be free himself. Scott, who could neither read nor write, had to sign the legal papers with an X.

The case was heard first in 1846 by a state court in Missouri, which granted Scott his freedom. The victory was short-lived, however, as the ruling was soon overturned by a higher court. Not until 1857 was the U.S. Supreme Court ready to rule on his case.

The Chief Justice at the time was Roger Brooke Taney, a Maryland native in his eighties whose parents had owned slaves of their own. A high-ranking public official since the days of Andrew Jackson, Taney had been Chief Justice for more than twenty years. Many critics thought him far too old and backward to continue serving.

Nonetheless, he still had great influence on his fellow justices. When Taney's Court ruled on Dred Scott's case, its judgment was that he remain a slave. Taney went beyond Scott's case to rule that no black descendant of any slave could ever be a U.S. citizen and declared that Congress had no right to pass laws to curtail the spread of slavery in federal territories.

Public reaction was swift and strong. Southerners expressed delight with the decision, claiming that it affirmed once and for all their right to keep slaves. Northerners expressed outrage, charging that the ruling was unjust and inhumane.

Ironically, Scott was freed later in 1857 when the army surgeon's widow married a congressman who opposed slavery. [Scott] died sixteen months after the Supreme Court's ruling, a free man.

It might be said that Dred Scott was used by those who opposed slavery to test how far the legal system would go to keep people in bondage. It is true that Scott probably understood little about the great impact of his case, but thanks in part to his quiet patience, opposition to slavery grew.

Retelling Protocol: The Decision That Led to Civil War (Level 9.0)

TOPIC: Dred Scott Decision

PRIOR	RECALL	
		1.* In 1857, the Supreme Court considered the question whether a slave living in a free state should be considered free.
		2. The Court's decision was no.
		3. This decision was known as the Dred Scott decision because it involved a slave named Dred Scott.
		4. Scott was sold by a St. Louis family to an army surgeon.
		5. The doctor first took Scott to Illinois, a free state, and then to the free territory of Wisconsin.
		6. Scott was eventually taken back to Missouri where his owner died.
		7. The former owners of Scott sued to have Scott declared a free man because he had spent so much time in free territory.
		8. A state court ruled that Scott was free.
		9. This ruling was overturned by a higher court.
		10. Eventually, the U.S. Supreme Court, under Chief Justice Roger Taney, ruled on the case.
		11. Southerners were delighted by the ruling; however, Northerners were outraged.
		12. Later in 1857, Scott's owner gave him his freedom.
		13. Scott died sixteen months after the ruling.
		14. Opposition to slavery grew in response to the Dred Scott decision.

*Stated main idea

OBSERVATIONS	Inadequate				Adequate
Has prior knowledge	1	2	3	4	5
Recalls information	1	2	3	4	5
Uses prior knowledge to infer	1	2	3	4	5
Recognizes stated main idea	1	2	3	4	5
	Verbatim				**In Own Words**
Restates text verbatim	1	2	3	4	5

OTHER FACTUAL INFORMATION GIVEN BY THE STUDENT

Who Helps Bear Cubs?

New bear cubs are so little. They can't see well. They can't get things to eat. But they are cute! When cubs are so little, they do not go out. The mother bear gives her cubs all that they need. Soon the cubs are not so little. They go out with their mother. Everything is new to the cubs! They want to see everything. The cubs have a good time jumping, rolling, and playing.

The mother bear is with her cubs all the time. She helps them find things to eat. She helps them know all about the things bears do. Someday, when the cubs are big, their mother will not need to help them.

Trees and Animals Need Each Other

Soil and trees are not the only things that depend on each other. Forest plants and animals need each other, too. The forest gives food and shelter to many animals. Squirrels and birds make their homes in tree branches. Raccoons live in holes in tree trunks. Insects live in tree bark. Many animals eat the seeds and nuts that grow on trees. Deer eat bark. Insects eat leaves, wood, and roots.

In return, the animals help more trees and plants to grow. How? Trees and plants grow from seeds and nuts. Birds scatter seeds that allow new plants to grow. Have you ever seen a squirrel bury an acorn? Squirrels bury more nuts than they can eat. Each nut they bury has a chance to become a new tree.

So forest animals and plants depend on each other in many ways. If whole forests are cut down, animals may lose their homes and die. If we learn how living things depend on each other, we can help forest life continue.

How Big Is Big?

Animals live in all parts of the world. They come in many sizes. Some animals are so tiny that you can't see them. Some are so huge that it's hard to even picture them in your mind. Find out just how big some animals are. Do you know which animal is the tallest of all? It is the giraffe. A giraffe is taller than any other animal on land. It is about as tall as three grown-up people. The giraffe has a very long neck and very long legs.

A giraffe is so tall that it can see things that are a long way off. If it sees something frightening, the giraffe has time to run away. The giraffe's long legs help it run very fast.

The giraffe is the tallest animal on land, but the elephant is the biggest. An elephant can weigh as much as sixty grown-up people!

Elephants live in herds. A herd is a group of animals that live together. They care for each other and look for food together. In some herds there are only four or five elephants, but in other herds there may be up to a thousand elephants!

Not all big animals live on land. Some live in the water. The whale shark is a very big fish. It is longer than four cars. It weighs as much as two elephants. Many people are afraid of sharks, but no one needs to be afraid of the whale shark. The whale shark is quite gentle and eats only small plants and fish.

The biggest animal that has ever lived on land or sea is the blue whale. The blue whale is huge. It weighs more than one thousand grown-up people. It is longer than seven cars.

Antarctica

Surrounding the South Pole is the continent of Antarctica. It is the coldest place on Earth. Even in summer, the average temperature is below freezing. However, in summer there are long periods of daylight.

Antarctica is covered with a solid ice cap. In some places it is a mile thick. Huge sheets of ice are called glaciers. They creep slowly down the mountains to the sea. When chunks of ice break off from glaciers, they form icebergs.

A large mountain range divides the continent in two. Some of these mountains rise over fourteen thousand feet. Some are completely buried in the ice cap. There is almost no life in the interior of the continent. In the surrounding waters and along the coasts, however, are fish, birds, whales, and six kinds of seals.

The leopard seal has strong jaws and sharp teeth. It sometimes preys on penguins and other seals. A more peaceful creature is the Weddell seal. The most common Antarctica seal is the crabeater. It does not eat crabs at all, but small sea animals called krill.

The birds that make Antarctica their home depend on the sea for food. Even those that fly, such as the blue-eyed shags and the southern giant fulmar, rarely venture far inland.

The most familiar Antarctica birds are penguins. They don't fly at all. A thick layer of fat protects penguins' bodies from the harsh Antarctic climate.

How the Electric Eel Makes Electricity

The electric eel does not have a fin along its back like most fish. It has a fin along its stomach. This "swimming" fin helps the eel move in a wavy motion. The eel also has smaller fins that help it steer. The electric eel spends much of its time lying quietly in the water. It moves only to come to the top for a breath of air. It would drown if it did not come up for air about every fifteen minutes.

All living things—including people—make electricity. This electricity is made in the nerves, glands, and muscles. Over millions of years, some of the electric eel's muscles have developed to make more electricity than normal muscles.

The muscles that produce electricity are known as electric organs. There are three electric organs: the main, the Sachs, and the Hunters. The main organ sends out a strong charge. The Sachs organ sends out a weak one. The Hunters organ seems to help the other two.

The electric eel is a blind, toothless, slow-moving fish. Without its electricity, it would have a hard time defending itself or catching its food.

The electric eel uses an electric field like a pilot uses radar. The Sachs organ sends a weak electric charge out the tail and back to receptor pits in the eel's head. This sets up a weak electric field around the eel. When something touches this field, the regular pattern is distorted. This change in the field tells the eel something is there. The eel can tell what is in its field and how far away it is.

If an object in its field is something the eel would like to eat, its main electric organ sends out a huge electric charge. Small fish and frogs are stunned or killed by the shock. The eel can catch them easily. Larger fish and animals are stunned or scared away.

Rice

Rice is the major food for at least half of the people in the world. Millions of farm families spend their lives growing this important food crop.

Rice is grown where there is plenty of water and a long, warm growing season. Over ninety percent of the world's rice is grown in Asia. The People's Republic of China grows the most rice. It is followed by India and Japan. In the United States, rice is grown mostly in Texas, California, Louisiana, and Arkansas. In Europe, Italy is where the most rice is grown. In Africa, it is grown mostly along the Nile River in Egypt.

There are two major kinds of rice. They are upland rice and lowland rice. Upland rice is grown in places where there is plenty of rain. Lowland rice is grown in fields that have been flooded with water. Most farmers grow this second kind of rice.

First, rice is planted in a muddy field. After about four weeks the young rice plants are ready to be moved to a plowed and flooded field. This field is called the rice paddy. When the leaves on the plants begin to turn from green to yellow, the field is drained. The rice becomes ripe in the sun. Then the rice is harvested.

A Mom with a Mission

To us, insects may not seem like the best parents. After mating, the female usually lays her eggs, then either leaves or dies. Without protection, many of the eggs and newly hatched young are eaten by predators. Other insects starve after hatching because they can't find enough food to eat. But moms of the treehopper species *Umbonia ataliba* give their young a better start in life.

Treehoppers are small insects that survive by sucking juices from living plants. Treehoppers are also called "thorn bugs," but they are not true bugs. Because of their body structure, they belong to the order *Homoptera* and are therefore related to cicadas, aphids, whiteflies, and scale insects. Although treehoppers are found all over the world, they are especially common in the warm tropics. This species lives along the edges of tropical forests in Central America.

One thing that makes treehoppers different from most other insects is that they often care for their eggs and young. After mating, a treehopper mom lays about ninety eggs near the tip of a tender branch. Then she sits silently below the eggs, guarding them against predators. If a hungry lizard, bird, or grasshopper comes along, the treehopper does her best to keep it away, standing in front of or over her eggs to protect them. Sometimes she'll even kick at the predator or spread her wings to startle the intruder and drive it off.

After the eggs hatch, the female treehopper continues her guard duty. But now she has other responsibilities as well. The young treehoppers, called nymphs, must feed on plant juices if they are to survive. Mom uses her sharp, beaklike mouth to drill feeding holes through the bark of the branch. The nymphs move to these feeding holes and start sucking juices.

The nymphs don't look anything like their brightly patterned mom. They are brown or yellow and blend in with the bark of their branch. This camouflage helps them hide from predators. As they grow, the young treehoppers molt four times. Each time they shed their skin, they look more like adult treehoppers. However, they still need their mom to guard against predators and drill feeding holes for them. If something happens to her before the nymphs reach adulthood, they usually die.

It takes *Umbonia* nymphs about six weeks to grow up. When they molt for the fourth time, the young treehoppers are finally adults. Now they can drill their own feeding holes. They also have a useful appendage called the pronotum, which projects like a crest above the treehopper's body—making the insect look like a thorn on a twig. The pronotum is hard and sharp and helps to keep the treehoppers from becoming a meal for a lizard or other animal.

As adults, the treehoppers are also ready to begin mating, and soon the females fly through the forest to lay their own eggs. Mom's mission is now accomplished. An *Umbonia* female only raises one clutch of young in her life, and then she dies. However, by giving her young a head start, Mom has helped make sure that the forest will be filled with treehoppers for generations to come.

The How and Why of Fingerprints

A young woman wandered into the police station in a small town in Maine. She told police that she did not know who she was or where she had come from. The woman was suffering from amnesia, a loss of memory.

The chief of police took a set of the woman's fingerprints. The prints were sent to the Federal Bureau of Investigation (FBI) fingerprint file in Washington, D.C., where they were matched with a set taken when the woman applied for a job with the government twenty years earlier. The woman's family was called, and they came to take her home.

Fingerprints are a sure, no-fail way of finding out who someone is. You can change your name, move to another country, get a new job, change your hairstyle, or put on or take off weight, but there is no way to change your fingerprints.

In earlier times, other means were used to make sure of someone's identity. For example, people might be branded for life to show that they had once committed crimes. In ancient Rome, soldiers who deserted the army were marked with a tattoo when they were found.

In later times, law officers depended on their memory or used photographs to identify criminals. But memories fail, and people's looks change.

Around 1870, a French scientist named Alphonse Bertillon found a way to measure and record the sizes of certain bones in the body. This method of identification was used for about thirty years. Then, around the beginning of the twentieth century, two men were found to have the same Bertillon measurements! This proved that the system was not foolproof.

During the 1900s, police began to accept fingerprints as the best method of identification. Police departments set up their own files of fingerprints. In 1924, the FBI formed a national fingerprint file, which now holds copies of the fingerprints of 200 million people. The fingerprints on file are not only of people who have been involved in crimes. For example, men and women applying for the armed services and for certain jobs are asked for their fingerprints. That is why the police in Maine were able to identify the woman with amnesia.

The Decision That Led to Civil War

Four years before the Civil War began, the first shots were fired—not on a battlefield, but in the Supreme Court. This occurred in 1857, when the Court considered a crucial question: Should a slave living in a free state be considered free?

The Court's answer to this question was no, and it sent shock waves through every state, slave and free alike. According to the ruling, which became known as the Dred Scott decision, a slave would always be regarded as property, no matter where he or she happened to be.

When the case began, Virginia-born Dred Scott had spent all of his fifty-one years in slavery. He had been owned by a St. Louis family, which had sold him to a local army surgeon. The doctor then took Scott from the slave state of Missouri to the free state of Illinois and later to the free territory of Wisconsin. Scott was then taken back to Missouri by his owner, who died there.

Automatically, the surgeon's widow inherited Scott. But when his former St. Louis owners learned what had happened, they launched a legal battle to have Scott and slaves like him declared free. They argued that he had spent so much time in free territory that he should now be free himself. Scott, who could neither read nor write, had to sign the legal papers with an X.

The case was heard first in 1846 by a state court in Missouri, which granted Scott his freedom. The victory was short-lived, however, as the ruling was soon overturned by a higher court. Not until 1857 was the U.S. Supreme Court ready to rule on his case.

The Chief Justice at the time was Roger Brooke Taney, a Maryland native in his eighties whose parents had owned slaves of their own. A high-ranking public official since the days of Andrew Jackson, Taney had been Chief Justice for more than twenty years. Many critics thought him far too old and backward to continue serving.

Nonetheless, he still had great influence on his fellow justices. When Taney's Court ruled on Dred Scott's case, its judgment was that he remain a slave. Taney went beyond Scott's case to rule that no black descendant of any slave could ever be a U.S. citizen and declared that Congress had no right to pass laws to curtail the spread of slavery in federal territories.

Public reaction was swift and strong. Southerners expressed delight with the decision, claiming that it affirmed once and for all their right to keep slaves. Northerners expressed outrage, charging that the ruling was unjust and inhumane.

Ironically, Scott was freed later in 1857 when the army surgeon's widow married a congressman who opposed slavery. [Scott] died sixteen months after the Supreme Court's ruling, a free man.

It might be said that Dred Scott was used by those who opposed slavery to test how far the legal system would go to keep people in bondage. It is true that Scott probably understood little about the great impact of his case, but thanks in part to his quiet patience, opposition to slavery grew.

First Grade

EXPOSITORY

(166 words)

Form B—

Teacher's Copy

Different Kinds of Bears

Bears are large animals with heavy fur. Some bears are black. Some are brown. Some are white. Most bears sleep in the winter. Bears can appear to be friendly. They can also be very dangerous. There are different kinds of bears.

Black bears live in the woods of North America. These bears are not always all black. Some have brown noses. Some have white fur on their chest. Black bears sometimes come close to houses or camps.

Grizzly bears are large bears. They live in western North America. They have gray hair growing in their brown fur. This makes them look grizzled. The word *grizzly* means "spotted with gray." These bears may be the most dangerous animals in North America.

Polar bears have heavy white fur. They live where it is very cold. They live where there is much ice and snow. Looking like snow helps protect these bears. Polar bears are good swimmers. They get much of their food from the sea.

Retelling Protocol: Different Kinds of Bears (Level 1.0)

TOPIC: Bears

PRIOR	RECALL	
		1. Bears are large animals with heavy fur.
		2. There are black, brown, and white bears.
		3. Most bears sleep in the winter.
		4. Bears can appear to be friendly, but they can be dangerous.
		5.* There are many different kinds of bears.
		6. Black bears live in the woods of North America.
		7. Some black bears have brown noses or white fur on their chests.
		8. Grizzly bears are very large bears that live in western North America.
		9. They look grizzly because they have gray hair growing in their brown fur.
		10. *Grizzly* means "spotted with gray."
		11. Grizzly bears are the most dangerous animals in North America.
		12. Polar bears have heavy white fur.
		13. They live where it is very cold and where there is much ice and snow.
		14. Looking like snow helps protect the polar bear.
		15. Polar bears are good swimmers.

*Stated main idea

OBSERVATIONS					
	Inadequate				**Adequate**
Has prior knowledge	1	2	3	4	5
Recalls information	1	2	3	4	5
Uses prior knowledge to infer	1	2	3	4	5
Recognizes stated main idea	1	2	3	4	5
	Verbatim				**In Own Words**
Restates text verbatim	1	2	3	4	5

OTHER FACTUAL INFORMATION GIVEN BY THE STUDENT

Second Grade

EXPOSITORY

(168 words)

Form B—

Teacher's Copy

Animal Homes

Animals live in many places. Caves, trees, and holes in the ground can be animal homes. In the day, some bats rest and sleep in caves. When it starts to get dark, they go out to get food. There are birds that live in caves, too. Like the bats, these birds go out of the cave to get food.

One animal that lives in a tree is a squirrel. You can see a squirrel as it runs from one tree to the next. There are many kinds of owls that live in trees. Some of these owls rest in the day. They fly about at night.

Moles live underground. They don't come out much. They get their food under the ground. A grasshopper mouse lives underground, too. It comes out at night to get food. There are other animals that live in caves, trees, or under the ground. You may want to find out about some other animals that live in these kinds of animal homes.

Retelling Protocol: Animal Homes (Level 2.0)

TOPIC: Animal Homes

PRIOR	RECALL	
		1.* Animals live in many places.
		2. Caves, trees, and holes in the ground can be animal homes.
		3. Bats rest and sleep in caves in the daytime.
		4. Bats go out to get food at night.
		5. Some birds live in caves.
		6. The birds go out of the cave for food.
		7. A squirrel lives in a tree.
		8. Many kinds of owls live in trees.
		9. Some owls rest in the daytime and fly around at night.
		10. Moles live underground.
		11. Moles get their food underground.
		12. The grasshopper mouse lives underground.
		13. The grasshopper mouse comes out at night to get food.

*Stated main idea

OBSERVATIONS

	Inadequate				Adequate
Has prior knowledge	1	2	3	4	5
Recalls information	1	2	3	4	5
Uses prior knowledge to infer	1	2	3	4	5
Recognizes stated main idea	1	2	3	4	5

	Verbatim				In Own Words
Restates text verbatim	1	2	3	4	5

OTHER FACTUAL INFORMATION GIVEN BY THE STUDENT

Third Grade

EXPOSITORY

(279 words)

Form B—

Teacher's Copy

Bird Migration

In the fall, as cold weather approaches, insects begin to disappear. Plants wither and die. Weed seeds are being blown away. The berries and food crops have all been picked or eaten. Fish are moving down to warmer, lower depths. There will not be much food left for birds who live where the seasons change. But the birds' bodies seem to know all this. As the days grow shorter, they prepare for winter.

Almost a third of the world's birds leave their homes each fall and return in the spring. Migrating birds store extra fat in their bodies for the journey. Some birds travel thousands of miles without stopping. They burn the stored fat for energy. The longer the distance a bird has to travel, the more fat it will store before it leaves.

The American golden plover lives in western Canada. It flies two thousand miles over the Atlantic Ocean to northern South America before stopping for food. Then it continues on. Its Alaskan cousin does the same thing on the West Coast, but its first stop is Hawaii, three thousand miles away.

When the golden plover starts its flight, it weighs about six ounces. It weighs just over three and a half ounces at the end of its flight. The plovers replace the fat quickly before they start again for their winter homes in Argentina.

Most birds fly north to south to reach a place where the weather is warm and there is plenty of food. They stay in their wintering places until spring comes back to their northern homes. Since the seasons are reversed below the equator, migrating birds have two summers and no winters.

Retelling Protocol: Bird Migration (Level 3.0)

TOPIC: Bird Migration

PRIOR	RECALL	
		1. There is not much food for birds in their northern homes in the winter.
		2.* One-third of the birds in the world leave their homes each fall and return each spring.
		3. Birds store extra fat in their bodies for energy.
		4. Some birds travel thousands of miles without stopping.
		5. The longer the distance, the more fat that will be stored.
		6. The American golden plover lives in western Canada.
		7. It flies over 2000 miles to northern South America before stopping.
		8. The Alaskan cousin of the plover flies to Hawaii, 3000 miles away.
		9. At the beginning of the journey, the plover weighs six ounces.
		10. At the end of the journey, the plover weighs three and one-half ounces.
		11. Argentina is the winter home of the golden plover.
		12. Migrating birds have two summers and no winters.

*Stated main idea

OBSERVATIONS

	Inadequate				Adequate
Has prior knowledge	1	2	3	4	5
Recalls information	1	2	3	4	5
Uses prior knowledge to infer	1	2	3	4	5
Recognizes stated main idea	1	2	3	4	5
	Verbatim				**In Own Words**
Restates text verbatim	1	2	3	4	5

OTHER FACTUAL INFORMATION GIVEN BY THE STUDENT

Fourth Grade

EXPOSITORY

(148 words)

Form B—

Teacher's Copy

Japan

Japan is a country in the Pacific Ocean. It is made up of four large islands and some smaller ones. Japan is only as large as the state of Montana. Over one hundred million people are crowded onto the islands. The mountains that cover Japan take up so much land. There is not much land on which people can live.

The highest mountains are called the Japanese Alps. The mountains are beautiful. They attract many tourists each year. The most famous peak is Mount Fuji. In winter, it is a skiing spot. In summer, people climb to the rim of its crater.

Because of these mountains, there is very little land that can be used for farming. The Japanese need to use every bit of their precious land carefully. Rice can be grown on the hillsides, as can tea. Wheat, barley, fruit, and vegetables are also grown in Japan.

Retelling Protocol: Japan (Level 4.0)

TOPIC: Japan

PRIOR	RECALL	
		1.* Japan is a country in the Pacific Ocean.
		2. It is made up of four large islands and some smaller ones.
		3. Japan is the size of Montana.
		4. The population is over 100 million.
		5. The highest mountains in Japan are called the Japanese Alps.
		6. The most famous peak is Mount Fuji.
		7. Because of these mountains, there is very little land that can be used for farming.
		8. Rice and tea can be grown on the hillsides.
		9. Other crops are wheat, barley, fruit, and vegetables.

*Stated main idea

OBSERVATIONS					
	Inadequate				**Adequate**
Has prior knowledge	1	2	3	4	5
Recalls information	1	2	3	4	5
Uses prior knowledge to infer	1	2	3	4	5
Recognizes stated main idea	1	2	3	4	5
	Verbatim				**In Own Words**
Restates text verbatim	1	2	3	4	5

OTHER FACTUAL INFORMATION GIVEN BY THE STUDENT

Fifth Grade

EXPOSITORY

(241 words)

Form B—

Teacher's Copy

Nocturnal Animals

When you go to sleep at night, one part of the animal world is just getting up. It is the world of nocturnal animals. Nocturnal animals are animals that are active at night.

Most nocturnal animals come out at night to look for food. The dark of the night helps keep nocturnal animals safe. Even if an enemy is near, the nocturnal animal is hard to see.

The raccoon is one kind of nocturnal animal. Some raccoons live on the ground, and some live in trees. Raccoons like to eat fruit and fish. They also like to eat corn and all kinds of seeds. Because of this, farmers do not like to have raccoons in their fields. The raccoon has dark fur with light circles on its tail. The dark circles around its eyes look like a mask.

The possum is another animal that moves about at night and sleeps during the day. It eats small animals, insects, and all kinds of plants. The possum is about the size of a cat. It can hang upside down by its tail. The possum is a good climber and often lives in trees. The possum has a special way of helping itself. When an enemy is near, the possum rolls over on its back and stays very still. When the possum does this, the enemy thinks the possum is dead and goes away.

Retelling Protocol: Nocturnal Animals (Level 5.0)

TOPIC: Nocturnal Animals

PRIOR	RECALL	
		1.* Nocturnal animals are animals that are active at night.
		2. Nocturnal animals come out to look for food at night because they are hard to see at night.
		3. The raccoon is one kind of nocturnal animal.
		4. Some raccoons live on the ground, and some live in trees.
		5. Raccoons eat fruit, fish, corn, and all kinds of seeds.
		6. The raccoon has dark fur with light circles on its tail.
		7. The dark circles around the raccoon's eyes look like a mask.
		8. The possum is another nocturnal animal.
		9. Possums eat small animals, insects, and all kinds of plants.
		10. The possum is about the size of a cat.
		11. The possum can hang upside down by its tail.
		12. The possum is a good climber and often lives in trees.
		13. When an enemy is near, the possum rolls over on its back and stays very still; the enemy thinks the possum is dead.

*Stated main idea

OBSERVATIONS

	Inadequate				Adequate
Has prior knowledge	1	2	3	4	5
Recalls information	1	2	3	4	5
Uses prior knowledge to infer	1	2	3	4	5
Recognizes stated main idea	1	2	3	4	5

	Verbatim				In Own Words
Restates text verbatim	1	2	3	4	5

OTHER FACTUAL INFORMATION GIVEN BY THE STUDENT

Sixth Grade

EXPOSITORY

(241 words)

Form B—

Teacher's Copy

How Tornadoes Behave

No storm is more violent than a tornado. A tornado is much different from a hurricane. A hurricane is made up of spiraling rain clouds. They swirl about a calm center, or eye. Its winds blow about 100 miles an hour. Compare this to the winds of the tornado. They have been measured at up to 300 miles an hour.

Scientists have several theories about how tornadoes are formed. They do know that the Gulf of Mexico is their breeding ground. Warm, moist air from the Gulf is carried north to the Rocky Mountains. Cold, dry air from the Rockies collides with the warm, moist air from the South. Troublesome weather is the result.

The conditions that bring about tornadoes are the same as those that cause thunderstorms. Tornadoes often develop along with thunderstorms. As the thunderstorm moves, tornadoes may form along its path, traveling a few miles, then dying out.

The tornado funnel usually appears beneath the thunderstorm's dark, heavy clouds. Often it stretches down toward the ground, whirling and twisting as it moves. Sometimes the funnel never quite reaches the earth's surface. Other times it touches down briefly, then rises.

On the average, the tornado path is a quarter of a mile wide and 16 miles long. Some tornadoes have caused heavy damage for as many as 200 or 300 miles. The forward speed of the tornado is about 40 miles an hour. However, speeds of up to 70 miles an hour have often been recorded.

Retelling Protocol: How Tornadoes Behave (Level 6.0)

TOPIC: Tornadoes

PRIOR	RECALL	
		1.* No storm is more violent than a tornado.
		2. A hurricane is made of spiraling rain clouds that swirl about a calm center, or eye.
		3. Hurricane winds blow about 100 miles an hour.
		4. In comparison, the winds of a tornado have been measured at 300 miles an hour.
		5. The Gulf of Mexico is the breeding ground of tornadoes.
		6. Cold, dry air from the Rockies collides with the warm, moist air from the Gulf of Mexico.
		7. The conditions that bring about tornadoes are the same as those that cause thunderstorms.
		8. Tornadoes often develop along with thunderstorms.
		9. The tornado funnel usually appears beneath the thunderstorm's dark, heavy clouds.
		10. The funnel stretches down toward the ground, whirling and twisting as it moves.
		11. Sometimes the funnel never quite reaches the earth's surface.
		12. Sometimes the funnel touches down briefly, then rises.
		13. The average tornado path is a quarter of a mile wide and 16 miles long.
		14. Some tornadoes have caused heavy damage for as much as 200 to 300 miles.
		15. The forward speed of the tornado is about 40 miles an hour.
		16. Some tornadoes have been clocked up to 70 miles an hour.

*Stated main idea

OBSERVATIONS					
	Inadequate				**Adequate**
Has prior knowledge	1	2	3	4	5
Recalls information	1	2	3	4	5
Uses prior knowledge to infer	1	2	3	4	5
Recognizes stated main idea	1	2	3	4	5
	Verbatim				**In Own Words**
Restates text verbatim	1	2	3	4	5

OTHER FACTUAL INFORMATION GIVEN BY THE STUDENT

Seventh Grade

EXPOSITORY

(345 words)

Form B—

Teacher's Copy

Tsunami

When an earthquake takes place on one of the continents, it can do a great deal of damage. It might seem that a quake far out at sea, however, could be ignored. The water would shake a bit, but surely no one would be hurt. And yet an earthquake at sea can be more dreadful than one on land.

The seaquake will set up a wave that is not very high in mid ocean but stretches across the surface for an enormous distance. It therefore involves a large volume of water. Such a wave spreads outward in all directions from the point at which the quake took place. As it approaches land and as the ocean gets shallower, the stretch of water in the wave is compressed front and rear. Water then piles up higher, then much higher. If the wave moves into a narrowing harbor, its volume is forced still higher, sometimes fifty to one hundred feet high.

That tower of water, coming suddenly and without warning, can break over a city, drowning thousands. Before the wave comes in, the preceding trough arrives. The water sucks far out, like an enormous low tide. Then the wave comes in like a colossal high tide. Because of this out-and-in effect the huge wave has been called a *tidal wave.* This is a poor name. It has nothing to do with the tides.

In recent decades the name *tsunami* (tsoo-na-me) has been used more and more frequently. This is a Japanese word meaning "harbor wave," which is an accurate description. The Japanese, living on an island near the edge of our largest ocean, have suffered a great deal from tsunamis.

The largest in recent years was in 1883, when the volcanic island Krakatoa (krak′e-to′e) in the East Indies exploded and sent hundred-foot tsunamis crashing into nearby shores. About 1400 B.C. an Aegean island exploded and a tsunami destroyed the civilization on the nearby island of Crete. Still a third famous tsunami destroyed the city of Lisbon in 1755.

Retelling Protocol: Tsunami (Level 7.0)

TOPIC: Tidal Waves/Tsunamis

PRIOR	RECALL	
		1.* An earthquake at sea can be more dreadful than one on land.
		2. Seaquakes stretch across the surface of the ocean for an enormous distance and involve a large volume of water.
		3. As the wave approaches land, the surface of the water is compressed.
		4. Water piles up higher and higher.
		5. This tower of water can destroy cities and drown thousands.
		6. This wave is sometimes called a *tidal wave* because of its out-and-in motion.
		7. Tidal wave is not a good name because the wave has nothing to do with tides.
		8. Recently, these waves have been called *tsunami,* a Japanese word that means "harbor wave."
		9. The largest tsunami in recent years was in 1883.
		10. The 1883 tsunami was a result of the explosion of the volcanic island of Krakatoa.
		11. Around 1400 B.C., a tsunami destroyed the civilization on the island of Crete.
		12. In 1755, the city of Lisbon was destroyed by a tsunami.

*Stated main idea

OBSERVATIONS

	Inadequate				Adequate
Has prior knowledge	1	2	3	4	5
Recalls information	1	2	3	4	5
Uses prior knowledge to infer	1	2	3	4	5
Recognizes stated main idea	1	2	3	4	5

	Verbatim				In Own Words
Restates text verbatim	1	2	3	4	5

OTHER FACTUAL INFORMATION GIVEN BY THE STUDENT

Eighth Grade

EXPOSITORY

(388 words)

Form B—

Teacher's Copy

The Origin of Agriculture

According to a new theory, the beginning of agriculture was the result of a change in climate and the depletion of natural resources.

This all began in the region of the Jordan Valley about 12,000 years ago when the climate of the mild summer months changed, becoming hot and dry. The stress on the environment took the form of lakes drying up, a shorter growing season, and game becoming scarcer because there was less food and water.

The people in the region had always lived by hunting and by gathering foods they found growing in the wild. Now they, like the animals, were dramatically affected by the scarcity of food and water. As a result, they moved to areas near the Dead Sea, where food and water were more plentiful. However, the swelling population soon made food scarce there, also.

Some plants, primarily legumes and grains, were actually helped by the change in climate. The life cycle of these plants ends in the spring. Because of their husks, seeds for these plants survived the hot, dry summers, leaving them ready to germinate during the cool, wet winters. The flourishing grains became tougher, so that their seeds did not scatter when the plant was plucked. It was logical that people would learn to save some of the seeds of these wild grasses for planting, to cultivate the plants, and then to harvest these cereals.

Archaeologists have discovered that a sophisticated culture formed in this area about 10,000 years ago. These people, called the Natufians, were not nomads; they lived in well-built houses in a permanent settlement. The Natufians had a distinctive social structure indicated by seashell badges of rank. This would suggest that these people had a social organization that allowed them to control the storage and distribution of grain. They also had the technology of flint, sickles, and stone mortars.

The increased food supplies made possible by agriculture led to the expansion of human population and thus to the formation of cities. So many people living together in one place necessitated an organization that we have come to call civilization.

Soon a spreading population carried the idea of agriculture east and north into Mesopotamia and what is now modern Turkey. Both agriculture and Western civilization were well under way.

From *Writer's Workshop / Grade 8* (1993). Macmillan/McGraw-Hill.

Retelling Protocol: The Origin of Agriculture (Level 8.0)

TOPIC: Beginning of Agriculture

PRIOR	RECALL	
		1.* The beginning of agriculture was the result of a change in climate and the depletion of natural resources.
		2. This change began about 12,000 years ago in the Jordan Valley.
		3. The climate in the Jordan Valley changed from mild to hot and dry.
		4. The people in the region had lived by hunting and gathering foods.
		5. They began to save seeds from plants and to cultivate new plants.
		6. A sophisticated culture, the Natufians, formed in this area about 10,000 years ago.
		7. They had a distinctive social structure indicated by seashell badges of rank.
		8. They were able to control storage and distribution of grain.
		9. They had the technology of flint, sickles, and stone mortars.
		10. Agriculture led to the expansion of the population, to the formation of cities, and eventually to the development of civilization.
		11. A growing population began to spread the idea of agriculture to other areas.

*Stated main idea

OBSERVATIONS

	Inadequate				Adequate
Has prior knowledge	1	2	3	4	5
Recalls information	1	2	3	4	5
Uses prior knowledge to infer	1	2	3	4	5
Recognizes stated main idea	1	2	3	4	5
	Verbatim				**In Own Words**
Restates text verbatim	1	2	3	4	5

OTHER FACTUAL INFORMATION GIVEN BY THE STUDENT

Ninth Grade

EXPOSITORY

(555 words)

Form B—

Teacher's Copy

Brown v. *Board of Education:* Desegregating America's Schools

In 1954, a unanimous Supreme Court decision stated that racial discrimination no longer had a place in America's public schools. Black and white children should be taught in the same classrooms.

The case began when Oliver Brown, a black man, sued the Topeka, Kansas, Board of Education. He asked that his daughter, Linda, be admitted to their neighborhood grade school, which only white students attended, instead of being sent across town to an all-black school. Kansas was then one of seventeen states that had separate schools for black and white children.

The Court declared that separation of children by race was unconstitutional under the Fourteenth Amendment to the U.S. Constitution. This amendment was passed after the Civil War in 1868, and its purpose was to ensure that black citizens' civil rights were the same as those enjoyed by all Americans. The Fourteenth Amendment said that no state may "deny to any person within its jurisdiction the equal protection of the laws." It did not mention schools. This is not surprising because at that time there were very few public schools for whites in the South and few, if any, for blacks. The court interpreted the law as broad enough to mean that everyone was entitled to equality of education.

The Topeka Board of Education and other segregated school systems said that the schools they ran for black students were just as good as their schools for whites. Because the schools were equally good, though separate, the school boards insisted that they were complying with the equal protection law.

This "separate but equal" idea was based on an earlier Supreme Court decision, *Plessy* v. *Ferguson,* in 1896. This case was not about schools but about railroad trains. The court had said that it was legal for railroad companies to insist that whites and blacks travel in different cars, so long as the cars were "separate but equal." For half a century, this policy was applied to elementary schools, too.

Now, in *Brown* v. *Board of Education,* the Supreme Court decided this was no longer fair treatment. Chief Justice Warren wrote, "In the field of public education the doctrine of 'separate but equal' has no place. Separate educational facilities are inherently unequal."

It took the Court about three years to hear arguments on this important case and to come to a decision. Then it took even longer to make the law work. The Supreme Court ordered that compliance with its ruling should be accomplished with "all deliberate speed," but ten years later, not even 10 percent of southern black students had been assigned to integrated schools. Some cities faced real difficulties in changing their school systems, but others deliberately dragged their feet. A few towns even closed their public schools rather than obey the law.

The Civil Rights Act of 1964 speeded up the process. The U.S. Justice Department was given responsibility for enforcing the law, and schools were notified that if they did not integrate, they would not receive federal money. Gradually, the nation's schools came into compliance with the law.

Brown v. *Board of Education* was of great importance in making the American school system more democratic and fair for all citizens. It was a catalyst for other civil rights gains that brought about greater equality in public accommodations, housing, voting, recreation, and employment opportunities.

Adapted from *Important Supreme Court Cases.* Copyright © 1989, Cobblestone Publishing Company, 30 Grove Street, Suite C, Peterborough, NH 03458. Reprinted by permission of the publisher.

Retelling Protocol: *Brown* v. *Board of Education* (Level 9.0)

TOPIC: *Brown* v. *Board of Education*

PRIOR	RECALL	
		1.* In 1954, a unanimous Supreme Court decision stated that racial discrimination no longer had a place in America's public schools.
		2. Oliver Brown, a black man in Topeka, Kansas, sued the Board of Education so that his daughter could attend a whites-only neighborhood school.
		3. The Court's decision was based on the Fourteenth Amendment to the Constitution, which guarantees equal protection under the law.
		4. Although the Fourteenth Amendment did not mention schools, the Court used it to decide that everyone was entitled to an equal education.
		5. The Topeka School Board argued that their schools were "separate but equal."
		6. The "separate but equal" argument was based on an earlier court decision in *Plessy* v. *Ferguson.*
		7. Although the Court took three years to make its decision, implementing the ruling took even longer.
		8. The Civil Rights Act of 1964 speeded up the process.
		9. The *Brown* v. *Board of Education* case was a catalyst for other civil rights gains.

*Stated main idea

OBSERVATIONS	Inadequate				Adequate
Has prior knowledge	1	2	3	4	5
Recalls information	1	2	3	4	5
Uses prior knowledge to infer	1	2	3	4	5
Recognizes stated main idea	1	2	3	4	5
	Verbatim				**In Own Words**
Restates text verbatim	1	2	3	4	5

OTHER FACTUAL INFORMATION GIVEN BY THE STUDENT

Different Kinds of Bears

Bears are large animals with heavy fur. Some bears are black. Some are brown. Some are white. Most bears sleep in the winter. Bears can appear to be friendly. They can also be very dangerous. There are different kinds of bears.

Black bears live in the woods of North America. These bears are not always all black. Some have brown noses. Some have white fur on their chest. Black bears sometimes come close to houses or camps.

Grizzly bears are large bears. They live in western North America. They have gray hair growing in their brown fur. This makes them look grizzled. The word *grizzly* means "spotted with gray." These bears may be the most dangerous animals in North America.

Polar bears have heavy white fur. They live where it is very cold. They live where there is much ice and snow. Looking like snow helps protect these bears. Polar bears are good swimmers. They get much of their food from the sea.

Animal Homes

Animals live in many places. Caves, trees, and holes in the ground can be animal homes. In the day, some bats rest and sleep in caves. When it starts to get dark, they go out to get food. There are birds that live in caves, too. Like the bats, these birds go out of the cave to get food.

One animal that lives in a tree is a squirrel. You can see a squirrel as it runs from one tree to the next. There are many kinds of owls that live in trees. Some of these owls rest in the day. They fly about at night.

Moles live underground. They don't come out much. They get their food under the ground. A grasshopper mouse lives underground, too. It comes out at night to get food. There are other animals that live in caves, trees, or under the ground. You may want to find out about some other animals that live in these kinds of animal homes.

Bird Migration

In the fall, as cold weather approaches, insects begin to disappear. Plants wither and die. Weed seeds are being blown away. The berries and food crops have all been picked or eaten. Fish are moving down to warmer, lower depths. There will not be much food left for birds who live where the seasons change. But the birds' bodies seem to know all this. As the days grow shorter, they prepare for winter.

Almost a third of the world's birds leave their homes each fall and return in the spring. Migrating birds store extra fat in their bodies for the journey. Some birds travel thousands of miles without stopping. They burn the stored fat for energy. The longer the distance a bird has to travel, the more fat it will store before it leaves.

The American golden plover lives in western Canada. It flies two thousand miles over the Atlantic Ocean to northern South America before stopping for food. Then it continues on. Its Alaskan cousin does the same thing on the West Coast, but its first stop is Hawaii, three thousand miles away.

When the golden plover starts its flight, it weighs about six ounces. It weighs just over three and a half ounces at the end of its flight. The plovers replace the fat quickly before they start again for their winter homes in Argentina.

Most birds fly north to south to reach a place where the weather is warm and there is plenty of food. They stay in their wintering places until spring comes back to their northern homes. Since the seasons are reversed below the equator, migrating birds have two summers and no winters.

Japan

Japan is a country in the Pacific Ocean. It is made up of four large islands and some smaller ones. Japan is only as large as the state of Montana. Over one hundred million people are crowded onto the islands. The mountains that cover Japan take up so much land. There is not much land on which people can live.

The highest mountains are called the Japanese Alps. The mountains are beautiful. They attract many tourists each year. The most famous peak is Mount Fuji. In winter, it is a skiing spot. In summer, people climb to the rim of its crater.

Because of these mountains, there is very little land that can be used for farming. The Japanese need to use every bit of their precious land carefully. Rice can be grown on the hillsides, as can tea. Wheat, barley, fruit, and vegetables are also grown in Japan.

Nocturnal Animals

When you go to sleep at night, one part of the animal world is just getting up. It is the world of nocturnal animals. Nocturnal animals are animals that are active at night.

Most nocturnal animals come out at night to look for food. The dark of the night helps keep nocturnal animals safe. Even if an enemy is near, the nocturnal animal is hard to see.

The raccoon is one kind of nocturnal animal. Some raccoons live on the ground, and some live in trees. Raccoons like to eat fruit and fish. They also like to eat corn and all kinds of seeds. Because of this, farmers do not like to have raccoons in their fields. The raccoon has dark fur with light circles on its tail. The dark circles around its eyes look like a mask.

The possum is another animal that moves about at night and sleeps during the day. It eats small animals, insects, and all kinds of plants. The possum is about the size of a cat. It can hang upside down by its tail. The possum is a good climber and often lives in trees. The possum has a special way of helping itself. When an enemy is near, the possum rolls over on its back and stays very still. When the possum does this, the enemy thinks the possum is dead and goes away.

How Tornadoes Behave

No storm is more violent than a tornado. A tornado is much different from a hurricane. A hurricane is made up of spiraling rain clouds. They swirl about a calm center, or eye. Its winds blow about 100 miles an hour. Compare this to the winds of the tornado. They have been measured at up to 300 miles an hour.

Scientists have several theories about how tornadoes are formed. They do know that the Gulf of Mexico is their breeding ground. Warm, moist air from the Gulf is carried north to the Rocky Mountains. Cold, dry air from the Rockies collides with the warm, moist air from the South. Troublesome weather is the result.

The conditions that bring about tornadoes are the same as those that cause thunderstorms. Tornadoes often develop along with thunderstorms. As the thunderstorm moves, tornadoes may form along its path, traveling a few miles, then dying out.

The tornado funnel usually appears beneath the thunderstorm's dark, heavy clouds. Often it stretches down toward the ground, whirling and twisting as it moves. Sometimes the funnel never quite reaches the earth's surface. Other times it touches down briefly, then rises.

On the average, the tornado path is a quarter of a mile wide and 16 miles long. Some tornadoes have caused heavy damage for as many as 200 or 300 miles. The forward speed of the tornado is about 40 miles an hour. However, speeds of up to 70 miles an hour have often been recorded.

Tsunami

When an earthquake takes place on one of the continents, it can do a great deal of damage. It might seem that a quake far out at sea, however, could be ignored. The water would shake a bit, but surely no one would be hurt. And yet an earthquake at sea can be more dreadful than one on land.

The seaquake will set up a wave that is not very high in mid ocean but stretches across the surface for an enormous distance. It therefore involves a large volume of water. Such a wave spreads outward in all directions from the point at which the quake took place. As it approaches land and as the ocean gets shallower, the stretch of water in the wave is compressed front and rear. Water then piles up higher, then much higher. If the wave moves into a narrowing harbor, its volume is forced still higher, sometimes fifty to one hundred feet high.

That tower of water, coming suddenly and without warning, can break over a city, drowning thousands. Before the wave comes in, the preceding trough arrives. The water sucks far out, like an enormous low tide. Then the wave comes in like a colossal high tide. Because of this out-and-in effect the huge wave has been called a *tidal wave.* This is a poor name. It has nothing to do with the tides.

In recent decades the name *tsunami* (tsoo-na-me) has been used more and more frequently. This is a Japanese word meaning "harbor wave," which is an accurate description. The Japanese, living on an island near the edge of our largest ocean, have suffered a great deal from tsunamis.

The largest in recent years was in 1883, when the volcanic island Krakatoa (krak′e-to′e) in the East Indies exploded and sent hundred-foot tsunamis crashing into nearby shores. About 1400 B.C. an Aegean island exploded and a tsunami destroyed the civilization on the nearby island of Crete. Still a third famous tsunami destroyed the city of Lisbon in 1755.

The Origin of Agriculture

According to a new theory, the beginning of agriculture was the result of a change in climate and the depletion of natural resources.

This all began in the region of the Jordan Valley about 12,000 years ago when the climate of the mild summer months changed, becoming hot and dry. The stress on the environment took the form of lakes drying up, a shorter growing season, and game becoming scarcer because there was less food and water.

The people in the region had always lived by hunting and by gathering foods they found growing in the wild. Now they, like the animals, were dramatically affected by the scarcity of food and water. As a result, they moved to areas near the Dead Sea, where food and water were more plentiful. However, the swelling population soon made food scarce there, also.

Some plants, primarily legumes and grains, were actually helped by the change in climate. The life cycle of these plants ends in the spring. Because of their husks, seeds for these plants survived the hot, dry summers, leaving them ready to germinate during the cool, wet winters. The flourishing grains became tougher, so that their seeds did not scatter when the plant was plucked. It was logical that people would learn to save some of the seeds of these wild grasses for planting, to cultivate the plants, and then to harvest these cereals.

Archaeologists have discovered that a sophisticated culture formed in this area about 10,000 years ago. These people, called the Natufians, were not nomads; they lived in well-built houses in a permanent settlement. The Natufians had a distinctive social structure indicated by seashell badges of rank. This would suggest that these people had a social organization that allowed them to control the storage and distribution of grain. They also had the technology of flint, sickles, and stone mortars.

The increased food supplies made possible by agriculture led to the expansion of human population and thus to the formation of cities. So many people living together in one place necessitated an organization that we have come to call civilization.

Soon a spreading population carried the idea of agriculture east and north into Mesopotamia and what is now modern Turkey. Both agriculture and Western civilization were well under way.

Brown *v.* Board of Education: *Desegregating America's Schools*

In 1954, a unanimous Supreme Court decision stated that racial discrimination no longer had a place in America's public schools. Black and white children should be taught in the same classrooms.

The case began when Oliver Brown, a black man, sued the Topeka, Kansas, Board of Education. He asked that his daughter, Linda, be admitted to their neighborhood grade school, which only white students attended, instead of being sent across town to an all-black school. Kansas was then one of seventeen states that had separate schools for black and white children.

The Court declared that separation of children by race was unconstitutional under the Fourteenth Amendment to the U.S. Constitution. This amendment was passed after the Civil War in 1868, and its purpose was to ensure that black citizens' civil rights were the same as those enjoyed by all Americans. The Fourteenth Amendment said that no state may "deny to any person within its jurisdiction the equal protection of the laws." It did not mention schools. This is not surprising because at that time there were very few public schools for whites in the South and few, if any, for blacks. The court interpreted the law as broad enough to mean that everyone was entitled to equality of education.

The Topeka Board of Education and other segregated school systems said that the schools they ran for black students were just as good as their schools for whites. Because the schools were equally good, though separate, the school boards insisted that they were complying with the equal protection law.

This "separate but equal" idea was based on an earlier Supreme Court decision, *Plessy* v. *Ferguson,* in 1896. This case was not about schools but about railroad trains. The court had said that it was legal for railroad companies to insist that whites and blacks travel in different cars, so long as the cars were "separate but equal." For half a century, this policy was applied to elementary schools, too.

Now, in *Brown* v. *Board of Education,* the Supreme Court decided this was no longer fair treatment. Chief Justice Warren wrote, "In the field of public education the doctrine of 'separate but equal' has no place. Separate educational facilities are inherently unequal."

It took the Court about three years to hear arguments on this important case and to come to a decision. Then it took even longer to make the law work. The Supreme Court ordered that compliance with its ruling should be accomplished with "all deliberate speed," but ten years later, not even 10 percent of southern black students had been assigned to integrated schools. Some cities faced real difficulties in changing their school systems, but others deliberately dragged their feet. A few towns even closed their public schools rather than obey the law.

The Civil Rights Act of 1964 speeded up the process. The U.S. Justice Department was given responsibility for enforcing the law, and schools were notified that if they did not integrate, they would not receive federal money. Gradually, the nation's schools came into compliance with the law.

Brown v. *Board of Education* was of great importance in making the American school system more democratic and fair for all citizens. It was a catalyst for other civil rights gains that brought about greater equality in public accommodations, housing, voting, recreation, and employment opportunities.

Think-Alouds

Brief Directions for Administering Think-Aloud Passages

Step One. Select the beginning point for the think-aloud passages in one of two ways: use the highest *independent* level achieved with the retelling passages or use a level that is at least one grade level below the student's grade placement.

Step Two. Follow the teacher prompts in the chosen passage.

Step Three. Complete the Observations checklist at the end of the passage.

Think-Aloud Passages and Rubrics

First and Second Grade Think-Aloud

Teacher's Script

TEACHER **Read the following paragraphs to yourself.**

Long, long ago, there were some mice who lived in a house. They got along very well with each other. But there was someone else they did not like at all. That someone was the Cat.

Whenever she saw a mouse, the cat chased it. Sometimes, she caught one. The mice were never safe from the Cat.

They didn't know what to do about the Cat. They thought and thought. First, they thought alone. Next, they all thought together. Then, they had a meeting, to make plans.

TEACHER **This is the beginning of a story that you are going to read. What do you think the rest of the story will be about? [Allow the child to make predictions, which you write on a blank piece of paper.] What makes you think that this will happen in the story?**

Read this section of the story. When you are finished reading, we will talk about the story and see if any of your guesses (predictions) are in the story.

The biggest mouse stood up first. He said, "I know what we can do!"

All the other mice cheered. Then they asked, "What? What?"

"We can move to another house!" said the biggest mouse.

The other mice shook their heads. They didn't want to move away.

"Well, that was my best plan," said the biggest mouse.

One by one, all the mice who had plans talked about them. But no one had thought of anything that pleased all the other mice at the meeting.

At last, the smallest mouse got up. "I know what to do," he said.

"What?" asked some of the mice.

"Well, YOU KNOW WHO is always quiet when she chases us," he began.

"Of course, we should run away and hide, whenever we hear YOU KNOW WHO."

The other mice said, "Yes, yes!"

The lady mouse said, "We don't hear YOU KNOW WHO."

"That's true. But suppose we had a little bell. Suppose we put that bell on a ribbon, around the neck of YOU KNOW WHO. Wouldn't we hear the bell?" asked the smallest mouse.

"A bell! Yes, a bell would be just the thing!" the other mouse shouted.

The smallest mouse smiled proudly. "So all we have to do is get a bell," he said. "And a ribbon."

The other mice laughed and cheered. "What a good plan!" they said.

TEACHER **What happened in this section of the story? Which of your predictions do you want to erase? Why? Which ones do you want to keep? Why? Which ones do you want to change? Why? Do you have any new ideas about what might happen next? What has happened that makes you think so? [Record or erase responses as necessary.]**

Read this last section of the story. We will talk about this section as soon as you are finished. Keep your guesses in mind as you read.

Then the oldest mouse stood up. He said, "May I ask something?"

"Why, yes," said the smallest mouse.

"Who will put it on YOU KNOW WHO?" asked the oldest mouse.

The smallest mouse stopped smiling. The other mice stopped laughing.

"Not I," said the biggest mouse.

One by one, the other mice spoke up. And each mouse said the same thing, "Not I!"

Even the smallest mouse said, in a very small voice, "Not I!"

The oldest mouse spoke up again. He said, "You should all think before you talk! Just remember this:

"It is easy enough to talk about putting a bell on a cat. But it is a very different thing to do it."

TEACHER **Did you guess what was going to happen? Why or why not?**

Adapted from "A Bell on the Cat," in *Hilltop Trails*, Lyons Carnahan, 1965, pp. 70–76.

Think-Aloud Protocol

OBSERVATIONS

	Inadequate				Adequate
Uses prior knowledge to establish story line	1	2	3	4	5
Makes logical predictions	1	2	3	4	5
Discards inappropriate predictions as new information is presented	1	2	3	4	5
Connects pieces of text into a whole text that makes sense	1	2	3	4	5
Offers predictions willingly	1	2	3	4	5
Requires prompting	1	2	3	4	5

COMMENTS

Long, long ago, there were some mice who lived in a house. They got along very well with each other. But there was someone else they did not like at all. That someone was the Cat.

Whenever she saw a mouse, the cat chased it. Sometimes, she caught one. The mice were never safe from the Cat.

They didn't know what to do about the Cat. They thought and thought. First, they thought alone. Next, they all thought together. Then, they had a meeting, to make plans.

The biggest mouse stood up first. He said, "I know what we can do!"

All the other mice cheered. Then they asked, "What? What?"

"We can move to another house!" said the biggest mouse.

The other mice shook their heads. They didn't want to move away.

"Well, that was my best plan," said the biggest mouse.

One by one, all the mice who had plans talked about them. But no one had thought of anything that pleased all the other mice at the meeting.At last, the smallest mouse got up. “I know what to do,” he said.

“What?” asked some of the mice.

“Well, YOU KNOW WHO is always quiet when she chases us,” he began. “Of course, we should run away and hide, whenever we hear YOU KNOW WHO.”

The other mice said “Yes, yes!”

The lady mouse said, “We don’t hear YOU KNOW WHO.”

“That’s true. But suppose we had a little bell. Suppose we put that bell on a ribbon, around the neck of YOU KNOW WHO. Wouldn't we hear the bell?" asked the smallest mouse.

"A bell! Yes, a bell would be just the thing!" the other mouse shouted.

The smallest mouse smiled proudly. "So all we have to do is get a bell," he said. "And a ribbon."

The other mice laughed and cheered. "What a good plan!" they said.

Then the oldest mouse stood up. He said, “May I ask something?”

“Why, yes,” said the smallest mouse.

“Who will put it on YOU KNOW WHO?” asked the oldest mouse.

The smallest mouse stopped smiling. The other mice stopped laughing.

“Not I,” said the biggest mouse.One by one, the other mice spoke up. And each mouse said the same thing, “Not I!”

Even the smallest mouse said, in a very small voice, “Not I!”

The oldest mouse spoke up again. He said, "You should all think before you talk! Just remember this:

"It is easy enough to talk about putting a bell on a cat. But it is a very different thing to do it."

Third and Fourth Grade Think-Aloud

TEACHER **Read the following paragraph to yourself.**

The children in Mrs. Fuller's class were busy studying their spelling words for the day. Mrs. Fuller was correcting papers.

TEACHER **This is the beginning of a story that you are going to read. What do you think the rest of the story will be about? [Allow the child to make predictions, which you write on a blank piece of paper.] What makes you think that this will happen in the story?**

Read this section of the story. When you are finished reading, we will talk about the story and see if any of your guesses (predictions) are in the story.

The room was so quiet that you could hear the sound of the pencils scraping on paper.

Mrs. Fuller reached down and opened the drawer in her desk.

Then it happened!

TEACHER **What has happened in the story so far? Which of your guesses do you want to erase? Why? Which ones do you want to keep? Why? Which ones do you want to change? Why? Do you have any new ideas about what might happen in the story? What has happened that makes you think so? [Record or erase responses as necessary.]**

Read the next section of the story. We will talk about this section as soon as you are finished. Keep your guesses in mind as you read.

Inside the drawer was a mouse.

The mouse wiggled his nose at Mrs. Fuller. She jumped.

So did the mouse!

The mouse ran so close to Sally Brown that he brushed her leg with his long tail.

Sally Brown screamed.

The boys in the room ran after the mouse. The girls ran after the boys. Mrs. Fuller ran after them all.

But the mouse ran fastest. He found his hole and disappeared into the wall.

Mrs. Fuller rapped sharply on her desk and called the room to order.

"We must catch the mouse," she said. "School is no place for him. Be quiet, and watch for him!"

But the mouse was too smart to show himself again that day.

TEACHER **What happened in this section of the story? Which of your guesses do you want to erase? Why? Which ones do you want to keep? Why? Which ones do you want to change? Why? Do you have any new ideas about what might happen next? What has happened that makes you think so? [Record or erase responses as necessary.]**

Read the next section of the story. We will talk about this section as soon as you are finished. Keep your guesses in mind as you read.

Mrs. Fuller set a mouse trap.

The next day the cheese was gone, but there was no mouse.

"He is too smart," said Mrs. Fuller. "He will never come back."

But the next day the mouse came back.

He sat up and wiggled his nose.

No one jumped. No one screamed. No one was frightened.

Mrs. Fuller cleared her throat. "If we are going to have a mouse in this class, we should give him a name."

The class voted to call the mouse Jack.

Jack visited the class almost every day. He usually came during the spelling lesson, for a reason known only to him.

One fine day the class was going to graduate to the next grade.

What was to be done about Jack?

He had been very good. Mrs. Fuller said that he was the quietest one in the whole room.

One of the children painted a sign and put it over his hole. The sign read, "The House That Jack Built."

For one whole day everyone thought and thought about what to do about Jack.

TEACHER **What happened in this section of the story? Which of your guesses do you want to erase? Why? Which ones do you want to keep? Why? Which ones do you want to change? Why? Do you have any new ideas about what might happen next? What has happened that makes you think so? [Record or erase responses as necessary.]**

Read this last section of the story. We will talk about this section as soon as you are finished. Keep your guesses in mind as you read.

Finally Sally Brown said, "Why can't we take him with us?"

All the class thought this was a wonderful idea.

Mrs. Fuller offered to make a report card for Jack, so that he could graduate into the next class in good standing.

Jack's report card read: Deportment, good; Cooperation, good; Spelling, good.

This pleased everyone, for there were lots of other boys and girls in the class with report cards very much like Jack's.

TEACHER **Did you guess what was going to happen? Why or why not?**

Think-Aloud Protocol

OBSERVATIONS

	Inadequate				Adequate
Uses prior knowledge to establish story line	1	2	3	4	5
Makes logical predictions	1	2	3	4	5
Discards inappropriate predictions as new information is presented	1	2	3	4	5
Connects pieces of text into a whole text that makes sense	1	2	3	4	5
Offers predictions willingly	1	2	3	4	5
Requires prompting	1	2	3	4	5

COMMENTS

The children in Mrs. Fuller's class were busy studying their spelling words for the day. Mrs. Fuller was correcting papers.

The room was so quiet that you could hear the sound of the pencils scraping on paper.

Mrs. Fuller reached down and opened the drawer in her desk.

Then it happened!

Inside the drawer was a mouse.

The mouse wiggled his nose at Mrs. Fuller. She jumped.

So did the mouse!

The mouse ran so close to Sally Brown that he brushed her leg with his long tail.

Sally Brown screamed.

The boys in the room ran after the mouse. The girls ran after the boys. Mrs. Fuller ran after them all.

But the mouse ran fastest. He found his hole and disappeared into the wall.

Mrs. Fuller rapped sharply on her desk and called the room to order.

"We must catch the mouse," she said. "School is no place for him. Be quiet, and watch for him!"

But the mouse was too smart to show himself again that day.

Mrs. Fuller set a mouse trap.

The next day the cheese was gone, but there was no mouse.

"He is too smart," said Mrs. Fuller. "He will never come back."

But the next day the mouse came back.

He sat up and wiggled his nose.

No one jumped. No one screamed. No one was frightened.

Mrs. Fuller cleared her throat. "If we are going to have a mouse in this class, we should give him a name."

The class voted to call the mouse Jack.

Jack visited the class almost every day. He usually came during the spelling lesson, for a reason known only to him.

One fine day the class was going to graduate to the next grade.

What was to be done about Jack?

He had been very good. Mrs. Fuller said that he was the quietest one in the whole room.

One of the children painted a sign and put it over his hole. The sign read, "The House That Jack Built."

For one whole day everyone thought and thought about what to do about Jack.

Finally Sally Brown said, "Why can't we take him with us?"

All the class thought this was a wonderful idea.

Mrs. Fuller offered to make a report card for Jack, so that he could graduate into the next class in good standing.

Jack's report card read: Deportment, good; Cooperation, good; Spelling, good.

This pleased everyone, for there were lots of other boys and girls in the class with report cards very much like Jack's.

Fifth and Sixth Grade Think-Aloud

TEACHER **Read the following paragraph to yourself.**

It was fair time in Melonia. All the farmers were polishing their best melons, hoping to win the Grand Prize.

TEACHER **This is the beginning of a story that you are going to read. What do you think the rest of the story will be about? [Allow the child to make predictions, which you will write on a blank piece of paper.] What makes you think that this will happen in the story?**

Read this next section of the story. When you are finished reading, we will talk about the story and see if any of your guesses (predictions) are in the story.

There were red ones, yellow ones, green and orange ones. Some were long and thin, or short or fat, or round as a ball. But they all had seeds!

After the King of Melonia presented the Grand Prize to the winning farmer, he made a special announcement.

"I have grown very tired of spitting out watermelon seeds," said the King. "If someone will produce a seedless watermelon, I will give him a purple cape and a fancy gold cup engraved with his name."

"Hooray for the King," shouted the farmers, and they all rushed home to go to work.

TEACHER **What has happened in the story so far? Which of your guesses do you want to erase? Why? Which ones do you want to keep? Why? Which ones do you want to change? Why? Do you have any ideas about what might happen in the story? What has happened that makes you think so? [Record or erase responses as necessary.]**

Read the next section of the story. We will talk about this section as soon as you are finished. Keep your guesses in mind as you read.

Many years went by. All the farmers except Farmer Green gave up the job in despair. But every summer Farmer Green counted the seeds of each watermelon. He would save the seeds from the melon with the smallest number of them, and in the spring he would plant those seeds. At summer's arrival, he would start counting again.

One year, Farmer Green discovered a large melon in his field that had only one seed in it—a big flat seed right in the middle.

The next spring all the villagers came to view the planting of the giant seed. It took three men to lift it in its hole!

TEACHER **What happened in this section of the story? Which of your guesses do you want to erase? Why? Which ones do you want to keep? Why? Which ones do you want to change? Why? Do you have any new ideas about what might happen next? What has happened that makes you think so? [Record or erase responses as necessary.]**

Read the next section of the story. We will talk about this section as soon as you are finished. Keep your guesses in mind as you read.

When the seed sprouted, its leaves were the largest that anyone in Melonia had ever seen on a watermelon plant. The blossoms were so large that after a rain, the children of Melonia used them as swimming pools. But in spite of all the flowers, there was only one melon. By midsummer it was as big as a house, and still growing.

As Fair time grew near, the King declared that it would have to be held in Farmer Green's field. The melon was too big to be moved.

On the last day of the Fair, a special saw was going to rip the melon open. Would there be a seed inside? Farmer Green was excited almost beyond endurance. He could hardly wait.

TEACHER **What happened in this section of the story? Which of your guesses do you want to erase? Why? Which ones do you want to keep? Why? Which ones do you want to change? Why? Do you have any new ideas about what might happen next? What has happened that makes you think so? [Record or erase responses as necessary.]**

Read this last section of the story. We will talk about this section as soon as you are finished. Keep your guesses in mind as you read.

At last the great day came. The crowd gathered in a grandstand at the field's edge. Flags flew and gay music was played.

Suddenly, a hush fell. The saw had started! Up one side—across the top—down the other side. Everyone rushed aside as the melon split.

Cheers went up from the waiting throng as it broke in half. There lay a vast expanse of red watermelon, smooth and firm—and no seeds!

The King put the purple cape around Farmer Green's shoulders. Proudly he handed him the gold cup for which he had worked so long.

Then Farmer Green invited everyone present to eat his fill of watermelon. Everyone did!

There are no seedless watermelons now. The giant melon had no seed to plant the following spring, so Farmer Green had to get regular seeds and start all over again.

Maybe the next time he grows a seedless watermelon, you will be there to eat some of it too!

TEACHER **Did you guess what was going to happen? Why or why not?**

Think-Aloud Protocol

OBSERVATIONS

	Inadequate				Adequate
Uses prior knowledge to establish story line	1	2	3	4	5
Makes logical predictions	1	2	3	4	5
Discards inappropriate predictions as new information is presented	1	2	3	4	5
Connects pieces of text into a whole text that makes sense	1	2	3	4	5
Offers predictions willingly	1	2	3	4	5
Requires prompting	1	2	3	4	5

COMMENTS

It was fair time in Melonia. All the farmers were polishing their best melons, hoping to win the Grand Prize.

There were red ones, yellow ones, green and orange ones. Some were long and thin, or short or fat, or round as a ball. But they all had seeds!

After the King of Melonia presented the Grand Prize to the winning farmer, he made a special announcement.

"I have grown very tired of spitting out watermelon seeds," said the King. "If someone will produce a seedless watermelon, I will give him a purple cape and a fancy gold cup engraved with his name."

"Hooray for the King," shouted the farmers, and they all rushed home to go to work.

Many years went by. All the farmers except Farmer Green gave up the job in despair. But every summer Farmer Green counted the seeds of each watermelon. He would save the seeds from the melon with the smallest number of them, and in the spring he would plant those seeds. At summer's arrival, he would start counting again.

One year, Farmer Green discovered a large melon in his field that had only one seed in it—a big flat seed right in the middle.

The next spring all the villagers came to view the planting of the giant seed. It took three men to lift it in its hole!

When the seed sprouted, its leaves were the largest that anyone in Melonia had ever seen on a watermelon plant. The blossoms were so large that after a rain, the children of Melonia used them as swimming pools. But in spite of all the flowers, there was only one melon. By midsummer it was as big as a house, and still growing.

As Fair time grew near, the King declared that it would have to be held in Farmer Green's field. The melon was too big to be moved.

On the last day of the Fair, a special saw was going to rip the melon open. Would there be a seed inside? Farmer Green was excited almost beyond endurance. He could hardly wait.

At last the great day came. The crowd gathered in a grandstand at the field's edge. Flags flew and gay music was played.

Suddenly, a hush fell. The saw had started! Up one side—across the top—down the other side. Everyone rushed aside as the melon split.

Cheers went up from the waiting throng as it broke in half. There lay a vast expanse of red watermelon, smooth and firm—and no seeds!

The King put the purple cape around Farmer Green's shoulders. Proudly he handed him the gold cup for which he had worked so long.

Then Farmer Green invited everyone present to eat his fill of watermelon. Everyone did!

There are no seedless watermelons now. The giant melon had no seed to plant the following spring, so Farmer Green had to get regular seeds and start all over again.

Maybe the next time he grows a seedless watermelon, you will be there to eat some of it too!

Seventh Through Ninth Grade Think-Aloud

TEACHER **Read the following paragraph to yourself.**

Kakikko was an Eskimo boy. He lived in an igloo in the far away Northland. His father, Oskeewas, owned many fine dogs. Kakikko often asked him for a huskie puppy, but his father always shook his head.

TEACHER **This is the beginning of a story that you are going to read. What do you think the rest of the story will be about? [Allow the child to make predictions, which you write on a blank piece of paper.] What makes you think that this will happen in the story?**

Read this section of the story. When you are finished reading, we will talk about the story and see if any of your guesses (predictions) are in the story.

"Huskies," he would say, "are work animals. They must be trained to pull sleds through the snow."

One day Kakikko was playing with some other Eskimo boys near the forest. Suddenly they heard the howl of a wolf. All the boys were frightened. They were about to run away, when Kakikko spotted the animal. It was a little wolf puppy! He was crying because he was lost.

The boys laughed at the little wolf. But Kakikko did not laugh. Instead, he lifted the puppy into his arms. The wolf snarled and bristled, for he was not used to people. Kakikko ran to show him to his father.

TEACHER **What has happened in the story so far? Which of your guesses do you want to erase? Why? Which ones do you want to keep? Why? Which ones do you want to change? Why? Do you have any new ideas about what might happen in the story? What has happened that makes you think so? [Record or erase responses as necessary.]**

Read the next section of the story. We will talk about this section as soon as you are finished. Keep your guesses in mind as you read.

When Oskeewas saw the little wolf, he said, "Wolves are wild. They do not make good pets."

Kakikko was sad. Already he had learned to love the little furry puppy. "He is very small," he said. "If he is left alone in the cold, he will die."

Oskeewas thought for a moment, then he said, "You may keep him for a week. If he will eat from your hand by then, he will be your pet. If he will not, we must turn him loose in the forest."

TEACHER **What happened in this section of the story? Which of your guesses do you want to erase? Why? Which ones do you want to keep? Why? Which ones do you want to change? Why? Do you have any new ideas about what might happen next? What has happened that makes you think so? [Record or erase responses as necessary.]**

Read the next section of the story. We will talk about this section as soon as you are finished. Keep your guesses in mind as you read.

Kakikko named the puppy "Wolf." Every day he spent hours trying to tame him. But Wolf was afraid. Each time Kakikko went near him, he would growl and flatten his ears. Kakikko would offer pieces of meat to him. At first the pup would stand off and growl fiercely. Later on, Kakikko would toss the meat to him. Wolf would eat it then. All along, Kakikko talked very gently to him.

Soon the day came when his father stood beside him. Kakikko was worried, for Wolf had not yet eaten from his hand. If only he had more time!

TEACHER **What happened in this section of the story? Which of your guesses do you want to erase? Why? Which ones do you want to keep? Why? Which ones do you want to change? Why? Do you have any new ideas about what might happen next? What has happened that makes you think so? [Record or erase responses as necessary.]**

Read this last section of the story. We will talk about this section as soon as you are finished. Keep your guesses in mind as you read.

Again he held the meat in his hand. For nearly an hour he coaxed Wolf to come for it. His voice was soft and kind, and he never raised it. This time he refused to toss the meat.

The puppy's mouth watered. He wanted the meat but he was afraid. He took a step forward and growled. Still another step he took, and then another. He eyed the meat hungrily. Then he sniffed it. He looked up at Kakikko, who still spoke gently to him. Slowly he took the meat in his mouth, then gulped it quickly.

Wolf wagged his tail for the first time. He was no longer afraid. He wanted more! Kakikko patted him and gave him another piece. Then he turned to his father. Oskeewas was smiling.

"Wolf is yours," his father said.

Kakikko shouted happily. Wolf was his very own pet. Wolf wagged his tail and barked. He seemed to understand, and he was happy too!

TEACHER **Did you guess what was going to happen? Why or why not?**

Think-Aloud Protocol

OBSERVATIONS

	Inadequate				Adequate
Uses prior knowledge to establish story line	1	2	3	4	5
Makes logical predictions	1	2	3	4	5
Discards inappropriate predictions as new information is presented	1	2	3	4	5
Connects pieces of text into a whole text that makes sense	1	2	3	4	5
Offers predictions willingly	1	2	3	4	5
Requires prompting	1	2	3	4	5

COMMENTS

Kakikko was an Eskimo boy. He lived in an igloo in the far away Northland. His father, Oskeewas, owned many fine dogs. Kakikko often asked him for a huskie puppy, but his father always shook his head.

"Huskies," he would say, "are work animals. They must be trained to pull sleds through the snow."

One day Kakikko was playing with some other Eskimo boys near the forest. Suddenly they heard the howl of a wolf. All the boys were frightened. They were about to run away, when Kakikko spotted the animal. It was a little wolf puppy! He was crying because he was lost.

The boys laughed at the little wolf. But Kakikko did not laugh. Instead, he lifted the puppy into his arms. The wolf snarled and bristled, for he was not used to people. Kakikko ran to show him to his father.

When Oskeewas saw the little wolf, he said, "Wolves are wild. They do not make good pets."

Kakikko was sad. Already he had learned to love the little furry puppy. "He is very small," he said. "If he is left alone in the cold, he will die."

Oskeewas thought for a moment, then he said, "You may keep him for a week. If he will eat from your hand by then, he will be your pet. If he will not, we must turn him loose in the forest."

Kakikko named the puppy "Wolf." Every day he spent hours trying to tame him. But Wolf was afraid. Each time Kakikko went near him, he would growl and flatten his ears. Kakikko would offer pieces of meat to him. At first the pup would stand off and growl fiercely. Later on, Kakikko would toss the meat to him. Wolf would eat it then. All along, Kakikko talked very gently to him.

Soon the day came when his father stood beside him. Kakikko was worried, for Wolf had not yet eaten from his hand. If only he had more time!

Again he held the meat in his hand. For nearly an hour he coaxed Wolf to come for it. His voice was soft and kind, and he never raised it. This time he refused to toss the meat.

The puppy's mouth watered. He wanted the meat, but he was afraid. He took a step forward and growled. Still another step he took, and then another. He eyed the meat hungrily. Then he sniffed it. He looked up at Kakikko, who still spoke gently to him. Slowly he took the meat in his mouth, then gulped it quickly.

Wolf wagged his tail for the first time. He was no longer afraid. He wanted more! Kakikko patted him and gave him another piece. Then he turned to his father. Oskeewas was smiling.

"Wolf is yours," his father said.

Kakikko shouted happily. Wolf was his very own pet. Wolf wagged his tail and barked. He seemed to understand, and he was happy too!

Portfolio Checklists

The following section contains forms that may be used in a student portfolio. Included in this section are the CARP summary sheet, miscue analysis worksheet, portfolio analysis worksheet, reading goals record sheet, observation checklists—oral reading and generic retelling protocol.

CARP Summary Sheet

STUDENT ______________ GRADE ________ GENDER ________ AGE ________

SCHOOL ______________ TEACHER ______________

CARP GIVEN BY ______________ DATE OF ADMINISTRATION ______________

NARRATIVE RETELLING				EXPOSITORY RETELLING			
FORM A PASSAGES				FORM A PASSAGES			
Silent ___ Oral ___	Ind.	Inst.	Frust.	Silent ___ Oral ___	Ind.	Inst.	Frust.
GRADE ONE				GRADE ONE			
GRADE TWO				GRADE TWO			
GRADE THREE				GRADE THREE			
GRADE FOUR				GRADE FOUR			
GRADE FIVE				GRADE FIVE			
GRADE SIX				GRADE SIX			
GRADE SEVEN				GRADE SEVEN			
GRADE EIGHT				GRADE EIGHT			
GRADE NINE				GRADE NINE			

NARRATIVE RETELLING				EXPOSITORY RETELLING			
FORM B PASSAGES				FORM B PASSAGES			
Silent ___ Oral ___	Ind.	Inst.	Frust.	Silent ___ Oral ___	Ind.	Inst.	Frust.
GRADE ONE				GRADE ONE			
GRADE TWO				GRADE TWO			
GRADE THREE				GRADE THREE			
GRADE FOUR				GRADE FOUR			
GRADE FIVE				GRADE FIVE			
GRADE SIX				GRADE SIX			
GRADE SEVEN				GRADE SEVEN			
GRADE EIGHT				GRADE EIGHT			
GRADE NINE				GRADE NINE			

Miscue Analysis Worksheet

PASSAGE ______________________ STUDENT ______________________

FORM __________ LEVEL ______________ DATE ______________________

Text Word	Miscue	Is Miscue Graphically Similar? (Y/N) Beg. Mid. End.	Is Meaning Changed? (Y/N)	Is Miscue Corrected? (Y/N)

Portfolio Analysis Worksheet

STUDENT ______________________ DATE ______________________

MATERIALS ____

____

1. STRENGTHS

2. NEEDS

3. STRATEGIES TO ADDRESS NEEDS

Reading Goals Record Sheet

STUDENT ______________________________

Goals	Completed	How Did I Do?

Observation Checklist—Oral Reading

STUDENT________________ **TEXT**____________________________

	Appropriate	Needs Work
Automatic Decoding		
Phrasing		
Fluency		
Intonation		
Rate		
Text Pointing		

Generic Retelling Protocol

Purpose-Setting Statement:

Story Title:

CHARACTERS (_____ points each)

_____ 1. ______________________________
_____ 2. ______________________________
_____ 3. ______________________________
_____ 4. ______________________________
_____ 5. ______________________________

SETTING (_____ points each)

_____ 1. ______________________________
_____ 2. ______________________________
_____ 3. ______________________________

PLOT (_____ points each)

_____ 1. ______________________________
_____ 2. ______________________________
_____ 3. ______________________________
_____ 4. ______________________________
_____ 5. ______________________________
_____ 6. ______________________________
_____ 7. ______________________________
_____ 8. ______________________________

RESOLUTION (_____ points)

_____ 1. ______________________________

Character Total _____
Setting Total _____
Plot Total _____
Resolution Total _____
TOTAL POINTS _____

READING LEVELS	
Independent	Above 85 Points
Instructional	70–84 Points
Frustration	Below 70 Points

OBSERVATIONS

	Inappropriate				Appropriate
Includes detail	1	2	3	4	5
Uses prior knowledge to establish story line	1	2	3	4	5
Infers beyond text	1	2	3	4	5
	Out of Sequence				**In Sequence**
Tells story in correct sequence	1	2	3	4	5
	Verbatim				**In Own Words**
Restates story verbatim	1	2	3	4	5

Resources

Annotated Bibliography of Children's Literature

This listing of children's literature is provided as a resource to teachers who are interested in finding appropriate books for the children in their classrooms. This is, of course, not an exhaustive list. The books were selected from current lists of award-winning children's books, from favorite choices of children, and from books the authors have successfully used in their work with children. We paid particular attention to books that a large number of children could relate to and that were sensitive to the interests and needs of children at the specific grade levels.

The books are organized according to grade levels. Readability was established in a variety of ways. Fry's readability formula (1977) was used to establish a base readability level. However, the books were also examined for repetitive lines and phrases, familiar concepts for the age group, and high interest level, all of which can influence the readability of any text. These readability groupings are meant only as a guideline. Children should be encouraged to read and work with a variety of levels of materials.

First Grade

1. **Ahlberg, Janet,** & **Ahlberg, Allan.** *Each Peach Pear Plum.* New York: Viking Kestrel, 1978. 28 pages (unpaged).

   This easy rhyming book invites the readers to participate by giving them something to look for in each picture. All clues are related to famous fairy tale and nursery rhyme characters such as Cinderella, Old Mother Hubbard, and the Three Bears.

2. **Aliki.** *We Are Best Friends.* New York: Mulberry Books, 1982. 28 pages (unpaged).

   Peter and Robert are best friends, but Peter is moving away. At first, Robert is lonely and sad. A new boy, Will, moves to Robert's neighborhood and they discover that new friends can be found.

3. **Asch, Frank.** *Happy Birthday, Moon.* Upper Saddle River, NJ: Prentice-Hall, 1982. 28 pages (unpaged).

   Bear decides to give Moon a birthday present. He is excited to find out that he and Moon share the same birthday. Bear takes all of the money in his piggy bank and buys Moon a hat. What a surprise: Moon gives Bear an identical hat.

4. **Bennett, Jill.** *Teeny Tiny.* Illustrated by Tomie dePaola. New York: Trumpet Club, 1985. 28 pages (unpaged).

   A teeny tiny woman finds a teeny tiny bone in the graveyard. She takes the bone home to make soup. Before she makes the soup, she decides to take a nap. She is tormented by a voice asking for the bone. Finally, the teeny tiny woman tells the voice to take the bone.

5. **Carle, Eric.** *The Very Hungry Caterpillar.* New York: Philomel Books, 1987. 22 pages (unpaged).

   On a Sunday morning, a very hungry caterpillar hatches from a tiny egg on a leaf. He eats his way through the week. By the end of the week, he is a very fat caterpillar. He builds a cocoon around himself. When he emerges, he is a beautiful butterfly. Children love the actual "holes" the caterpillar eats through food in this book. The book is useful in studying the days of the week, the metamorphosis of caterpillars, and counting.

6. **Christopher, Matt.** *The Dog That Pitched a No-Hitter.* Illustrated by Daniel Vasconcellos. New York: Trumpet Club, 1988. 42 pages.

   Mike and his dog, Harry, have a special relationship: they can read each other's minds. Harry loves and knows baseball. He helps Mike pitch a no-hitter game.

7. **Cohen, Miriam.** *No Good in Art.* Illustrated by Lillian Hoban. New York: Dell Publishing, 1980. 29 pages (unpaged).

   In kindergarten, Jim's art teacher does not like his paintings because he forgets to give his men necks, and he makes his grass too fat. In first grade, Jim's class has a new art teacher. She tells the class to paint pictures of what they want to be when they grow up. Jim does not want to paint because he does not think he can. The art teacher persuades him to paint something he likes to do. Everyone in the class loves Jim's work, and he decides maybe he can do art.

8. **Fox, Mem.** *Hattie and the Fox.* Illustrated by Patricia Mullins. New York: Trumpet Club, 1986. 16 pages (unpaged).

   Hattie sees something suspicious in the bushes and tries to alert the other farm animals. No one particularly cares until the fox jumps out of the bushes.

9. **Galbraith, Kathryn O.** *Look! Snow!* Illustrated by Nina Montezimos. New York: Margaret K. McElderry Books, 1992. 27 pages (unpaged).

The limited text is supplemented by wonderful pictures. Children can use these pictures to tell their own stories of a snow day away from school.

10. **Giff, Patricia R.** *Spectacular Stone Soup.* Illustrated by Blanche Sims. New York: Dell Publishing, 1989. 76 pages.

Mrs. Zachary, Stacy Arrow's teacher, likes for her students to be people-helpers. Stacy wants to be a people-helper, but her good efforts backfire every time. Finally, Stacy learns what helping people is all about when she contributes to the class's spectacular stone soup.

11. **Giff, Patricia R.** *The Valentine Star.* Illustrated by Blanche Sims. New York: Dell Publishing, 1985. 72 pages.

Emily starts a feud with Sherri that threatens to ruin her entire year in school. Each one tries to do something worse to the other. A student teacher finally resolves the situation by enlisting their help in a joint project to create a card for their regular teacher.

12. **Hughes, Shirley.** *Bouncing.* Cambridge, MA: Candlewick Press, 1993. 16 pages (unpaged).

This book looks at all the ways children can bounce—on a bed, on a sofa, on pillows, etc. Children enjoy the humor and fun depicted in the beautiful pictures.

13. **Kalen, Robert.** *Jump Frog, Jump.* Illustrated by Byron Barton. New York: Mulberry Books, 1981. 30 pages (unpaged).

This cumulative story draws children in with its repetitive line, "Jump frog, jump." Frog escapes many dangers in the pond until he is captured by some young boys. Frog's only escape is to "Jump frog, jump!"

14. **Kraus, Robert.** *Leo the Late Bloomer.* Illustrated by José Aruego. New York: Crowell, 1971. 28 pages (unpaged).

Leo's father is worried because Leo can't read, write, or speak. His mother is not worried because she knows that Leo is just a late bloomer. Leo's father watches and watches for Leo to bloom. Leo finally blooms in his own way and time.

15. **Lobel, Arnold.** *Owl at Home.* New York: Harper & Row, 1975. 64 pages.

This easy chapter book shares Owl's experiences at home, for example, an uninvited guest, bumps in his bed, the making of tear-water tea, and becoming friends with the moon.

16. **Martin, Bill.** *Brown Bear, Brown Bear, What Do You See?* Illustrated by Eric Carle. Austin, TX: Holt, Rinehart & Winston, 1983. 24 pages (unpaged).

This is a repetitive chant in which one animal asks another what he sees. The rhythm and repetition provide for a fun read-aloud. Color words and words that follow basic word patterns make this an easy reader.

17. **Martin, Bill,** & **Archambault, John.** *Here Are My Hands.* Illustrated by Ted Rand. New York: Henry Holt and Company, 1987. 24 pages (unpaged).

Children from a variety of ethnic backgrounds help children learn various parts of the body. The rhythm and rhyme of the text make it an easy reader.

18. **Mayer, Mercer.** *I Was So Mad.* Racine, WI: Western Publishing Co., 1983. 23 pages (unpaged).

Monster was so mad because he could not do what he wanted. He packs his things to run away until his friends invite him to go to the park. He decides to run away tomorrow.

19. **Minarik, Else Holmelund.** *A Kiss for Little Bear.* Illustrated by Maurice Sendak. New York: Trumpet Club, 1988. 32 pages.

Hen takes a picture to Grandmother for Little Bear. Grandmother asks Hen to thank Little Bear for the gift by giving him a kiss. On her way back to Little Bear, Hen asks various forest creatures to pass the kiss on.

20. **Minarik, Else Holmelund.** *Little Bear.* Illustrated by Maurice Sendak. New York: Trumpet Club, 1988. 63 pages.

This simple chapter book for young readers details several episodes in Little Bear's life. In the chapter "What Will Little Bear Wear?" Little Bear continuously asks Mother Bear for something additional to wear because he is so cold. In "Birthday Soup" Little Bear is convinced that Mother Bear has forgotten his birthday. He prepares birthday soup for his friends who arrive to help him celebrate. Little Bear realizes that Mother Bear has not forgotten his birthday when she arrives with the birthday cake. The third chapter, "Little Bear Goes to the Moon," tells the story of what happens to Little Bear when he decides that he can fly to the moon. The final chapter, "Little Bear's Wish," brings closure to the book by summarizing all of Little Bear's adventures.

21. **Numeroff, Laura J.** *If You Give a Mouse a Cookie.* Illustrated by Felicia Bond. New York: Scholastic Inc., 1985. 28 pages (unpaged).

What happens when you offer a cookie to a mouse? Lots of things. In fact, the mouse will take over your home and one thing leads to another. This is a fun, rhythmic story that children find wonderfully humorous.

22. **Rylant, Cynthia.** *Henry and Mudge and the Wild Wind.* Illustrated by Suçie Stevenson. New York: Trumpet Club, 1993. 40 pages.

    Henry is afraid of thunderstorms, but Mudge is even more afraid. He circles the kitchen table, hides his head in the couch cushions, or sits in the bathroom. During one storm, Henry's parents try to keep Henry entertained with games and food. It works for Henry but not for Mudge.

23. **Stevenson, James.** *Quick! Turn the Page!* New York: Greenwillow Books, 1990. 29 pages (unpaged).

    The repetitive phrase keeps children turning the pages of this easy reader. The teacher has many opportunities to engage students in predicting what will be on the next page.

24. **Ward, Leila.** *I Am Eyes. Ni Macho.* Illustrated by Nonny Hogrogian. New York: Scholastic, 1978. 27 pages (unpaged).

    On each page, the African child describes something he sees in his environment. The book is illustrated with both black-and-white drawings and soft color pictures.

25. **Wood, Audrey.** *The Napping House.* Illustrated by Don Wood. Orlando, FL: Harbrace Juvenile Books, 1984. 29 pages (unpaged).

    This is a cumulative tale of a napping granny who is joined in her nap by a child, a dog, a cat, a mouse, and a flea. The result is hilarious. Children enjoy the repetition. The pictures are breathtaking.

Second Grade

1. **Adler, David A.** *Cam Jansen and the Mystery of the Stolen Diamonds.* Illustrated by Susanna Natti. New York: Viking Press, 1980. 58 pages.

    Cam Jensen and her friend Eric Shelton are sitting in the mall watching Eric's baby brother when they hear the alarm go off in the jewelry store. They witness a man run from the store and through the mall. Cam and Eric follow the man and discover who really committed the crime.

2. **Allard, Harry,** & **Marshall, James.** *Miss Nelson Has a Field Day.* Boston: Houghton Mifflin, 1985. 32 pages.

The children in Horace B. Smedley School are depressed because their football team is awful. The team will not listen to the coach. When the coach is absent for a few days, Viola Swamp appears and whips the team into shape. They win the big game with the Central Werewolves. The surprise in this book is that Miss Nelson has a twin.

3. **Allard, Harry,** & **Marshall, James.** *Miss Nelson Is Missing.* Boston: Houghton Mifflin, 1982. 32 pages.

When Miss Nelson has her tonsils out, Mr. Blandsworth, the principal, substitutes. He is so boring that the children develop a plan to convince him that Miss Nelson is back. Miss Nelson stops the class's fun when she becomes Viola Swamp, their new substitute. The children are truly glad when Miss Nelson returns.

4. **Bogart, Jo Ellen.** *Daniel's Dog.* Illustrated by Janet Wilson. New York: Scholastic, 1990. 32 pages.

When Daniel's mother brings home a new baby sister, Daniel feels left out. He compensates by playing with and reading to an imaginary dog.

5. **Buchanan, Ken.** *This House Is Made of Mud.* Illustrated by Libba Tracy. Flagstaff, AZ: Northland Publishing Company, 1994. 30 pages (unpaged).

This story describes the simplicity of a dwelling in the desert. English and Spanish versions are printed side by side.

6. **Calmenson, Stephanie.** *The Principal's New Clothes.* Illustrated by Denise Brunkus. New York: Scholastic Inc., 1989. 36 pages (unpaged).

This is a modern version of *The Emperor's New Clothes.* In this case, Mr. Bundy, the principal, is tricked by a couple who promise to make him a one-of-a-kind new suit. Only smart people and people who are doing their jobs well can see the new suit. An honest kindergarten student helps the principal face the truth.

7. **Cleary, Beverly.** *Two Dog Biscuits.* Illustrated by DyAnne DiSalvo-Ryan. New York: Dell Publishing, 1961. 30 pages (unpaged).

Jimmy and Janet are twins. Their neighbor, Mrs. Robbins, gives each twin a dog biscuit. Their mother takes them on a walk to find a dog who might want the dog biscuits. However, the twins cannot find a dog that they want to have the biscuits. They decide, instead, to give their dog biscuits to a cat.

8. **Cleary, Beverly.** *Janet's Thingamajigs.* Illustrated by DyAnne DiSalvo-Ryan. New York: William Morrow & Co., 1987. 30 pages (unpaged).

Janet and Jimmy are twins. Janet loves to collect little things, "thingamajigs," put them in brown paper bags, and put them in her crib. Jimmy wants Janet to share, but she refuses. Mother does not know what to do. One day she surprises the twins with new beds. Janet's thingamajigs will not stay on the new beds, so she decides they are not important anymore.

9. **Cushman, Doug.** *Aunt Eater's Mystery Vacation.* New York: HarperCollins, 1992. 64 pages.

Aunt Eater goes on a vacation to Hotel Bathwater. While on vacation, she is called on to solve three mysteries. All she really wants to do is read her mystery book. In the end, she meets the author of her favorite books.

10. **dePaola, Tomie.** *Oliver Button Is a Sissy.* Illustrated by the author. Orlando, FL: Harcourt Brace, 1979. 43 pages (unpaged).

Oliver Button does not like to do the things that other little boys like to do. His father wants him to play ball, but he is too clumsy. His parents decide to let him go to dancing school for the exercise. The boys at school make fun of Oliver every day. Oliver participates in a talent show, and the other kids realize that he is a star.

11. **Freeman, Don.** *Corduroy.* Illustrated by the author. New York: Scholastic Inc., 1968. 32 pages.

Corduroy is a little stuffed bear who lives in a department store. He dreams of a home of his own. One day a little girl sees Corduroy in the store and wants to buy him. At first, her mother refuses, but she finally allows the little girl to use her savings to buy Corduroy.

12. **Hoban, Russell.** *A Bargain for Frances.* Illustrated by Lillian Hoban. New York: Scholastic Inc., 1970. 63 pages.

Frances wants a new china tea set with blue pictures painted on it. Her friend Thelma convinces her that such a tea set is unavailable, and that Frances should buy Thelma's plastic tea set instead. Frances later learns that Thelma takes the money and buys herself the china tea set. Frances successfully changes the situation to her favor.

13. **Hughes, Shirley.** *The Snow Lady.* New York: Lothrop, Lee & Shepard Books, 1990. 24 pages (unpaged).

Sam lives on Trotter Street next door to Mrs. Dean. Mrs. Dean is always stopping Sam and her dog, Mick, or her friends from playing. They call her Mrs. Mean. After the first snowfall, Sam and her friend Barney build a snowlady and name her Mrs. Mean. Luckily the rain washes it away before Mrs. Dean can see it.

14. **Isadora, Rachel.** *Over the Green Hills.* New York: Trumpet, 1992. 29 pages (unpaged).

    Zolani, his mother, and his baby sister, Norma, walk to a nearby village to visit Grandma Zindzi. The story and illustrations provide a window into life in small African villages.

15. **Lawlor, Laurie.** *Second-Grade Dog.* Illustrated by Gioia Fiammenghi. Morton Grove, IL: Albert Whitman & Co., 1990. 37 pages (unpaged).

    Bones is a lucky dog; he has everything a dog could want. But Bones wants to go to school. He searches through the attic and finds clothes that he hopes will disguise him as a little boy. The next day he joins the second grade. The children realize he's a dog, but the teachers and the principal do not notice until a fire fighter points it out. Bones is not allowed to return to school, but his new friends promise to visit him every day.

16. **Lobel, Arnold.** *Frog and Toad Together.* New York: Harper & Row, 1972. 64 pages.

    This easy chapter book details the daily activities of two friends, Frog and Toad. In Chapter 1, "A List," Toad makes a to-do list for the day and marks off activities as they are completed. In Chapter 2, "The Garden," Frog helps Toad grow a flower garden. Chapter 3, "Cookies," finds the two friends trying to develop will power so they won't eat too many cookies. In Chapter 4, "Dragons and Giants," Frog and Toad prove they are brave. In Chapter 5, "The Dream," Toad dreams that Frog goes away.

17. **Pickett, Anola.** *Old Enough for Magic.* Illustrated by Ned Delaney. New York: HarperTrophy, 1989. 64 pages.

    Peter gets a magic set for his birthday. His sister, Arlene, accidentally turns herself into a frog because she fails to read the directions. Peter asks everyone he meets how they solve problems. By following their advice, he is able to undo the spell.

18. **Porte, Barbara A.** *Harry's Birthday.* Illustrated by Yossi Abolafia. New York: Greenwillow Books, 1994. 47 pages.

    Harry's birthday is coming up. He's wishing for a cowboy hat. His dad will not hire a clown or take the guests to get pizza. Harry settles for cake and ice cream at home. Uncle Leo and Aunt Rose provide the entertainment. All the guests have a great time, and Harry gets his wish—seven cowboy hats!

19. **Rodgers, Frank**. *Doodle Dog.* New York: Dutton, 1990. 29 pages (unpaged).

Sam wants a dog, but his mother says he cannot have one in an apartment. She and Sam draw a picture of a dog. Sam names him Doodle. In Sam's imagination Doodle becomes alive, and they share an adventurous trip to a farm.

20. **Rylant, Cynthia.** *Henry and Mudge and the Best Day of All.* Illustrated by Suçie Stevenson. New York: Trumpet Club, 1995. 40 pages.

    It's May 1 and Henry's birthday. Henry has a party and invites all his friends. Mother and Father have set up games such as ringtoss, potato sack races, and a piñata in the backyard. After playing the games, the children eat cake and ice cream and watch Henry open his gifts. It's the best day of the year.

21. **Rylant, Cynthia.** *Miss Maggie.* Illustrated by Thomas DiGrazia. New York: Dutton, 1983. 26 pages (unpaged).

    Maggie Ziegler, an old woman, lives next to Nat Crawford's farm. Although Nat goes to Miss Maggie's house often, he never goes in because he has heard that she keeps a snake hanging from the rafters. The two become close friends after Nat rescues Miss Maggie from a very cold cabin with no fire.

22. **Sharmant, Marjorie W.** *Nate the Great and the Mushy Valentine.* Illustrated by Marc Simont. New York: Bantam Doubleday Dell Publishing Group, 1994. 44 pages.

    In this easy chapter book, Nate the Great has two mysteries to solve. Who sent the mushy valentine to Sludge, his dog? Who stole the valentine that Annie was making? After collecting all the clues, Nate the Great solves the mystery in his usual, careful manner.

23. **Sharmant, Marjorie W.,** & **Weinman, Rosalind.** *Nate the Great and the Pillowcase.* Illustrated by Marc Simont. New York: Bantam Doubleday Dell Publishing Group, 1993. 48 pages.

    Rosamond calls Nate the Great in the middle of the night to tell him that the pillowcase that her cat, Big Hex, sleeps on is missing. Because Nate is a serious detective, he throws on his bathrobe and proceeds to investigate the mystery. After talking with Annie, Rosamond's friend, Nate the Great solves the mystery and returns home to bed.

24. **Turner, Ann.** *Sewing Quilts.* Illustrated by Thomas B. Allen. New York: Macmillan, 1994. 28 pages (unpaged).

    This book shares the heritage one little girl gets from her mother's quilting. The little girl and her sister begin their own quilts. Soft pictures add to the warm feeling from this book.

Third Grade

1. **Adler, David A.** *Cam Jansen and the Mystery of the Stolen Corn Popper.* Illustrated by Susanna Natti. New York: Viking Penguin, 1986. 58 pages.

   Cam Jansen and her best friend, Eric Shelton, go to Binky's Department Store to shop for school supplies. The store is very crowded because Binky's is having big sales in every department. While they are shopping, they are witness to the theft of several shopping bags. Cam, with her photographic memory, and Eric set about to solve the mystery.

2. **Baker, Barbara.** *Third Grade Is Terrible.* Illustrated by Roni Shepherd. New York: Dutton, 1989. 106 pages.

   Liza knows that third grade will be wonderful because she has been assigned to Mrs. Lane's room. Her reassignment to Mrs. Rumford's room is only one of many things that go wrong. Her best friend makes friends with someone else, she has no friends in Mrs. Rumford's class, and Amy Cutter, Miss Perfect, sits right in front of her. Through all of her trials during the first week of school, Liza finally makes friends with a new girl and mends her relationship with her best friend.

3. **Blume, Judy.** *Freckle Juice.* Old Tappan, NJ: Four Winds Press, 1971. 40 pages.

   Andrew Marcus wants to have freckles just like Nicky Lane. Sharon sells him a secret formula for freckle juice for fifty cents. The concoction makes Andrew sick, and he realizes that Sharon has tricked him. When he returns to school, he puts blue marks on his face and tells the class that the formula gave him blue freckles. Miss Kelly has a magic formula, and Andrew uses it to rid himself of his freckles.

4. **Bunting, Eve.** *Fly Away Home.* Illustrated by Ronald Himler. Boston: Clarion Books, 1991. 32 pages.

   Andrew and his father have been homeless since Andrew's mother died. They live at the airport. Andrew works hard at not being noticed because they would have to leave the airport. He hopes that one day his father will be able to find them a place to live.

5. **Bunting, Eve.** *Night Tree.* Illustrated by Ted Rand. New York: Trumpet Club, 1991. 28 pages (unpaged).

   A little boy with his father, mother, and sister, Nina, look for their tree on Christmas Eve. Instead of cutting it down, they decorate it with seeds, popcorn chains, and fruit for the creatures of the forest. After decorating the tree, they sit under the moonlit sky and sing favorite Christmas songs. This is an especially beautiful story for the holiday season because it deals with the joys of giving.

6. **Catling, Patrick S.** *The Chocolate Touch.* Illustrated by Margot Apple. New York: Bantam, 1952. 87 pages.

   This older book is still delightful. John Midas loves candy better than anything, and his favorite candy is chocolate. He discovers a unique coin and an unusual candy store. He spends the coin to buy a box of chocolate. After eating the chocolate, John discovers that everything he puts into his mouth turns to chocolate. At first, he is thrilled, but his excitement is short lived. John learns his lesson about being selfish and greedy, and his life returns to normal.

7. **Cleary, Beverly.** *Ellen Tebbits.* New York: Bantam Doubleday Dell Publishing Group, 1979. 160 pages.

   Ellen Tebbits and Austine Allen become best friends in third grade. They share ballet, horseback riding, and a terrible secret—their mothers make them wear long woolen underwear. On the first day of fourth grade, Ellen slaps her best friend and is miserable until she figures out a way to say she's sorry.

8. **Cleary, Beverly.** *Muggie Maggie.* New York: Avon Books, 1990. 70 pages.

   Maggie Schultz's third grade teacher tells them that this will be a wonderful year. Maggie is doubtful because she dreads cursive writing. The grown-ups in her life do not understand her reluctance to write. Their pressure forces Maggie to vow to herself that she will never write cursive. Only Maggie can decide when the time is right to learn this new skill.

9. **Dahl, Roald.** *The Enormous Crocodile.* New York: Bantam, 1988. 42 pages.

   The Enormous Crocodile is hungry for children. As he walks through the jungle to the village, he tells his plans to several of the jungle inhabitants. In the village, the Enormous Crocodile attempts to implement his various plans for catching children. Each time he is thwarted by one of the jungle beasts he had met on his journey. The elephant flings the Enormous Crocodile into outer space, where he collides with the sun.

10. **dePaola, Tomie.** *The Legend of the Bluebonnet.* Illustrated by the author. New York: G. P. Putnam, 1983. 27 pages (unpaged).

    The People have been suffering from drought and famine. The Great Spirits say that an offering of the most valued possession is the only way to stop the drought. She-Who-Is-Alone gives up her warrior doll, the only thing she has left to remind her of her family. As a reward, the Great Spirits cover the hillsides with bluebonnets and end the drought.

11. **Duffey, Betsy.** *How to Be Cool in the Third Grade.* Illustrated by Janet Wilson. New York: Trumpet Club, 1993. 69 pages.

    Robbie York wants to be "cool" for the first day of third grade. Unfortunately, his day gets off to a bad start. He has to wear shorts instead of the jeans he's sure everyone else will be wearing. His mother walks him to the bus stop and gives him a big kiss before he gets on the bus. Then Robbie trips on the bus and lands in the lap of the school bully, Bo Haney. The worst part of the day is when Robbie finds out that he has to be a reading buddy to Bo Haney, who is assigned to the same third grade classroom. Robbie resolves to change some of these things so he can be cool. He learns that the changes are not that difficult but also that being cool is not the most important thing in life.

12. **Fleischman, Paul.** *Time Train.* Illustrated by Claire Ewart. New York: Trumpet Club, 1991. 29 pages (unpaged).

    Miss Pym's students are riding a train to Dinosaur National Monument to study dinosaurs over spring break. This is a very unusual train. By the time they arrive at the park, they have traveled millions of years back in time to the age of dinosaurs. They are able to study dinosaurs in very real settings. The author, however, includes some unrealistic activities, such as playing football, with the dinosaurs as well. All too soon, their time is up and they travel the time train back to reality.

13. **Fleischman, Sid.** *The Case of the 264-Pound Burglar.* Illustrated by Bill Morrison. New York: Random House, 1982. 62 pages.

    The Bloodhouse Gang is called in to solve the mystery of Mrs. Tolliver's missing money. They investigate evidence at the scene and narrow the suspects to twin nephews of Mrs. Tolliver.

14. **Friedman, Tracy.** *Henriette: The Story of a Doll.* Illustrated by Vera Rosenberry. New York: Scholastic Inc., 1986. 63 pages.

    Henriette is a porcelain doll who has belonged to three generations of little girls. She has never met her current owner, and she feels she must travel the long distance to Atlanta to find her owner, who lives in an orphanage. This book details the incredible efforts of the doll as she endures dangers and unruly children.

15. **Gondosch, Linda.** *The Monsters of Marble Avenue.* Illustrated by Cat Bowman Smith. New York: Little, Brown, 1988. 60 pages.

Luke Palmer has a big problem. He has promised to do a puppet show for Erin Bozwell's birthday party, but his mother sold all of his puppets at a garage sale. Luke's friends help him make some new puppets and then help him put on the puppet show.

16. **Hoffman, Mary.** *Amazing Grace.* Illustrated by Caroline Binch. New York: Dial Books for Young Readers, 1991. 24 pages (unpaged).

    Grace loves stories, and she loves to act them out. Grace's teacher announces that the class will be doing the play *Peter Pan*, and Grace decides to try out for the lead. Her classmates tell her she cannot play Peter Pan because she is a girl and because she is black. Grace practices and practices for the part. Her hard work pays off when she lands the lead.

17. **Johnson, Paul B.** *The Cow Who Wouldn't Come Down.* Illustrated by the author. New York: Trumpet Club, 1993. 28 pages (unpaged).

    Miss Rosemary's cow, Gertrude, decides to become a flying cow. Nothing that Miss Rosemary does persuades Gertrude to come back down and act like a normal cow. Miss Rosemary places a sign advertising for a new cow on her gate. The next morning a "new" cow appears. This brings Gertrude back to the ground in a hurry. What will she think of next? The author gives a pictorial hint that will encourage children to compose a sequel.

18. **Kerby, Mona.** *38 Weeks Till Summer Vacation.* New York: Scholastic Inc., 1989. 90 pages.

    With Mrs. Carter as her teacher, Nora Jean is sure that fourth grade will be lots of fun. Unfortunately, Jimmy Lee Drover, the school bully, has also been assigned to her class. Despite Jimmy Lee's constant harassment, Nora Jean has a good year. She and Jimmy Lee even become friends in the end.

19. **MacLachlan, Patricia.** *Sarah, Plain and Tall.* New York: HarperTrophy, 1985. 58 pages. Newbery winner.

    After Anna and Caleb's mother dies, their father advertises for a wife and mother. Sarah, a native of Maine, applies by writing letters to Anna, Caleb, and their father. After Sarah arrives at their prairie home, Anna and Caleb learn to love their new mother.

20. **MacLachlan, Patricia.** *Three Names.* Illustrated by Alexander Pertzoff. New York: HarperCollins, 1991. 31 pages.

    This is the story of Grandfather and his dog, Three Names. Three Names goes to the prairie school with Grandfather. The story describes what one-room schools were like during the first part of this century.

21. **Markham, Marion M.** *The April Fool's Day Mystery.* Illustrated by Paul Estrada. Gainesville, FL: Camelot Books, 1991. 58 pages.

Mickey and Kate Dixon are twins, and they like to solve mysteries. Mickey is a detective, and Kate is a scientist. In this book, they have to find out who put a snake in the cafeteria's flour bin. Everyone suspects Billy Wade, but the twins find evidence to the contrary.

22. **Myers, Bernice.** *Sidney Rella and the Glass Sneaker.* New York: Macmillan, 1985. 30 pages (unpaged).

In this modern version of Cinderella, a young boy is ridiculed and made to work by his two mean brothers. What Sidney really wants to do is play football. His fairy godfather grants him his wish, but Sidney must be home by six o'clock. Sidney wins the game but has to leave before receiving his trophy. The coach goes door to door to locate the boy who can wear the glass sneaker. Sidney becomes famous and grows up to own his own company.

23. **Myers, Laurie.** *Garage Sale Fever.* Illustrated by Kathleen Collins Howell. New York: HarperCollins, 1993. 86 pages.

Will decides to have a garage sale after the contents of his closet fall on top of him and almost injure his dog. Once the word gets around school, all of his friends want to participate. The garage sale is a success until Will's friend Pete sells a gift he received from Louise to her best friend, Jan. Jan plans to give the gift to Louise for her birthday. Will's solution to the problem is brilliant.

24. **Naylor, Phyllis R.** *One of the Third Grade Thonkers.* Illustrated by Walter Gaffney-Kessell. New York: Atheneum, 1988. 136 pages.

Jimmy Novak, Sam Angelino, and Peter Nilsson are Thonkers. Thonkers have proven their bravery in outstanding ways such as living through operations, bone breaks, and car wrecks. When Jimmy's young cousin comes to stay with Jimmy's family when his mother has heart surgery, Jimmy learns a new meaning of bravery.

25. **Steig, William.** *Sylvester and the Magic Pebble.* New York: Trumpet Club, 1969. 30 pages (unpaged). Caledecott winner.

Sylvester Duncan collects unusual pebbles. One day he finds a magic pebble. Unfortunately, he runs into a lion and wishes to himself that he was a rock. Unable to touch the stone and wish himself normal, Sylvester has to stay as a rock. His parents, on a picnic the following spring, find the magic pebble and Sylvester is rescued.

Fourth Grade

1. **Blume, Judy.** *Here's to You, Rachel Robinson.* New York: Dell Publishing, 1993. 196 pages.

   Rachel's big brother is expelled from boarding school and is causing a lot of worries for Rachel and her friends. Although Rachel is a straight A student, she still has many problems: seventh grade, boys, her sister's problems, but mostly her brother.

2. **Blume, Judy.** *Iggie's House.* New York: Dell Publishing, 1970. 117 pages.

   Winnie's best friend, Iggie, moves away, and a new family has moved into the house. Winnie hopes they will be as good friends as she and Iggie were. The family is the only black family on the block. Will this be a problem for Winnie?

3. **Blume, Judy.** *Starring Sally J. Freeman as Herself.* New York: Dell Publishing, 1977. 298 pages.

   Set in the time of World War II, ten-year-old Sally must move to Florida for the winter so her brother doesn't get sick again. She meets a lot of new friends and has her daydreams to keep her occupied. But could the man in her building be Adolf Hitler?

4. **Byars, Betsy.** *The Not-Just-Anybody Family.* New York: Dell Publishing, 1986. 149 pages.

   This is the first book in a very humorous series based on the unusual Blossom family. The three young children live with grandpa, who is a real character, because mother is on the rodeo circuit. The zany adventures these children experience are very authentic and entertaining.

5. **Byars, Betsy.** *Wanted: Mud Blossom.* Illustrated by Jacqueline Rogers. New York: Dell Publishing, 1991. 148 pages.

   Scooty, the school hamster, is missing. Mad Mary's cane and bag are found on the side of the road. Is Pap's dog, Mud, responsible? Is that why he stays under the porch? And is someone out to murder Vern and Michael?

6. **Cleary, Beverly.** *Dear Mr. Henshaw.* New York: Dell Publishing, 1983. 133 pages.

   This story is told through letters written to Mr. Henshaw, a writer, from Leigh Botts and a diary kept by Leigh. Leigh is trying to deal with the divorce of his parents and the absenteeism of his father. Leigh's mother is a caterer who is raising Leigh by herself and taking courses at the community college to become a nurse.

7. **Cleary, Beverly.** *Strider.* Illustrated by Paul O. Zelinsky. New York: Trumpet Club, 1991. 179 pages.

   The great sequel to *Dear Mr. Henshaw*, *Strider* continues the adventures of Leigh Botts and his new dog, Strider. Both have had the feeling of abandonment but rise above it and become the best friends either one ever had. But can Strider really read?

8. **Conrad, Pam.** *Pedro's Journal.* New York: Scholastic Inc., 1991. 80 pages.

   This is a journal of a young boy's adventures aboard Christopher Columbus's *Santa Maria.*

9. **Draper, Sharon M.** *Ziggy and the Black Dinosaurs.* Illustrated by James Ransome. Orange, NJ: Trumpet Club, 1994. 86 pages.

   Ziggy and his friends form a club called the Black Dinosaurs.

10. **Farmer, Nancy.** *Do You Know Me?* New York: Scholastic Inc., 1993. 104 pages.

    Tapiwa's Uncle Zeka is visiting Zimbabwe. Tapiwa used to be bored, but with her uncle she is having great fun. She hopes he will stay.

11. **Fleischman, Sid.** *The Whipping Boy.* Mahwah, NJ: Troll Associates, 1986. 89 pages.

    This is the story of Jemmy, the whipping boy, and Prince Brat. Jemmy must take any whippings for Prince Brat when the prince misbehaves, which is all the time. Together Prince Brat and Jemmy run away from the palace to start new lives. During their adventures, Jemmy and Prince Brat are taken by outlaws and rescued by Betsy and Petunia, the dancing bear.

12. **Gardiner, John Reynolds.** *Stone Fox.* New York: Trumpet Club, 1980. 81 pages.

    When his grandfather cannot pay his back taxes and risks losing his farm, Little Willy decides to spend his college money to enter a sled race. Willy later discovers that Stone Fox, an Indian, and his five Samoyeds have entered the race as well. They have never lost a race. Nevertheless, Little Willy has his trusty dog Searchlight and he is determined to win.

13. **Haun, Mary Downing.** *The Doll in the Garden.* Boston: Houghton Mifflin, 1989. 128 pages.

    After her father's death, Ashley and her mother rent a room in the house of Miss Cooper. Ashley later finds a doll in the garden with a note attached. Is the garden haunted by a young girl who died seventy years ago? And what does Miss Cooper have to do with it?

14. **Hesse, Karen.** *Letters from Rifka.* New York: Puffin Books, 1992. 148 pages.

Rifka's family must flee Russia. Her letters to family tell her story.

15. **Lester, Julius.** *Black Cowboy, Wild Horses.* Illustrated by Jerry Pinkney. New York: Dial Books, 1998. 36 pages.

Bob Lemmons was a former slave who moved to Texas and became a famous cowboy. This story tells of his adventures tracking a group of wild mustangs.

16. **MacLachlan, Patricia.** *Baby.* New York: Dell Publishing, 1993. 132 pages.

Larkin comes home to find a baby on her front porch with a note saying the baby's name is Sophie. Although unable to care for the baby now, the mother says she will be back for her someday. Sophie becomes one of the family. But what if the mother comes back? Will she take Sophie away?

17. **MacLachlan, Patricia.** *Journey.* New York: Dell Publishing, 1991. 83 pages.

Journey is left to stay with his grandparents after his mother's unexplained need to leave. She writes to them, but there is no return address. Journey searches to find the answers as to why his mother felt she had to leave and discovers much more.

18. **MacLachlan, Patricia.** *Sarah, Plain and Tall.* New York: HarperTrophy, 1985. 58 pages.

Sarah moves to Kansas to be the wife of a widowed farmer and the mother of his children after answering the father's ad for a bride. Sarah changes the lives of this family for the better.

19. **Namioka, Lensey.** *Yang the Youngest and His Terrible Ear.* New York: Dell Publishing, 1992. 134 pages.

This is a wonderful story of friendship. Yingtao is the youngest in a family of musicians, except for Yingtao. After moving to Seattle, he finds a friend who helps him discover something he loves and is good at. Now to tell his family.

20. **Naylor, Phyllis Reynolds.** *Shiloh.* New York: Dell Publishing, 1991. 144 pages.

When Marty discovers that Old Man Judd is abusing his dog, he decides he is going to buy, steal, or do anything to keep the dog safe from harm.

21. **Sachar, Louis.** *There's a Boy in the Girls' Bathroom.* New York: Alfred A. Knopf, 1987. 195 pages.

Not only is Bradley the oldest fifth grader, he is the worst fifth grader ever. But the new school counselor sees a different side of Bradley. Will Bradley ever straighten up?

22. **San Souci, Robert D.** *Fa Mulan.* Illustrated by Jean & Mou-Sien Tseng. New York: Hyperion Books, 1998. 28 pages.

    This is a traditional Chinese tale of a young girl who disguises herself as a boy to serve in the Khan's army. Fa Mulan distinguishes herself as a warrior and a leader and is allowed to return home as a reward. Only then does she reveal that she is a woman.

23. **Smith, Robert Kimmel.** *The War with Grandpa.* New York: Dell Publishing, 1984. 140 pages.

    When Peter's grandmother dies, Peter's parents ask his grandfather to move in with them. Peter's grandfather, though, cannot climb the stairs to the guest room, so Peter is moved out of his room and into the guest room. Peter is quite unhappy about this, and he decides to declare war on his grandfather. Initially, Grandpa ignores Peter's attempt to start the war, but then he joins in the fighting until Peter does something that brings the war to a sudden end.

24. **Spinelli, Jerry.** *Wringer.* New York: HarperTrophy, 1997. 229 pages.

    A boy's tenth birthday marks an event he would rather ignore: the day that he is ready to take his place as a "wringer" at the annual family fest, Pigeon Day. When an unwanted visitor—in the form of a trusting pigeon—arrives on his windowsill, the boy realizes that it is a sign to stand up for what he believes.

25. **Taylor, Mildred D.** *Roll of Thunder, Hear My Cry.* New York: Dell Publishing, 1976. 210 pages.

    An African-American girl is forced to learn the truth about life and what being black means.

Fifth Grade

1. **Alexander, Lloyd.** *The Book of Three.* New York: Dell Publishing, 1964. 224 pages.

    Join Taran, the assistant pig keeper, on his magical adventures to save his beloved Prydain. With the help of friends and determination, Taran is unstoppable.

2. **Babbitt, Natalie.** *Tuck Everlasting.* New York: Trumpet Club, 1975. 139 pages.

    The Tuck family is no ordinary family, and something strange is going on behind their house. What is it, and will the Tucks be taken in by it?

3. **Cooney, Caroline.** *The Face on the Milk Carton.* New York: Dell Publishing, 1990. 184 pages.

   One day Janie is forced to ask herself who she is, when she discovers her own face on a milk carton. If the Johnsons are not her real parents, who are? Was she kidnapped by the Johnsons?

4. **Cooney, Caroline.** *Whatever Happened to Janie?* New York: Dell Publishing, 1993. 199 pages.

   Janie discovers she was kidnapped, and her real parents want her back. Yet the Johnsons are not giving up. What will Janie (or is it Jennie) do?

5. **Dorris, Michael.** *Sees Behind Trees.* New York: Scholastic, 1996. 104 pages.

   This is the story of how Walnut, a young boy of the Powhatan tribe, earns the name Sees Behind Trees.

6. **Fenner, Carol.** *Yolanda's Genius.* New York: Scholastic, 1995. 211 pages.

   Yolanda is convinced that her young brother, Andrew, has a great musical gift, but she must use her brains and strength to convince others.

7. **Fox, Paula.** *Western Wind.* New York: Dell Publishing, 1993. 201 pages.

   Elizabeth feels her new brother is taking her parents away. She is to spend the summer with her grandmother. Even though she loves her grandmother, who is very understanding, she wants to be home. Then Elizabeth meets Aaron, and things begin to change.

8. **George, Jean Craighead.** *My Side of the Mountain.* New York: Trumpet Club, 1988. 177 pages.

   Sam runs away from home into the Catskill Mountains. With only his wits, a few supplies, and information he read in a survival book, he sets out to live his own life. Will he stay there or come home?

9. **Hobbs, Will.** *Bearstone.* New York: Avon Books, 1989. 154 pages.

   Cloyd Atcitty is sent by his tribe from his home in Utah to live with Walter, a rancher, in Colorado where he finds a carved turquoise bear in the mountains. This story tells how Cloyd and Walter find a way to live together.

10. **Hobbs, Will.** *Kokopelli's Flute.* New York: Avon Books, 1995. 165 pages.

    Tepary Jones finds an ancient bone flute in an ancient cliff dwelling. Tepary soon discovers that this flute is a magic flute.

11. **Konigsburg, E. L.** *From the Mixed-up Files of Mrs. Basil E. Frankweiler.* New York: Dell Publishing, 1967. 159 pages.

Tired of life at home, Claudia and her brother decide to run away and live in the Metropolitan Museum of Art. But just when they get comfortable, strange things start to happen. Told by Mrs. Frankweiler, this book is full of mysteries and surprises.

12. **Laird, Elizabeth.** *Kiss the Dust.* New York: Penguin, 1991. 279 pages.

Twelve-year-old Tara lives in Iraq. Her family are Kurds who must flee Iraq for the safety of the Kurdistan mountains. They find themselves in a refugee camp in Iran.

13. **L'Engle, Madeleine.** *A Wrinkle in Time.* New York: Dell Publishing, 1962. 190 pages.

Meg and Charles Murray's father is missing. With the help of three very strange ladies, they set off on a strange and wild experience. How do these ladies know so much, and who is their father, anyway?

14. **Lisle, Janet Taylor.** *Afternoon of the Elves.* New York: Scholastic Inc., 1989. 122 pages.

Sara-Kate doesn't fit in very well at school. Hillary likes her but is also a little unsure. Then the two girls discover an elf village in Sara-Kate's backyard. The elves teach the girls wonderful things.

15. **Lowry, Lois.** *Number the Stars.* New York: Dell Publishing, 1989. 137 pages.

Set in Denmark in 1943, this is the story of Annemarie and Ellen. Ellen is Jewish, and her family is facing "relocation" to a concentration camp. Annemarie's family must help Ellen's family make their way to freedom in Sweden.

16. **Naylor, Phyllis Reynolds.** *Night Cry.* New York: Dell Publishing, 1984. 154 pages.

After Ellen's brother is killed and another boy kidnapped, she wonders what is in the woods behind her house. Can Ellen uncover the secret of the woods and the night cries?

17. **O'Dell, Scott.** *Sing Down the Moon.* New York: Dell Publishing, 1970. 134 pages.

Bright Morning and Running Bird must think fast before Spanish slavers threaten the peaceful valley. Will they escape this terrible fate?

18. **O'Dell, Scott,** & **Hall, Elizabeth.** *Thunder Rolling in the Mountains.* New York: Dell Publishing, 1992. 128 pages.

In 1877, the miners come to the Wallowa River to pan for gold. Knowing her people are outnumbered, a young Indian girl must come to grips with her life and what that means.

19. **Paterson, Katherine.** *Bridge to Terabithia.* New York: HarperCollins, 1987. 128 pages.

Jess has been practicing all summer to be the fastest boy in the fifth grade. When a strange new girl decides to join the boys and beats Jess, he is bent on getting back at her. But he will never forget the friendship he finds with her at the bridge to Terabithia.

20. **Paterson, Katherine.** *Jacob, Have I Loved.* New York: Harper & Row, 1980. 175 pages.

Louise is the healthier twin, but Caroline gets all the attention. Louise learns how to live as a waterman would. Watching Caroline get everything Louise dreamed of, Louise gathers her strength, accomplishes more than her sister ever could, and gains the respect of all.

21. **Paulsen, Gary.** *Canyons.* New York: Dell Publishing, 1990. 184 pages.

Brennan Cole finds the 100-year-old skull of an Apache boy, Coyote Runs. Brennan finds an incredible journey ahead of him in his quest to return the skull to its rightful place.

22. **Paulsen, Gary.** *Hatchet.* New York: Trumpet Club, 1987. 195 pages.

On the way to see his father, Brian is in a plane crash in which the pilot dies. He is forced to live in the Canadian woods for fifty-four days with only a hatchet his mother gave him.

23. **Paulsen, Gary.** *The Winter Room.* New York: Dell Publishing, 1989. 103 pages.

When Uncle David begins to tell stories, Eldon and Wayne listen anxiously. When Uncle David tells the story of the Woodcutter, things aren't the same.

24. **Savin, Marcia.** *The Moon Bridge.* New York: Scholastic Inc., 1992. 231 pages.

When Mitzi Fujimoto moves to San Francisco, she immediately becomes friends with Ruthie Fox. But when the U. S. government forces all Americans of Japanese ancestry to move to internment camps, Mitzi disappears. It is three long years before the friends are reunited.

25. **Spinelli, Jerry.** *Maniac Magee.* New York: HarperCollins, 1990. 184 pages.

Wild stories are being spread about Jeffrey Magee. He's a legend in his town. When a real situation occurs, will Maniac Magee measure up?

26. **Winthrop, Elizabeth.** *The Castle in the Attic.* New York: Bantam Publishing, 1989. 179 pages.

William's nanny is going home to England to be with her brother. She gives William a toy castle that has been in her family for years. William does not want her to leave. Through the magic of the castle, William forces her to stay. But when he is forced to fight for her freedom and his, will he be brave enough?

Sixth Grade

1. **Avi.** *The True Confessions of Charlotte Doyle.* New York: Franklin Watts, 1990. 215 pages.

   A thirteen-year-old girl boards a ship and discovers she is the only passenger. She learns the captain is a murderer, but Charlotte is accused and convicted. Can she get out of it?

2. **Bunting, Eve.** *Sharing Susan.* New York: HarperTrophy, 1991. 122 pages.

   At birth, two baby girls are mixed up and the parents take home the wrong child. This mistake is not discovered for twelve years. The problem is even more complicated because one child has died. Now the two sets of parents must decide how they are going to share Susan.

3. **Curtis, Christopher Paul.** *The Watsons Go to Birmingham—1963.* New York: Scholastic, 1995. 210 pages.

   This humorous award-winning book (Newbery Honor Book, Coretta Scott King Honor Book) tells the story of the Weird Watson's family trip to Birmingham, Alabama, during a turbulent time in its history.

4. **Cushman, Karen.** *Catherine, Called Birdy.* New York: HarperCollins, 1994. 212 pages.

   Catherine's father wants to marry her off to the richest suitor. She manages to dissuade several suitors. Then an ugly, old man comes to town. Unfortunately for Catherine, he is the richest suitor yet. Will she escape?

5. **Danziger, Paula.** *Not for a Billion Gazillion Dollars.* New York: Dell Publishing, 1992. 121 pages.

   Three teenagers create a business together to make a lot of money. Can they do it?

6. **Eckert, Allan W.** *Incident at Hawk's Hill.* New York: Bantam Publishing, 1987. 191 pages.

This is a true story about an autistic boy who gets lost and is cared for by a mother badger who just lost her pups. Ben is able to communicate with the badger.

7. **Eisenberg, Lisa.** *Mystery at Bluff Point Dunes.* Mahwah, NJ: Troll Associates, 1990. 150 pages.

   Kate is staying with her good friend, Bonnie, on Cape Cod for the summer. Things start to disappear. When Kate begins to investigate, she may not want to accept what she finds.

8. **George, Jean Craighead.** *Julie of the Wolves.* New York: HarperCollins, 1992. 170 pages.

   Running away from an arranged marriage, thirteen-year-old Julie takes off to be with her friend in San Francisco. But she is lost in the Arctic wilderness with no food or shelter. All seems lost until she wins over the affections of a wolf pack and the leader, Amaroq. With their help, she is able to eat, learns more about herself, and reflects on her life. She is later reunited with her father.

9. **Gordon, Sheila.** *Waiting for the Rain.* New York: Bantam Books, 1987. 214 pages.

   This is the story of Tengo and Frikkie, two South African boys, one black and one white, who are friends during a time in South Africa when apartheid still existed.

10. **Hamilton, Virginia.** *Anthony Burns: The Defeat and Triumph of a Fugitive Slave.* New York: Alfred A. Knopf, 1988. 193 pages.

    Anthony Burns is an escaped slave. After he is captured, he must await trial. Will Anthony ever be free?

11. **Hamilton, Virginia.** *M. C. Higgins, The Great.* New York: Macmillan, 1974. 278 pages.

    Two strangers are able to help M. C. live and realize his greatest dream.

12. **Hamilton, Virginia.** *Plain City.* New York: Scholastic Inc., 1993. 194 pages.

    When a girl discovers that what she knows about her father is all lies, her mother refuses to help her discover the truth. But she is determined to find out for herself.

13. **Lowry, Lois.** *The Giver.* New York: Dell Publishing, 1993. 180 pages.

    In a world where only the Giver possesses true feelings and emotions, Jonas finds he is next to possess this ability. Is he ready?

14. **Paterson, Katherine.** *Lyddie.* New York: Lodestar Books, 1991. 182 pages.

Lyddie is a poor farm girl living in Vermont. She goes to Lowell, Massachusetts, to work in a factory. She gains her independence and fights for a better life for everyone.

15. **Paulsen, Gary.** *Island.* New York: Dell Publishing, 1988. 202 pages.

When Will finds an island where he can be alone, he may never come back. Can Will face his fears or will he stay on the island?

16. **Paulsen, Gary.** *The River.* New York: Dell Publishing, 1991. 129 pages.

The sequel to *Hatchet.* Brian is asked to go back to the situation he returned from. This time it is in a different place and with Derek. Derek is a man who is interested in teaching survival to others by observing how Brian was able to survive. But when things go wrong, can Brian bring them both back to safety?

17. **Rawls, Wilson.** *Summer of the Monkeys.* New York: Dell Publishing, 1976. 283 pages.

When Jay and his dog are out exploring, they discover a monkey in the middle of nowhere, and their summer becomes quite exciting.

18. **Rawls, Wilson.** *Where the Red Fern Grows.* New York: Dell Publishing, 1961. 249 pages.

A young boy has two dogs who bring him more happiness and love than he ever dreamed of. In the end, however, all his love lies where the red fern grows.

19. **Roberts, Willo Davis.** *Baby-Sitting Is a Dangerous Job.* New York: Atheneum, 1985. 161 pages.

Darcy has agreed to baby-sit Melissa, Jeremy, and Shana Foster. The three young children are ill behaved, though that is the least of Darcy's problems when one afternoon she and the three children are kidnapped. The kidnappers are the father and brothers of a girl Darcy knows from school. She knows that the man is violent because his daughter has run away several times to escape his abuse. Unfortunately, Darcy lets the kidnappers know that she knows their names and thus puts her own life in danger.

20. **Sachs, Marilyn.** *A Pocket Full of Seeds.* New York: Scholastic Inc., 1973. 137 pages.

Being Jewish in occupied France is not easy. Now Nicole and her family must find each other again and manage to survive.

21. **Selden, George.** *The Cricket in Times Square.* New York: Dell Publishing, 1960. 151 pages.

A boy, a cricket, a mouse, and a cat become friends and overcome an obstacle that brings joy to a family in need.

22. **Speare, Elizabeth George.** *The Witch of Blackbird Pond.* New York: Dell Publishing, 1958. 249 pages.

Moving from paradise to the bleak shore of Connecticut, Kit feels isolated in this new world. Befriending an old woman makes her feel less lonely, but it leads her to big trouble.

23. **Staples, Suzanne Fisher.** *Shabanu: Daughter of the Wind.* New York: Random House, 1989. 240 pages.

Shabanu lives in the Cholistan Desert of Pakistan. At eleven, she is asked to make the greatest sacrifice of her life.

24. **Voigt, Cynthia.** *Dicey's Song.* New York: Ballantine Books, 1982. 211 pages.

Forced to hold her family together at the age of thirteen, Dicey grows up a little too fast. She finds it hard to live for herself and accept things from others. In the end, Dicey learns something very important.

25. **Yep, Laurence.** *Dragonwings.* New York: HarperCollins, 1975. 248 pages.

Moon Shadow sails from China to visit the golden land where the father he has never seen lives. Although in a strange land, he comes to love his father and learns to live in this new world.

Seventh Through Ninth Grade

1. **Amos, Berthe.** *Lost Magic.* New York: Hyperion Books for Children, 1993. 184 pages.

Ceridwen is the heroine of this fairy tale–type story set in the Middle Ages. She survives a series of events that include being placed in a basket as an infant and floating in a moat, being accused of witchcraft, and causing a plague. Can she herself survive this plague that she has been accused of causing?

2. **Avi.** *Beyond the Western Sea.* New York: Avon Books, 1996. 325 pages.

With only their belongings in bundles, Maura O'Connel (fifteen), her brother, Patrick (twelve), and Sir Laurence Kirkle (eleven), try to escape their lives in Ireland with their tickets for ocean passage. Fate brings these three together, and they begin their daring scheme that may lead to glory, and freedom, or dire consequences.

3. **Bloor, Edward.** *Tangerine.* San Diego: Scholastic, 1997. 294 pages.

   Paul Fisher and his family move to Tangerine, Florida. Paul lives in the shadow of his older brother Erik, an all-star football player. Everyone is blinded by his superstardom except for Paul, who knows the horrible truth about Erik.

4. **Bosse, Malcolm.** *Deep Dream of the Rain Forest.* New York: Farrar, Straus & Giroux, 1993. 179 pages.

   While on an expedition with his uncle in the jungles of Borneo in 1920, fifteen-year-old Harry Windsor is captured by Bayang, a young Iban tribesman, who believes that Harry has some power to help him and an outcast Iban girl on their dream quest.

5. **Brooks, Martha.** *Bone Dance.* New York: Orchard Books, 1997. 192 pages.

   When Alexandra's father dies, the man she never knew leaves his legacy—a cabin on prairie land he purchased from the LaFreniere family. Lonny LaFreniere's father sold the land to Alexandra's father after Lonny rejected it. Now Lonny is tormented by guilty memories and dreams and visions he can't shake. How could Lonny have known the land would end up in the hands of a city girl like Alexandra Sinclair?

6. **Buffie, Margaret.** *The Dark Garden.* Buffalo: Kids Canadian Press, 1997. 240 pages.

   Sixteen-year-old Thea is suffering from traumatic amnesia. As she begins to discover who she is—and who she is not—the empty places of her mind fill up with shadowy memories. Thea finds herself caught between two worlds. In one, her unhappy family seems to be falling apart. In the other, spirits haunt her with their tragic passion. She must find out what these ghosts want of her!

7. **Charnas, Suzy McKee.** *The Kingdom of Kevin Malone.* San Diego: Harcourt Brace, 1993. 272 pages.

   Amy's cousin has died and relatives have gathered at her family's apartment. Amy goes skating in Central Park where she encounters a bully from school, Kevin Malone. Amy is drawn into Kevin's dangerous fantasy world. She soon realizes that only she and her friends can save Kevin.

8. **Cole, Brock.** *Celine.* New York: Farrar, Straus & Giroux, 1989. 216 pages.

   Before Celine, a sixteen-year-old artist, can take a promised trip to Europe, she must show a little maturity, finish an overdue term paper, and support her seven-year-old neighbor during his parent's separation.

9. **Cole, Brock.** *The Goats.* Orange, NJ: Trumpet Club, 1987. 184 pages.

   Laurie and Howie are picked to be the "goats" by the kids at their camp. They just want to disappear, and that's what they do.

10. **Cooper, Susan.** *The Boggart.* London: Puffin Books, 1993. 208 pages.

    The Boggart is an ancient spirit who has lived in Castle Keep for centuries. He delights in playing tricks on the castle's owners. When Emily and Jessup's father inherits the castle, they travel from Toronto to Scotland to visit it. The Boggart returns to Toronto with them and mayhem abounds. With the help of a computer, can they send the Boggart back to Castle Keep?

11. **Cormier, Robert.** *Beyond the Chocolate War.* New York: Doubleday Dell Books, 1985. 278 pages.

    School is almost out for the students at Trinity School. Obie has decided to part ways from a secret organization at Trinity called the Vigils. Obie has a surprise for the leader of the Vigils, Archie, and also seeks revenge on those who have it coming.

12. **Creech, Sharon.** *Chasing Red Bird.* New York: HarperTrophy, 1997. 261 pages.

    Thirteen-year-old Zinny has an entire summer to uncover a trail to understand her family and find her place in her backyard that will help her in the world.

13. **Dickinson, Peter.** *A Bone from a Dry Sea.* New York: Laureleaf, 1993. 199 pages.

    Two parallel stories present a young prehistoric female who is instrumental in advancing her people and a modern-day girl who joins her father, a paleontologist, in discovering important fossil remains in Africa.

14. **Fine, Anne.** *Step by Wicked Step.* Boston: Little, Brown, 1996. 144 pages.

    Five children find they have a lot in common after discovering an old diary in a haunted house.

15. **Gantos, Jack.** *Joey Pigz Swallowed the Key.* New York: Farrar, Straus & Giroux, 1998. 192 pages.

    To the constant disappointment of his mother and his teachers, Joey has trouble paying attention or controlling his mood swings when his prescription medications wear off and he starts getting worked up and acting wired.

16. **Griffin, Peni R.** *Switching Well.* New York: Puffin, 1993. 218 pages

Two twelve-year-old girls in San Antonio, Texas, Ada in 1891 and Amber in 1991, switch places through a magic well and try desperately to return to their own times.

17. **Grove, Vicki.** *The Crystal Garden.* New York: Putnam, 1995. 217 pages.

Eliza moves to a new town and starts junior high. Like everyone, she wants to be popular, but becoming friends with her loner next-door neighbor makes her afraid this won't happen.

18. **Hautzig, E.** *The Endless Steppe.* New York: HarperCollins Publishers, 1968. 243 pages.

The Rudomin family is arrested in June 1941, by the Russians. Taken from their home and friends in Vilna, Poland, in cattle cars, they head for Siberia. Working in exile, weeding potato fields, and working in the mines, struggling for survival, Esther and her family only have each other to hold on to. Can the strength of their family sustain them and give them hope for the future?

19. **Hayes, Daniel.** *Flyers.* New York: Simon & Schuster, 1996. 203 pages.

While filming a movie for a school project, Gabe and his friends discover mysterious activities at a supposedly vacant house.

20. **Hesse, Karen.** *Out of the Dust.* New York: Scholastic Trade, 1997. 160 pages.

In a series of poems, fifteen-year-old Billie Jo relates the hardships of living on her family's wheat farm in Oklahoma during the dust bowl years of the Depression.

21. **Highwater, Jamake.** *Anpao.* Philadelphia: Lippincott, 1977. 133 pages.

On a long and dangerous quest to the realm of the Drowned Ones, Anpao, a young Native American man, experiences thrilling and magical experiences that reflect the rich heritage of his people.

22. **Hobbs, Will.** *The Big Wander.* New York: Simon & Schuster, 1992. 181 pages.

Clay and his big brother Mike take a cross-country trip from Seattle to Monument Valley in the southwest to find their lost uncle. Mike decides to give up the search and heads home, but Clay decides to go on and find him.

23. **Hobbs, Will.** *Far North.* New York: Avon Books, 1996. 216 pages.

From the window of the floatplane, Gabe Rogers and his roommate, Raymond Providence, are getting their first look at Canada's Northwest territories. With the brutal subarctic winter approaching, the boys soon find themselves stranded in Deadmen Valley. In a frozen world of moose, wolves, and bears, the two boys, from vastly different cultures, come to depend on each other for their survival.

24. **Holt, Kimberly Willis.** *My Louisiana Sky.* New York: Henry Holt & Company, Inc., 1998. 176 pages.

    Set in the South of the 1950s, this tender coming-of-age novel explores a twelve-year-old girl's struggle to accept her grandmother's death, her mentally deficient parents, and the changing world around her. This story is filled with unforgettable characters and it emphasizes the importance of family and home.

25. **Ingold, Jeanette.** *The Window.* San Diego: Harcourt Brace & Co., 1996. 181 pages.

    Mandy is blinded in a car accident that kills her mother. She is sent to live with her great aunt and uncle, whom she has never met. She chooses to attend the local high school instead of the school for the blind. She faces challenges every day that give her the ability to see things without the use of her eyes.

26. **Johnson, Angela.** *Toning the Sweep.* New York: Orchard Books, 1993. 103 pages.

    Fourteen-year-old Emily learns the ritual of "toning the sweep," a way of drumming a plow to create a sound that honors the deceased, in this tale of mourning and healing. Emily, her mother, and her terminally ill grandmother, Ola, meet at Ola's home in the desert to pack her up for a move to Cleveland, where Ola will live out the rest of her days.

27. **Keller, Beverly**. *The Amazon Papers.* San Diego: Harcourt Brace, 1996. 150 pages.

    Athletic, straight A student Iris finds herself in trouble for the first time in her life when her mother's vacation gives way to a wrecked car, two unlikely boyfriend prospects, and a zany scheme to fix everything.

28. **Kherdian, David.** *The Road from Home.* New York: Beech Tree Books, 1979. 238 pages.

    This is a biography of the author's mother, concentrating on her childhood in Turkey before the Turkish government deported its Armenian population.

29. **Krisher, Trudy.** *Spite Fences.* New York: Laureleaf, 1994. 283 pages.

    As she struggles with her troubled relationship with her mother during the summer of 1960, a young girl is also drawn into the violence, hatred, and racial tension in her small Georgia town.

30. **Lasky, Katherine.** *Beyond the Burning Time.* New York: Pointe Publications, 1994. 272 pages.

When, in the winter of 1691, accusations of witchcraft surface in her small New England village, twelve-year-old Mary Chase fights to save her mother from execution.

31. **L'Engle, Madeleine.** *Troubling a Star.* New York: Farrar, Straus & Giroux/Harcourt Brace Jovanovich, 1994. 296 pages.

As she tries to stay alive after being left on an iceberg in the Antarctic, sixteen-year-old Vicky recalls the series of events that brought her to the bottom of the world and involved her in a dangerous mystery.

32. **Levine, Ellen.** *Freedom's Children: Young Civil Rights Activists Tell Their Own Stories.* New York: Avon, 1992. 224 pages.

Southern blacks who were young and involved in the civil rights movement during the 1950s and 1960s describe their experiences.

33. **Levine, G. C.** *Ella Enchanted.* New York: HarperCollins Publishers, 1997. 232 pages.

Ella of Frell was cursed at birth by a foolish fairy whose gift to Ella was the "gift" of obedience. Ella must obey any order that is given to her, no matter how silly it may be. She sets out to break the curse and be rid of it forever.

34. **Marsden, John.** *Letters from the Inside.* Boston: Houghton Mifflin Company, 1994. 146 pages.

The relationship between two teenage girls who become acquainted through letters intensifies as their correspondence reveals some of the terrible problems of their lives.

35. **Matchek, Diane.** *The Sacrifice.* New York: Farrar, Straus & Giroux, 1998. 224 pages.

When her father's death leaves her orphaned and an outcast among her people, a fifteen-year-old Apsaalooka (Crow) Indian girl sets out to avenge his death and prove that she, not her dead twin brother, is destined to be the Great One.

36. **McCaughrean, Geraldine.** *The Pirate's Son.* New York: Scholastic Trade, 1998. 224 pages.

It is the year 1717 in England when Nathan and his sister, Maud, find themselves orphaned. Tamo White, the son of a pirate, offers them refuge and extraordinary adventure in a new life on the high seas.

37. **McGraw, Sharon.** *The Moorchild.* New York: Aladdin, 1996. 241 pages.

Mogl was sent to live with humans after being banished from her homeland. With humans, she is called Saaski.

She wants to go back to her homeland, but is afraid they will reject her, so she must stay and fit in with the humans.

38. **Mead, Alice.** *Adem's Cross.* New York: Laureleaf, 1996. 132 pages.

    Seeing his sister being shot to death for reading a poem at a demonstration against Serbian control of largely Albanian Kosovo changes forever the life of thirteen-year-old Adem.

39. **Meyer, Carolyn.** *Jubilee Journey.* San Diego: Harcourt Brace, 1997. 270 pages.

    Thirteen-year-old Emily Rose Chartier receives a letter from her great grandmother Rose Lee Jefferson asking her to visit her in Texas for the Juneteenth celebration. Emily has never met her great grandmother, so she and her mother and two brothers get on a bus and go to Texas to visit with her and do some much-needed catching up.

40. **Meyer, Carolyn.** *White Lilacs.* San Diego: Harcourt Brace, 1993. 242 pages.

    Based on a true story set in 1921, this thought-provoking novel chronicles the response of a Texas town's black community when they learn that local whites plan to raze their section of town in order to build a park.

41. **Morpurgo, Michael.** *Waiting for Anya.* New York: Puffin Books, 1990. 172 pages.

    Jo places his life in danger when he helps protect a growing number of Jewish children who have sought refuge at a reclusive widow's farm.

42. **Myers, W. D.** *Slam!* New York: Scholastic, 1996. 266 pages.

    Greg "Slam" Harris can do it all on the basketball court. He knows he's got what it takes to go all the way to the top. Slam's grades aren't so hot, though, and when his teachers jam his troubles in his face, he blows up.

43. **Napoli, D. J.** *The Magic Circle.* New York: Puffin, 1993. 128 pages.

    This is the story of Hansel and Gretel told from the point of view of the Ugly One, the witch in the fairy tale. The story begins long before Hansel and Gretel appear on the scene and ends with the redemption of the witch.

44. **Nixon, J. L.** *Whispers from the Dead.* New York: Delacorte Press, 1989. 192 pages.

    After nearly drowning, Sarah believes she is being followed by a stranger. She feels relieved when she and her family move from Missouri to Houston. Sarah thinks she will be able to put the frightening experience behind her. Then she begins to feel uneasy in her new house. Sarah hears someone whispering in Spanish. Is someone stalking Sarah or is it all in her imagination?

45. **Orr, Wendy.** *Peeling the Onion.* New York: Laureleaf, 1997. 176 pages.

Following an automobile accident in which her neck is broken, a teenage karate champion begins a long and painful recovery with the help of her family.

46. **Paterson, Katherine.** *Lyddie.* New York: Lodestar Books, 1991. 182 pages.

Impoverished Vermont farm girl Lyddie Worthen is determined to gain her independence by becoming a factory worker in Lowell, Massachusetts, in the 1840s.

47. **Paulsen, Gary.** *The Crossing.* New York: Orchard, 1987. 114 pages.

In Juarez, Mexico, there is much hunger and fear—hunger in the stomachs of many and fear in their hearts. Manny Bustos is a homeless street rat who dreams of fleeing to the United States. He decides to make his dreams come true by crossing the border to El Paso, Texas.

48. **Pausewang, Gudrun.** *The Final Journey.* Australia: Penguin Books, 1996. 153 pages.

Hiding in the basement of her former home after Hitler comes to power, Alice finds herself on the run with her grandfather after her grandmother is taken prisoner, and she begins to understand the horrors of Hitler's Germany.

49. **Pfeffer, S. B.** *The Year without Michael.* New York: Bantam Books, 1987. 164 pages.

Somewhere between home and the softball field, Jody's brother, Michael, disappeared. From that moment, Jody's world falls apart. This is a novel of separation and coming together, of breaking apart and becoming whole.

50. **Potok, Chaim.** *Zebra and Other Stories.* New York: Knopf, 1998. 128 pages.

Potok tells six stories in which children face moments of crisis or grief and see themselves, their parents, and the world around them anew. In the title story, Adam Zebrin—known as Zebra—takes an art class with a disabled Vietnam vet the summer that he himself suffered a crippling accident. Seeing the world through drawing and sculpture, Zebra begins to see himself and others with a new clearness.

51. **Pullman, Phillip.** *The Golden Compass.* New York: Knopf, 1996. 416 pages.

In an alternative world in which every human being is accompanied by an animal familiar, the disappearance of several children prompts Lyra and her bear protector to undertake a journey to the frozen Arctic in pursuit of kidnappers.

52. **Rapp, Adam.** *The Buffalo Tree.* Asheville, NC: Front Street Press, 1997. 112 pages.

    Serving a six-month sentence at Hamstock Juvenile Detention Center, thirteen-year-old Sura befriends his vulnerable bunkmate, Coly Jo, only to watch in dismay as Coly Jo loses himself to the pressures and predators of the institution and must draw on his own inner strength to survive.

53. **Roberts, Willo Davis.** *Nightmare.* New York: Atheneum, 1989. 216 pages.

    Nick has a terrible day. In this adventure story, his girlfriend drops him, a man falls off an overpass onto Nick's car and dies, and that evening someone breaks into his house and shoots his dog. Nick decides to go visit his brother, Mickey, to try to forget his horrible day. As Nick travels to Texas to see Mickey, things only seem to get worse before they get better.

54. **Ryan, Mary Elizabeth.** *Alias.* New York: Aladin Paperbacks, 1997. 160 pages.

    Fifteen-year-old Toby, who has spent his entire life traveling from place to place with his mother as she constantly changes her identity, discovers that she is a political fugitive from justice.

55. **Sachar, Louis.** *Holes.* New York: Orchard Books, 1993. 103 pages.

    Stanley Yelnats's family has a history of bad luck, so he isn't too surprised when a miscarriage of justice sends him to a boys' juvenile detention center, Camp Green Lake. There is no lake—it has been dry for over a hundred years—and it's hardly a camp. As punishment, the boys must each dig a hole a day, five feet deep, five feet across, in the hard earth of the dried-up lake bed. The warden claims that this pointless labor builds character, but she is really using the boys to dig for loot buried by the Wild West outlaw Kissin' Kate Barlow.

56. **Shusterman, Neil.** *The Dark Side of Nowhere: A Novel.* Boston: Little, Brown, 1997. 192 pages.

    Fourteen-year-old Jason faces an identity crisis after discovering that he is the son of aliens who stayed on earth following a botched invasion mission.

57. **Skurzynski, Gloria.** *Virtual War.* New York: Simon & Schuster, 1997. 152 pages.

    In a future world where global contamination has necessitated limited human contact, three young people with unique genetically engineered abilities are teamed up to wage a war in virtual reality.

58. **Slepian, Jan.** *Back to Before.* New York: Philomel Books, 1993. 170 pages.

Cousins Linny and Hilary are accidentally transported back one year in time. They seize this opportunity to try to prevent Linny's mother from dying and Hilary's father from leaving her family.

59. **Smith, Roland.** *Jaguar.* New York: Hyperion Press, 1998. 256 pages.

In the sequel to *Thunder Cave,* Jacob finds that he has become involved in a frightfully dangerous mystery after his father attempts to open a jaguar preserve in Brazil and is met with one violent attack after another.

60. **Smith, Roland.** *Thunder Cave.* New York: Hyperion, 1997. 256 pages.

Determined, after his mother's accidental death, to foil his stepfather's plans for his future, fourteen-year-old Jacob travels alone to Africa in search of his father, a biologist studying elephants in a remote area of Kenya.

61. **Snyder, Z. K.** *Fool's Gold.* New York: Yearling Books, 1993. 224 pages.

Rudy and his friends have just gotten out of school for the summer. There is an old gold mine nearby that they have been warned to stay away from, but Rudy's friends want to spend the summer secretly searching for gold. Rudy volunteers to baby-sit for his younger sister while his mom works to keep from having to tell his friends that he is afraid to go down into the dark tunnel. Then he must devise a plan to keep his friends out of the tunnel.

62. **Stanley, Jerry.** *Children of the Dust Bowl.* New York: Crown, 1992. 180 pages.

This photo album tells the stories of "The Okie" migration from Oklahoma to California. The story is told by pictures and also in the words of the migrants.

63. **Staples, S. F.** *Dangerous Skies.* New York: HarperTrophy, 1996. 232 pages.

Buck and Tunes have been best friends since birth. They could be brother and sister if it weren't for their different skin colors. One afternoon, something horrible happens and they try to hold on to their friendship.

64. **Staples, S. F.** *Haveli.* New York: Knopf Paperback, 1993. 320 pages.

Having relented to the ways of her people in Pakistan and married the rich older man to whom she was pledged against her will, Shabanu is now the victim of his family's blood feud and the malice of his other wives. This is the sequel to *Shabanu: Daughter of the Wind.*

65. **Taylor, Mildred.** *Let the Circle Be Unbroken.* New York: Puffin Books, 1991. 394 pages.

    The Logan family, their friends, and their neighbors are living through a frightening time. With some trying to stand up for their right to vote, some trying to pass for white, some facing an all-white jury, and some dealing with greedy landowners, times are turbulent. Cassie and the Logans stand together with courage, love, and understanding. This is the sequel to *Roll of Thunder, Hear My Cry.*

66. **Temple, Frances.** *Tonight, by Sea: A Novel.* New York: Orchard Books, 1995. 152 pages.

    As governmental brutality and poverty become unbearable, Paulie joins with others in her small Haitian village to help her uncle secretly build a boat they will use to try to escape to the United States.

67. **Thesman, Jean.** *The Ornament Tree.* Boston: Houghton Mifflin, 1996. 170 pages.

    When fourteen-year-old Bonnie moves to her cousin's boardinghouse in Seattle in 1918, she learns about life from the boarders and progressive women who live and work there.

68. **Tolan, Stephanie.** *Welcome to the Ark.* New York: Beech Tree Books, 1996. 256 pages.

    Miranda and three other gifted people are removed from their violent surroundings in the real world and brought to a special place, where they learn about their gift to make people change the way they behave in order to make good use of their gift in their society.

69. **Turner, Megan Whalen.** *The Thief.* New York: Puffin, 1996. 224 pages.

    Because of his great skill at thievery, Gen lands in the King's prison. After months of isolation, kept sane only by his sharp intelligence, Gen is released by the King's Scholar, the Magus, who believes that Gen knows the site of an ancient treasure. The Magus needs the best thief in the land to help him steal it, and that thief is Gen. But Gen is also a survivor and a trickster—and he has ideas of his own.

70. **Vick, Helen Hughes.** *Walker of Time.* Tucson: Harbinger House, 1993. 205 pages.

    A fifteen-year-old Hopi boy and his freckled companion travel back 800 years to the world of the Sinagua culture, a group of people beset by drought and illness and in need of a leader.

71. **Vick, Helen Hughes.** *Walker's Journey Home.* Tucson: Harbinger House, 1995. 182 pages.

Still trapped in ancient times, fifteen-year-old Walker reluctantly accepts the responsibility of leading a group of Indians on a difficult and dangerous journey across the high desert country of northern Arizona to a new home on the Hopi mesas.

72. **Voigt, Cynthia.** *When She Hollers.* New York: Scholastic Trade, 1994. 177 pages.

Tish, a teenager who has been enduring abuse from her stepfather since she was a small child, finally decides she must do something to stop him.

73. **Wisler, G. Clifton.** *Caleb's Choice.* New York: Puffin, 1996. 160 pages.

While living in Texas in 1858, fourteen-year-old Caleb faces a dilemma in deciding whether to assist fugitive slaves in their run for freedom.

74. **Woodson, Jacqueline.** *I Hadn't Meant to Tell You This.* New York: Delacorte Press, 1994. 115 pages.

In a quiet, beautiful friendship story, two young teenagers resist the bigotry in their school and the sorrow in their families and help each other find the strength to go on.

75. **Zeinert, Karen.** *The Amistad Slave Revolt and American Abolition.* New Haven, CT: Linnet Books, 1997. 89 pages.

Traces the 1839 revolt of Africans aboard the slave ship Amistad, their apprehension, and long trial, which ended in their acquittal by the Supreme Court.

Grateful acknowledgment to Amazon.com, the source of many of these summaries.

Glossary

Authentic reading assessment
Reading assessment that involves actual reading tasks in a natural environment such as a classroom; should parallel regular instruction.

Automaticity
A theory developed by LaBerge and Samuels (1974) that suggests that as a reader practices reading, the decoding of words becomes more instantaneous and reading becomes more fluent.

Concurrent validity
Validity established by statistically correlating results of one assessment instrument to a second, recognized standardized instrument.

Content validity
The degree to which the test materials include content from specific domains (in this case, reading) as judged by experts in the field.

Expository text
Text that provides information to the reader; it may be organized in a variety of structures; most classroom textbooks are expository text.

Frustration reading level
The level at which a reader experiences extreme difficulty with decoding and/or comprehension.

Independent reading level
The level at which a reader can easily read materials without help from the teacher; few or no problems with decoding or comprehension.

Instructional-assessment cycle
An instructional model in which instruction is planned from informal assessments, and students' performances, behaviors, and processes are assessed during instruction; essentially, instruction and assessment tools are derived from the same reading strategies (that is, retellings, think-alouds, K-W-Ls).

Instructional reading level
The level at which a reader benefits from instruction regarding decoding and comprehension strategies; decoding and comprehension are still high.

K-W-L
A study strategy developed by Ogle (1986) in which readers are asked what they know before reading, what questions might be answered by the text, and, after the reading, what was learned.

Miscue
Oral word errors that occur when a reader deviates from the printed text; examples include mispronunciations, substitutions, omissions, repetitions, and teacher-provided words.

Miscue analysis
A systematic examination of a reader's oral word errors to determine what specific decoding strategies the reader uses when reading.

Narrative text
Text that is organized around a story structure that includes characters, setting, plot episodes, and resolution of problem.

Protocol
Worksheet on which the examiner marks responses given by the student, indicates performance levels, and/or writes notations regarding student responses and reading behaviors.

Retelling
A recounting of a story, either in written or oral form, after it has been read.

Schemata
The collection of ideas and concepts that a person knows about any particular topic.

Think-aloud
A strategy in which a reader is asked to talk about thoughts and ideas regarding a text during the reading act.

Traditional reading assessment
Typically, assessment in a multiple choice or simple answer format; most often requires literal knowledge and results in a numerical score.

Zone of Proximal Development
The gap between what a person knows and what the person is ready to learn; the area in which instruction is needed to advance to a higher level of learning.

Brief Guide to Administering the CARP

TO ASSESS . . .	ADMINISTER . . .
Independent, instructional, and/or frustration reading levels	• Narrative retelling passages • Expository retelling passages
Understanding of story structure	• Narrative retelling passages
Use of prior knowledge	• Narrative retelling passages • Expository retelling passages • Think-aloud passages
Metacognitive skills	• Think-aloud passages
Decoding strategies	• Narrative retelling passages with a miscue analysis • Expository retelling passages with a miscue analysis
Differences between oral and silent reading levels	• Narrative retelling passages • Expository retelling passages
Differences in ability to handle a variety of text	• Narrative retelling passages *and* • Expository retelling passages
Ability to construct meaning	• Narrative retelling passages • Expository retelling passages • Think-aloud passages